T. C. Lethbridge:

The Man Who Saw the Future

T. C. Lethbridge:

The Man Who Saw the Future

Terry Welbourn

BOOKS

Winchester, UK
Washington, USA

First published by O-Books, 2011
O-Books is an imprint of John Hunt Publishing Ltd., Laurel House, Station Approach,
Alresford, Hants, SO24 9JH, UK
office1@o-books.net
www.o-books.com

For distributor details and how to order please visit the 'Ordering' section on our website.

ISBN: 978 1 84694 500 7

A CIP catalogue record for this book is available from the British Library.

Design: Stuart Davies

Printed in the UK by CPI Antony Rowe
Printed in the USA by Offset Paperback Mfrs, Inc

CONTENTS

I have mentioned this before in some other book,
but will do so again, for I find it takes about twenty years
before people believe anything I say.
T. C. Lethbridge

'Having been inspired by T.C. Lethbridge after reading my best-seller 'Mysteries' (Hodder and Stoughton, 1978), Terry Welbourn took up the mantle and has revealed that there were more strings to Lethbridge's bow than we could ever have imagined. His investigations into psychical research sit comfortably alongside his Arctic adventures, archaeological discoveries and his love of the ocean; for after all his enquiring mind knew no boundaries.

Colin Wilson

'In his role as Honorary Keeper of Anglo-Saxon Antiquities, T.C. Lethbridge substantially contributed to the development of the Cambridge University Museum of Archaeology and Anthropology. Artefacts from Lethbridge's archaeological excavations in the Fens, the Western Isles and from his Arctic expeditions alongside Sir James Wordie are still displayed in the museum today. He is remembered as a congenial, well-informed lecturer and a fine artist. Terry Welbourn's well-researched biography sheds light on the life of this controversial yet crucial figure in the history of twentieth-century British archaeology.'

Professor Thurstan Shaw

'In 1973 I took curator care of a very substantial collection of T.C. Lethbridge's notebooks, artwork and associated correspondence. In spring 2007 I was contacted by Terry Welbourn who had become aware of my collection through his ongoing research into Lethbridge's life. Through the forthcoming years, I had pleasure in assisting Terry with his research which enabled him to add further 'meat to the bones' of his splendid biography, 'T.C. Lethbridge: The Man Who Saw the Future'. My archive, 'The Gadd Collection' is now housed in the University Library, Cambridge.'

John Gadd

'An engaging and well researched account of one of the most extraordinary and at times inspiring people who have pursued the pattern of superstition and story-telling in the Hebrides.'

Adam Nicolson

Acknowledgements

Simon Brighton; Wendy Brown and the University Museum of Archaeology and Anthropology, Cambridge; Elizabeth Clark; W.A. Clark, former Head Warden of Wandlebury Estate; Julian Cope; Janet Cornish, Properties Manager/Secretary at Cambridge Past, Present and Future; Jacqueline Cox at the Cambridge University Archives; Andrew and Jackie David; Jo Erskine-Collins & Patric Nestcher; Hilary Everitt; Dr. Steven Roger Fischer; John & Barbara Gadd; Peter Gathercole; Dave Goudsward; Robert Halliday; Barbara Heath; Emma Higginbotham; Bill Holcomb; Lesa Holcombe; Dr. Matthias Alfred Jaren; Joy Kiddle; Nicholas & Barbara Leadbitter; Susan Lee; Mairi MacGregor; Daniel Martin; Chris McGrail; Neil Mortimer; Paul Newman; Mike Pitts, Jonathan Rhys-Lewis; Mary Rose Rogers; Dr. Pamela Jane Smith; Peter Swete; Jeff Pathe; Jeffrey Simmons; Michael Smith; Michael Turner; Mark Walford; Geoff Ward; Colin & Joy Wilson and Peter and Alice Wordie.

For Sue and Katie

Preface

On the morning of Thursday 19 November 1987, I found myself on Newark Station about to board an Inter City train destined for London King's Cross. The journey would have been typical of any grey, autumnal commute had it not been for an unfolding drama at the scene of my destination. The previous evening, a fire had swept through the underground section of King's Cross Station, causing massive devastation and resulting in the death of 31 passengers. As my train neared its destination, the atmosphere on board became tense and restless and an apprehensive silence overwhelmed the carriage. Disembarking onto the platform, I met with a sombre scene: the normal clatter and chatter of the busy station had been replaced by a respectful orderliness. Smoke still shrouded the canopies of the terminal and a pungent smell of burning permeated the morning air. Travellers diligently exited the busy thoroughfare, silently bypassing the cordoned underground entrance and onto the busy streets and patiently began making alternative arrangements for their onward journeys.

The experience of that fateful morning, if not significant enough for me already, had further implications in store. I had taken the opportunity of the journey to begin reading Colin Wilson's *Mysteries,* a weighty, intriguing tome that had been recommended to me by my friend, the author and photographer Simon Brighton. During my two-hour journey, I had become engrossed with Wilson's masterwork and on arrival at King's Cross I carefully marked my page and closed the book. I was unaware that the previous two hours of reading were destined to change my life. My train of thought was briefly interrupted by the mundane nature of my working day, but the return journey home to Lincoln provided me with another opportunity to continue my literary indulgence.

Published in 1978, *Mysteries* is a tantalising sequel to Wilson's previous study *The Occult* in which he attempts to provide the *Principia* of psychic science by exploring a whole variety of occult phenomena including hauntings, demonic possession and precognition. However, the underlying theme focuses on mankind's own ability to utilise and harness its own untapped and neglected potential. *Mysteries* is split into three parts, but it was the first section that had intrigued me, for it was almost entirely dedicated to the ideas and investigations of a remarkable man called Thomas Charles Lethbridge.

Perhaps it would be an overstatement to say that *Mysteries* changed my life, but it did provide for me a portal into another world – a parallel universe. The following year, I would stumble upon the magnificent stone circle of Avebury, a chance visitation that would lead to an ongoing preoccupation with prehistoric culture. As I progressed around the megalithic sites of Britain, Wilson's mind-expanding theories became even more pertinent to my own researches, but it was the ideas and pragmatic approach of T.C. Lethbridge that proved to be the most resounding and relevant to my own undertakings.

I acquired my first T.C. Lethbridge book from a secondhand bookshop in Winchester whilst visiting the West Country over the August Bank Holiday weekend of 1988. *The Essential T.C. Lethbridge* edited by Tom Graves and Janet Hoult, is an assemblage of Lethbridge's later works and contains a foreword written by Wilson. The significance of this find was further enhanced by the fact that I began reading the volume while sitting in a deckchair overlooking the sea on the Devonshire cliffs. I had paid no attention to the place I had chosen to camp until I began reading Lethbridge's encounter with ghoul phenomena at a place near his Branscombe home called Ladram Bay. The place name immediately rang alarm bells as I glanced up at the parking sticker affixed to my car windscreen that read: 'Ladram Bay Campsite'. The synchronicity of this encounter further enhanced the mystery of this enigmatic writer.

Along with a stream of coincidences, I encountered others along the way that had been equally influenced by Lethbridge. The fact that I was not alone in my discovery added to the esoteric nature of this intriguing figure.

On 24 September 1992, I was leafing through a copy of *The Independent* newspaper when I encountered a photograph of the rock musician Julian Cope leaning against the megalithic tomb known as The Devil's Den near Marlborough, Wiltshire. In the corresponding article, Cope discussed his recent interest in megalithic culture and his discovery of T.C. Lethbridge through the writings of Colin Wilson. By 1996, I had become acquainted with Cope, and the consequences of this union resulted in the release of *A Giant – The Definitive T.C. Lethbridge* in 2003. The work consisted of a double CD long-box set that included a 36-page booklet containing my own anthological review of Lethbridge's entire published works. The first disc contained rock music inspired by Lethbridge and the second consisted of spoken-word contributions from Colin Wilson, the man who had first initiated my fixation.

Since the release of *A Giant* and the launch of an associated website dedicated to Lethbridge (www.tc-lethbridge.com), there now appears to be a growing audience who find his ideas even more pertinent and relevant in this new millennium.

Lethbridge, like Wilson, revealed to me that there is more to the world than we are led to believe. The odd and the extraordinary are there to be disentangled and deciphered, not hidden away, or swept under the carpet. The significance of events on that November day in 1987 become even more pertinent when I explain how I had missed the train down to King's Cross the previous evening due to a sudden and inexplicable change of heart. It was a journey that would have seen me entering the King's Cross underground system at the time of the fire. My possibly life-saving decision is an occurrence that happens to someone, somewhere everyday of the week, but it is during these moments of intense significance when we feel glad to be alive. It is these crucial moments, or 'glimpses' as Wilson refers to them, that enable us to readjust our focus away from everydayness, onto the fundamentals of existence. It is this train of thought that motivated Lethbridge to test the barriers of his own comprehension.

Terry Welbourn - Lincoln – July 2010

Foreword

T.C. Lethbridge by Colin Wilson

Tom Lethbridge died of a virus infection in Exeter Hospital on September 30th, 1971. Three weeks earlier, on September 3rd, my book the *The Occult* had been published, and a correspondent suggested to me that I ought to get in touch with Lethbridge, who lived in Devon, only about a hundred miles away from my home in Cornwall. That seemed a good idea, for I had been acquainted with his work since 1965 when I had come across *Witches: Investigating an Ancient Religion* in a second-hand bookshop. Accordingly, I sent off a copy of *The Occult* by way of his publisher, Routledge and Kegan Paul. A couple of weeks later, I received a letter from his wife, Mina, saying that Tom had just died, and asking me whether she should return the book to me. I wrote immediately, saying, 'Please keep it by all means.' And we began to correspond.

It was pity I had left it so late. At least a year earlier, my wife Joy had started reading his *Ghost and Ghoul,* and began to tell me about his amazing theories on dowsing. The more she told me, the more I realised that I should have devoted a long section to him in *The Occult.* For Lethbridge's dowsing experiments had led him to the conclusion that the universe has many dimensions, and that the 'time world' in which we live is only one of the many possible worlds.

Expressed in that way, it sounds almost commonplace. We have been hearing something of the sort ever since Einstein created the theory of Relativity in the first decade of the twentieth century. But the way in which Lethbridge approached the matter was altogether more empirical and down-to-earth. Although his work could be used – and indeed I have used it –

as the foundation of a complex theory of the paranormal, he was not, particularly, interested in 'the occult'. As Terry Welbourn explains in this book, even Lethbridge's fascination with dowsing was only the outcome of his interest in archaeology. Archaeology, after all, means looking for things under the ground, and when Lethbridge was taking part in an archaeological dig on the Island of Lundy, he decided to try dowsing for volcanic dykes, now hidden under centuries of earth. At that point, Lethbridge, like most dowsers, was using a hazel twig. For the benefit of those who have never tried it, I should explain that the dowser begins by cutting a forked hazel twig, and then holding it by the two ends. As he walks above underground water, the dowsing rod twists upwards – or sometimes downwards – in his hands.

The strange thing about this is that the dowsing rod will find many things besides water. I have seen a dowser in my own dining room locating various coins which we had hidden under the carpet. He was a man named Robert Leftwich, and he explained to us that he could simply program his mind to look for anything. We tested this by placing copper coins and silver coins under the carpet, and he first of all demonstrated that he could find all the copper coins, then all the others.

This also explains the curious fact that 'map dowsing' is equally effective. It should of course be a nonsensical superstition, but the fact remains that it is not. Any good dowser can use a map to locate underground springs, as I discovered when one of them did precisely that at our remote farm cottage in Cornwall in 1957. It was not even a printed map – just one I had drawn with a pencil on a sheet of paper.

Lethbridge explained that the mind seems to have an extraordinary capacity for locating virtually anything. I am afraid there is nothing for it but to accept that we appear to possess some kind of paranormal faculty that can be tapped into with the use of dowsing rod – or, as Lethbridge later preferred, a pendulum, consisting of some sort of wooden bob on the end of a piece of string.

When the Lethbridges moved from Cambridge to the village of Branscombe in Devon in 1957, they made the acquaintance of an old lady who lived down the hill, and who was a 'witch'. She could charm warts, heal sick cattle and do various other things that are extremely useful to people living in country districts, and it was the 'witch' who advised Tom to use a pendulum rather than a dowsing rod.

Tom was fairly certain that the garden of their home, Hole House, must contain all kinds of artefacts that had accumulated over the centuries, and he found that he was able to locate all sorts of things with his dowsing rod. He soon found, however, that the 'witch' was right, and that a pendulum was just as effective. All he had to do was to hold it between finger and thumb, and it would go into a kind of circular swing whenever it had detected something.

Having the temperament of a scientist, Lethbridge then decided to try and experiment. Instead of a short length of string, he used a long piece wound around a wooden rod, so that it could be extended or shortened at will. Then, by testing various substances, he quickly reached the conclusion that the pendulum would react to various substances at different lengths. For example, it reacted to slate and concrete at 13 inches, glass at 14, running water at 26.5, gold at 29 and copper and brass at 30.5.

He soon devised an interesting method of exploring his garden. He would stand with the pendulum in one hand, stretch out his other arm, and move it slowly in an arc across the garden. As soon as the pendulum began to swing, he would draw a line from the spot where he was standing straight across the garden. Then he would move to another spot, and do the same thing. Where the two lines crossed, he would dig, and he invariably found something. If what he was looking for was silver or lead (which reacted at the same length) he would simply adjust the length of the string to 22 inches.

In this way, he discovered that all substances react at some length between nought and forty inches.

It was then that he made his most interesting discovery so far. He recalled that a colleague back in Cambridge had told him that a pendulum can tell whether a skull is male or female, and he demonstrated this by dangling one over an ancient skull. The pendulum swung back and forth which meant – apparently – that it was a man's skull. If it had swung round in a circle, the skull would have been female. (Midwives sometimes use the same method in determining the sex of an unborn baby.) In that case, it seemed to him that the pendulum was reacting to ideas as much as to material substances. And he quickly found that if he held an idea very clearly in his mind – like anger, evolution, male, female or death – the pendulum would once again react at a definite length. Death, typically enough, was precisely 40 inches. Male was 24 inches and female 29. He tested this by throwing stones at a wall and getting Mina to do the same thing. He then discovered that he could tell which stone either of them had thrown by whether it reacted at 24 inches or 29.

But what, he wondered, happened beyond 40? He tried testing a pile of sulphur, which reacts at 7 inches. He discovered that when the pendulum was 47 inches long, it once again reacted. And, in fact, the same was true of the lengths associated with various other substances: graphite (10), carbon (12) and so on. But there was a small difference. The pendulum no longer reacted directly above the substance, but slightly to one side.

Was it possible, Lethbridge wondered, that when the pendulum registers something beyond 40 inches, it registers a world beyond death – another dimension? He remembered an experience of being at the dentist under anaesthetic, and finding himself outside his body, hovering up in the air and slightly to the left – just like the 'displacement' reaction of the pendulum to the heap of sulphur.

He noticed another odd thing. Below 40 inches, there is no 'rate' for the concept of time; the pendulum will simply not respond. But when he lengthened the pendulum to 60 inches, he got a strong reaction for time. He reasoned that because 'our world' – that is the world that is registered below 40 – is 'in' time, there is no reaction to the idea of time itself, just as you could not appreciate the speed of a river if you were drifting down it in a boat. The fact that there was a reaction for time, 20 inches 'beyond death', seemed to indicate that there is a sense in which this a timeless realm.

Moreover, Lethbridge found that if he lengthened the pendulum beyond 80 inches (he had to stand on a flight of steps to do it), he got the same result all over again, as if there is yet another world – or dimension – beyond that one. And this 'third world' also has the reaction for time. But when Lethbridge lengthened the pendulum beyond 120 inches, he discovered that the world beyond that had no reaction for time.

Lethbridge's explanation of the strange 'power of the pendulum' is that there is a part of human mind – the unconscious perhaps – that knows the answer to all questions. Unfortunately, it cannot convey these answers to the 'everyday self', the busy conscious being that spends its time coping with practical problems. This 'other you' can convey its message via the dowsing rod or pendulum by the simple expedient of controlling the muscles.

Lethbridge, of course, was pragmatic enough to recognise that it was perfectly possible that his pendulum was not reacting to 'other dimensions'. But there could be absolutely no doubt that it was reacting to *something*.

In 1962, five years after the move to Devon, Lethbridge's ideas began to crystallize into a coherent theory, which he outlined in a book called *Ghost and Divining Rod*. This appeared in 1963, and aroused more interest than anything he had published so far. It deserved to be popular for its central theory was original, exciting and well-argued.

He suggested that nature generates fields of static electricity in certain places, particularly near running water. These 'fields' are capable of picking up and recording the thoughts and feelings of human beings and other living creatures. But human beings are also surrounded by a mild electric field, as the researches of Harold Burr of Yale University revealed in the 1930s. So if someone goes into a room where a murder has taken place and experiences a distinctly unpleasant feeling, all that is happening is that the emotions associated with the crime (such as fear, pain and horror) are being transferred to the visitor's electrical field, in accordance with the laws of electricity. If we are feeling full of energy, excitement, misery or anger, the emotional transference may flow the other way, and our feeling will be recorded on the field.

It was quite clear to Lethbridge that human beings are surrounded by 'hidden information' – in the form of impressions on an electrical field, exactly analogous to tape recordings. In fact, this idea had been suggested at the beginning of the twentieth century by the researcher Sir Oliver Lodge, who had suggested that the unpleasant 'atmosphere' in certain haunted houses is simply a kind of recording on the walls of the house. Lethbridge came to feel that this is particularly true in the presence of damp.

During his years at Hole House, Lethbridge stumbled upon an incredible number of interesting theories. One of these concerned the nature of time. In May 1964, a BBC camera team went to Hole House to record an interview with Lethbridge about dowsing. A young cameraman looked so dazed and startled as he got out of the car that Lethbridge asked him, 'Have you been here before?' The cameraman shook his head, 'No, but I've dreamed about it.' He asked if he could look behind the house. Pointing to the wall that Lethbridge had knocked down and rebuilt, he said, 'That wasn't like that years ago. There used to be buildings against it.' Lethbridge knew this was true – but not in his own time.

In the Herb Garden, the cameraman said, 'There used to be buildings there, but they were pulled down.'

Lethbridge knew about the 'time theories' of J.W. Dunne, which had caused a great sensation in the 1930s. Dunne was an aeronautic engineer who, around the turn of the century, had a number of impressive dreams of the future – for example, he dreamed accurately about the forthcoming eruption of the volcano, Mount Pelee, on Martinique. Dunne had suggested that time is like a tape or film which may get twisted and tangled, so that we can catch glimpses of other times. He used to keep a notebook and pencil by his bed and jot down his dreams the moment he woke up. He was convinced that we all dream about the future – probably every night of our lives – but that we forget it almost as soon as we wake up. J.B. Priestley went on to write a series of remarkable plays in the 1930s based upon his theories.

From then, Lethbridge also kept a notebook and pencil at the side of his bed, and made a note of his dreams, particularly if they were exceptionally clear. One night, he dreamed about the face of a man who seemed to be looking at him out of a mirror. He was doing something with his hands which seemed to be moving in the area of his chin. Lethbridge thought he might be shaving.

The next day, Lethbridge was driving slowly along a narrow lane when a car came round the corner, and at the wheel was the same man he'd seen in his dream. His face was framed by a windscreen – which was why Lethbridge had mistaken it for a mirror – and his hands were moving in the area of his chin on top of the steering wheel. Lethbridge was certain that he had never seen the man before. In due course, these remarkable discoveries also went into another of Lethbridge's books.

What I've said here can only a give a brief and hasty glimpse of some of the remarkable ideas that can be found in Lethbridge's eight books. (I am not including *Gogmagog: the Buried Gods*/ (1957) because this is an account of an archaeological quest.)

None of the Lethbridge's books are much over a hundred pages long, and none of them attempt to create a full and comprehensive theory of the paranormal. I have attempted to do something of the sort in my sequel to *The Occult (1971), Mysteries* (1978).

Yet, he ended with one firm conviction – that there is a meaning in human existence and that it is tied up with the concept of our personal evolution.

I would add, by way of commentary, that I have become convinced that all living creatures are being driven to evolve whether they like it or not. There is something in us that dislikes mere plodding, everyday existence and that experiences a craving for a more powerful form of consciousness.

Lethbridge's books certainly generate an excitement which produces precisely this effect.

Colin Wilson, Gorran Haven - July 2010

Introduction

The Man Who Saw the Future

At first glance, a story based upon the life and times of a one-time Keeper of Anglo-Saxon Antiquities in the University Museum of Archaeology and Ethnology, Cambridge is unlikely to whet many appetites. However, further investigation reveals to us that Thomas Charles Lethbridge was one of the most remarkable, yet overlooked men of the twentieth century. As well as being a respected archaeologist who wrote a number of well-received books based on his passion and understanding of British history, he was also a talented artist, an Arctic explorer and an experienced offshore sailor. However, his wide-ranging pursuits progressed far beyond the remits of his vocation into areas that challenge our very understanding of the universe. Mention his name today and it is likely that you will draw only blank expressions. Occasionally, however, you may hear the reply, 'Isn't he the pendulum man?' It is sadly ironic that Lethbridge, like many great writers, should solely be remembered for a single, specific aspect of their illustrious careers.

Lethbridge's story is unique, for not only did he live during an era that led to a golden age of archaeology at one of the great seats of learning; he also witnessed the world on the verge of a technological revolution. It was, however, his ability to recognise and then document his own unique role during this watershed period that has left us with a vital legacy. He was indeed a man who glimpsed the future and realising his own privilege and as a consequence, embarked upon a unique voyage of discovery. His approach and direction were considered too radical for his peers and many eventually chose to distance themselves from a colleague considered a loose cannon and maverick.

It would therefore be remiss to state that Lethbridge was simply an archaeologist, for there were many strings to his complex bow. He was a born explorer with an intensely inquisitive mind. This rational approach to his vocation enabled him to apply commonsense and intelligent solutions to historical conundrums that he encountered in the field. During his time at Cambridge, he accompanied his friend, the polar explorer Sir James Wordie, on three expeditions into the northern waters beyond Britain. These journeys fuelled his growing interest in ancient mariners and exposed him to unfamiliar prehistoric cultures and traditions. They also provided him with a wealth of experiences that he was able to draw upon for his own studies. It was this reliance upon primary research that was to be the key to his undertakings.

Lethbridge's tale is widely encompassing and, as well as the Arctic adventures, his colourful story includes groundbreaking archaeological excavations on Hebridean Islands, a controversial discovery of lost chalk-cut figures on a Cambridgeshire hillside, through to the pendulum experiments and investigations into dowsing, ESP and precognition at his final home in Branscombe, Devon. It was, however, the repercussions of his discovery of the hill-figures at Wandlebury Camp in the Gogmagog hills south of Cambridge that proved to be a turning point in his career. I have therefore considered it appropriate to separate this study into two parts, for it is a divide that reflects Lethbridge's own personal watershed.

Lethbridge was an astute observer and through his own experiences he was able to bring to life the lives of the people he chose to study. All of his books all have a strong personal flavour. He was also never afraid to challenge generally accepted notions. He threw off dozens of fresh ideas and possibilities, leaving it to less original minds to prove him wrong. When the latter occasionally happened, he was always the first to acknowledge any misjudgements, for he believed that dogma was the curse of sound learning. He often found the trade unionism of the academic world stifling and deadening and seized every opportunity to stretch the boundaries of his profession. He believed that without this kind of challenging enquiry, the intellectual evolution of the human race was doomed.

Throughout his work, Lethbridge demonstrated shrewdness and a canny understanding of his subjects and delivered his discourses with dry wit and humour. His vast general knowledge, combined with an enquiring mind, enabled him to perceive the world, not as a specialist, but as a champion of commonsense. He understood that to fully comprehend, one has to rid oneself of preconceived barriers and agendas. He believed in the middleman, the 'Jack-of-all-trades' approach, for he considered this position advantageous in his desire to test the waters of the academic hinterland. Unshackled by the dogma often associated with profession, he acknowledged that individuals who had a grounding in commonsense were better placed to facilitate and piece together the jigsaw from their concurrent position.

In retrospect, Lethbridge's genius is perfectly clear to us. Yet immediately after his death in a nursing home in 1971, it seemed likely that his lifetime's achievements might be forgotten. Fortunately, this injustice was avoided by virtue of a number of coincidences that would lead to him being recognised as a leading figure not just in the world of archaeology, but also in the field of psychical research. It is therefore ironic to commence Lethbridge's story with his untimely death, but as is often the case with such controversial figures, it is with the benefit of hindsight that we can best comprehend their story.In his foreword, Colin Wilson has already described how his introduction to Lethbridge was initially ignited by a recommendation by his wife Joy which eventually led to a meeting with Mina Lethbridge shortly after her husband's death. Mina's association with him also resulted in him contributing the foreword to Lethbridge's final, posthumous work *The Power of the Pendulum*. Credit is therefore due to Wilson, for acknowledging him as a major figure in the study of the paranormal. It is likely that he perceived Lethbridge as a 'like mind', for he too had found the need to move to the West Country to 'escape' the hostile glare of the media that labelled him as one of the 'Angry Young Men' after the release of his first book *The Outsider* in 1956.

Wilson once remarked how Lethbridge's breezy willingness to admit that he might be quite wrong always remained basically reassuring to him. Many have criticised his work for being repetitive, but Wilson believed that this was necessary, for his ideas were constantly changing and he often felt the necessity to revisit topics in the advent of new evidence. By reading Lethbridge, we are privy to a developing and evolving mind, which Wilson suggests is akin to the working journals of Leonardo, or any important discoverer. It would therefore be foolish to simply divide his published work into two camps, the 'historical' and the 'occult', for to do so would conceal the subtle but profound evolution that occurred throughout his writing. What we witness in his work is the development of an astonishing and original mind.

Lethbridge never set out to be a radical, although his pragmatic approach to his vocation often saw him at odds with his peers. He was a natural writer and his books stand out for their precision and erudite worth, but, unfortunately, many modern-day scholars still choose to steer clear of him due to the 'controversial' nature and subject matter of his later writings. However, their reticence is misguided, for his early works provide us with a unique study of British history. Ironically, it is for his final sequence of eight extraordinary books, which he wrote during the final decade of his life, documenting his investigations into 'occult' matters, that he is best remembered.

Lethbridge utilised the pendulum as a tool for divination. He believed that every inanimate object had the ability to store information, to somehow capture its history within itself. By using the pendulum as an instrument of detection, he believed he could unlock information 'recorded' within any given object. His explanation of ghosts and ghouls was based on a similar theory; in that rooms, places or atmospheres, could, in the right given conditions, somehow 'record' themselves onto the ether. For these 'recordings' to be replayed, it would, of course, require the right person and appropriate conditions to be present.

He believed that 'mind' was distinct from brain and that intellectual consciousness was a faculty that we had developed in our own evolution. He had problems with both the Darwinian vision of evolution and the view expressed by the theologians. He believed that a middle way was the more likely solution to the conundrums of human development and the growth of consciousness. The pendulum seemed to him an almost magical tool for detecting the 'recordings' imprinted on the world of matter. He truly believed that magic and the paranormal were simply powers of the mind that had yet to be explained by science. Throughout his work, he was always thorough in his own experimentation and meticulously recorded his findings. During the course of his work, he was quick to realise that 'hands on' research was the real key to discovery, while placing a reliance on other people's ideas lead to the perpetuation of heresy and dogma.

The body of work left behind by Tom Lethbridge reveals a man not content with accepting the limitations generally accepted by his fellows. His findings and discoveries must be viewed in the context of their time, that is; we must recognise that he was standing on the threshold of a brave new world. His originality is due to him stepping beyond the boundaries of his profession, and striding boldly into the dark. The result was a legacy of findings that are often startling, but never less than exciting.

Only today, four decades after his death, science is finally beginning to acknowledge that he was one of the most remarkable investigators of his time. His publishers, Routledge and Kegan Paul, are to be congratulated for their vision and foresight. Collectively, his later works build into a remarkable and unique study and demonstrate an enquiring mind unshackled by dogma and convention. Lethbridge did not set out to be controversial, he viewed his approach as being simply 'commonsense', something that he believed was lacking not just in his own in his vocation, but in the wider field of academia. He perceived this inability to see beyond the literal as an affliction that he termed 'the block'. It was an obstacle that inhibited not only his profession, but also one that transcended all aspects of comprehension. He believed that mankind's true potential could only be released once we had rid ourselves of preconceived ideas and agendas.

Terry Welbourn, Grantham, Lincolnshire – July 2010

PART ONE

Chapter One

A Silver Spoon

Thomas Charles Lethbridge was born at 4.00am on 23 March 1901. His parents, Ambrose and Violet (nee Murdoch) were a well-to-do couple in their mid-twenties who, at the time of their son's birth, were living at *Knowle House,* in the parish of Timberscombe in Somerset. Tom's father Ambrose was a prolific diarist and on the day of his son's birth, he recorded the details of his wife's difficult four-hour labour.[1] Ambrose was a man in possession of considerable wealth and the national census undertaken a month after Tom's arrival reveals that the Lethbridge household boasted six servants and a housemaid. Born with a silver spoon in his mouth, the young Tom Lethbridge was always destined to live a privileged existence.

The Lethbridge family line extends back to the twelfth century and boasts an ancestry of explorers, soldiers, sailors, members of parliament and churchmen renowned for their eccentricity. The family fortune was largely attributable to Tom's grandmother, Susan Anne Yarburgh – a local coal heiress, who married Tom's grandfather Charles at St. Lawrence Church, Heslington in Yorkshire on 25 January 1865. It is apparent that the family wealth enabled the Lethbridge men-folk to pursue their dreams without the worry of day-to-day subsistence. Tom's father, Ambrose, was acknowledged as a man of 'independent means' and was known to be a fine watercolour artist who specialised in painting insects and tiny landscapes. He had served as a Lieutenant in the Grenadier Guards, but on leaving the army had developed an interest in archaeology, botany and zoology. The Lethbridges were country folk who were unfamiliar and unconcerned with the workings of towns and cities.

Tom's grandfather once paid a visit to London with the objective of marrying-off one of his daughters, but was arrested at his lodgings for shooting dead a crowing cock that had awoken him from his slumber. When Tom was older, he reflected on his grandfather's folly, explaining: he had not been a stupid man, but just one who liked peace and quiet in his own domain. In fact, the whole of the Lethbridge family appears to have suffered from a 'devil may care' attitude, which often led them to pay the consequences for their riotous and insubordinate behaviour.

In contrast to the eccentric Lethbridges, his mother's side of the family appear to have adopted a more pragmatic approach to life. It was, in fact, Tom's great uncle John Hanning Speke who was honoured by the National Geographic Society for his discovery of the source of the Nile in 1863.

By 1907, the Lethbridge family had moved to *Lewell Lodge* in Dorchester where, on 7 June 1907, Violet gave birth to a daughter, Jacintha. The family appeared to have itchy feet, for on the birth of their second son, Ambrose William Speke (Bill), on 6 April 1907, they had moved yet again to *Trevissome* in the village of Flushing in Cornwall. It was here that the nearby harbours of Penryn and Falmouth became places of pilgrimage for the young Tom Lethbridge who soon became beguiled by the colourful flotillas in the marinas.

Towards the end of the decade, Tom's father contracted Tuberculosis and for practical reasons, the family moved in with his grandfather Charles who owned a house in Heytesbury, Wiltshire. Charles Lethbridge had gained enormous wealth by selling family-owned land in Somerset. He utilised his wealth to rent out a number of properties including *Trafalgar House* in Salisbury, *Firle Place* in Sussex, *Sherford Manor* in Berkshire and *Langton House* near Blandford. Tom recalled that his grandfather was often prone to hire a train that would take him, his family and staff, along with his rolled-top desk and hip-bath, to one of his many residences.[2] Verification of Ambrose's considerable wealth was confirmed by the sale of Sherfield House, Hampshire for £41,000 in 1899.[3]

It was, however, at his father's home in Heytesbury that Ambrose Lethbridge became consumed by his Tuberculosis and died on 11 September 1909. He was aged only 34. Tom was only eight years old and Violet was left to bring up her young family alone. In his will, Ambrose bequeathed Tom a princely sum of £15,000 (about £440,000 equivalent today) to be made payable to him on his 21st birthday.

By the time he was a teenager, Tom had already developed a love of the sea and once boasted that as a child he knew every vessel in *Jane's Fighting Ships*. Even when he was older, he claimed that he was still able to identify their silhouettes and armaments. It is likely that his fascination for ships was triggered by his boyhood visits to Falmouth harbour. A love of the ocean wasn't Tom's only passion; as a schoolboy he became intrigued by nature. Often accompanied by his good friend, Humphrey David; the pair would spend their leisure time out in the fields, studying birds, or collecting beetles. Their school museum housed a very fine collection of insects and Tom and David spent many industrious hours pulling out the drawers in the cabinets and learning the different species off-by-heart. By the time he was 16, Tom had taken an interest in art and, like his late father, he also developed fascination for drawing insects. It was a pastime that later developed to see him specialising in the rendering of landscapes and ships. Having been exposed to his father's work, it came as no surprise to him in later life to discover that his artwork bore a striking resemblance to his father's efforts.

At school, Tom developed an interest in archaeology and it was his enthusiasm for the subject that later inspired his school friend, William Syer 'Whiskers' Bristowe – who eventually became a leading authority on spiders – to eventually pursue the vocation at Cambridge. Even at school, Tom was influential, displaying virtues that would later prompt Bristowe to comment upon his, '...toughness, experience and self assurance.'[4] These were qualities that inspired confidence in his friend. Tom had grown up amongst men who the Victorians referred to as 'mighty hunters before the Lord'. They had taught him to observe detail in nature, for it was considered an essential weapon in the huntsman's arsenal. They not only taught him to scrutinise, but also installed in him the skills of recall. His mother's side of the family had boasted men who had become politicians and it is from them that Tom developed an insatiable curiosity and inquisitiveness. It was an aptitude that he grew to perfect, for he realised that primary knowledge was far more valuable than a lifetime of peering down microscopes and reading books. His grandfather once claimed: 'Nothing will induce me to believe that there are such things as microbes. They are not in the Bible.'[5] Tom considered that this statement demonstrated an inflexible indifference to learning and installed in him at an early age, a loathing of dogma and uncompromising principles.

In 1913, arrangements had been made for Tom to join the Royal Navy, but family plans were thrown into disarray when he failed his entrance medical due to poor eyesight. In later life, he once claimed that he had never been required to wear glasses and that his eyesight was as good as any man's. One can only speculate, but his desire to enlist might have simply been a façade to appease his family. His failure to join the Royal Navy resulted in him being ordained into the Rifle Brigade and four years later, with the outbreak of the First World War, he was sent to Wellington College. It would have been appropriate for a boy of his standing to be sent to Eton, but Tom's mother had once been told that it was an unhealthy place to send her child. After the war, Tom was destined for Sandhurst, but many, including his mother, believed that the Great War had been the war to end all wars and with this in mind, she chose not to enlist her son.

During the First World War, Violet and her young family moved into her mother's home at Buckhurst near Wokingham. Her mother, Sophia Murdoch, was the widow of Tom's grandfather, the late conservative MP for Reading, Charles Townshend Murdoch. After the death of her husband in 1898, Sophia had thrown herself into public service. As well as becoming President of the Reading Women's Conservative Association, a member of the Grand Council of the Primrose League, Honorary Private Secretary to H.R.H. Princess Christian in connection with the Soldiers' and Sailors' Help Society, Honorary Private Secretary to H.R.H. Princess Helena Victoria and President of the League of Mercy, she also found time to act as president of the Berkshire Operatic Club. In addition, she was secretary to the Waifs and Strays Society and often placed her home at the disposal of those deserving assistance. In light of her dedication, it appears that the accommodation of her daughter and her young family would not have proved too big an imposition on the kind-hearted Sophia.

It was just after the First World War that Tom had an encounter with what he would later describe as 'the odd'. On a winter's day, early in 1919, he and his mother took a walk from his grandmother's house at Buckhurst. The amble had taken them through the Great Wood and on to the road that joins the main entrance of the park, to the village of Easthampstead and past a covert known as Golden Ball. Tom and Violet walked up a ride into the thicket to enjoy the winter colours of the leafless trees. A few minutes had passed when they both experienced, what Tom would later describe as: '...a horrible feeling of gloom and depression, which crept upon us like a blanket of fog over the surface of the sea.'[6] Unable to shake off their experience, the couple hurriedly departed the wood. Two days later, the pair received news that the keeper of the Easthampstead estate, whilst out searching for a missing man, had discovered a dead body in the Golden Ball covert. The man had apparently committed suicide and his corpse must have lain only feet from where Tom and his mother had walked days earlier.

By February of the same year, Violet Lethbridge and her three children had moved to the Manor House in nearby Finchampstead, but only 10 years after the death of her husband, Violet was beset by yet another tragedy. During early spring, whilst Tom was away at Wellington College, a flu epidemic spread across Britain. Back home in Finchampstead his brother and sister both became seriously ill and although Jacintha's condition improved, Bill's health deteriorated and he eventually contracted meningitis. He never recovered from his illness and died at the family home on 15 March 1919.

Still reeling from the death of his brother, Tom returned to Wellington College to complete his schooling. Amidst her grief back home in Finchampstead, Violet was conscious that immediate decisions had to be made about her eldest son's future education. She was aware that the Lethbridge family had a long association with Oxford and Tom was relieved to discover that that the college he had been earmarked to attend, was not the one that his grandfather had once left in disgrace. Once again, things didn't go to plan and realising that her son had never been taught Greek, Violet sent Tom on a month-long course to instil in him the basic required knowledge. The intensive tuition was not a success and although Greek was compulsory for entry into Oxford, the same was not so at Cambridge. During his schooling at Wellington, Tom had acquired a fundamental knowledge of Latin and this was considered an acceptable entry requirement for the East Anglian university.

Tom formally enrolled in the university on 21 October 1921, having been admitted to Trinity College. It was his intention to study geology and geography for a 'Special' – an Ordinary BA without honours. On arrival, the famous buildings of Cambridge made little impression on him and he found the flat Cambridgeshire landscape boring and uninspiring compared to his previous homes in the West Country. However, things soon began to change and after witnessing the fields ripe with corn, he began to realise that Cambridgeshire had a unique charm all of its own. Tom was enrolled into Trinity College, although the objective of obtaining a degree during his time there did not dawn on him until fairly late in the day. The family wealth, which appears to have been a contributory factor to the previous lack of academic motivation in the Lethbridge family, was apparently rubbing off on Tom. As well as a private income that was paid into his bank account each quarter, he was soon to be eligible to access the funds bequeathed to him by his late father. He considered this money his own entitlement and not his family's money and he believed that any responsibility to education lay fairly-and-squarely upon his own shoulders. He realised that in the event of his failure, the money that many might have considered squandered, would have been his and his alone.

Tom soon realised that there were no penalties for the non-attendance of lectures and as he found most of them of little interest he often chose to not to grace them with his presence. However, on occasions when he did decide to make an appearance, it was mainly due to the industry demonstrated by his fellow students, who realised that their own diligence was crucial to their future subsistence. As a countryman, he found spending time alone in the city unappealing and therefore reluctantly chose to accompany his fellow students to lectures. His attendance was therefore due to the need for companionship rather than a desire to learn. His own attitude to a university education appears to have been almost nonchalant and no one was more surprised than Tom when, having sat examinations in 1922, he was placed in the second class.

The following year, he progressed to the third class before eventually graduating BA by proxy on 16 June 1923.[7] His further education continued with his subscription to embark on an MA, but his commitment to this or any other recognisable qualification was, to say the least, indifferent. The desire to be a perpetual student suited his immediate needs and his tuition fees provided mutual reciprocation for the university administrators. Fourteen years would pass before Tom was eventually awarded his MA by proxy on 19 June 1937.[8]

For a man who later demonstrated a passionate curiosity for all aspects of knowledge, his contempt for the Cambridge curriculum appears surprising. He claimed that: 'Geology was crushingly dull',[9] but his view of most subjects appears to have been influenced and prejudiced by those who tutored the given subjects. He was often critical of the lecturers and despaired at the futility of their archaic technique and approach to learning. He often pondered on the rationale of copying a drawing of a fossil from a blackboard when he could quite easily look up an example in a textbook. One subject, however, that did catch Tom's imagination was archaeology. His obsession became a distraction from his actual studies and he spent many long hours in the library mugging up on the subject. It was not long before his newfound interest brought him into contact with a group of men planning a journey to the Arctic island of Jan Mayen.

Chapter Two

The Cold North

In January 1921, whilst studying at Caius College Cambridge, a young botanist, aptly named James Chaworth-Musters, had a notion to assemble a party to visit Jan Mayen.[10] The island, situated within the Arctic Circle, is a small 'cutlet-shaped' landmass that lies 300 miles off the east coast of Greenland. Only 35 miles long, many believe that it was the island of *Svalbard* described in the Norwegian Sagas – a fact often disputed by Norsemen. In 1607, it became known as *Hudson's Tutches* after its 'discoverer', Henry Hudson. In 1614, a Dutch captain, Jan Cornelius May, claimed territorial rights for Holland and as a consequence of this tenure, the island was renamed after him. The first fully authenticated English visit was in 1615 by Robert Fotherby who referred to it as *Sir Thomas Smith's Island*. Other pioneers were soon to call it *Young's Foreland, Mauritius, Pico* and the *Isle de Richeliou*. The island was used by the Dutch and possibly the English, who kept its name and whereabouts secret mainly due to illicit whaling activities.

Aged only 19, Chaworth-Musters was an unusual looking character. He had light mustard-coloured hair and wore a darker mustard-coloured suit to match. He was a long lean character who drifted through the courts of Caius like a solitary bird. He was of a friendly disposition and had small blue eyes and a long protruding nose. His family were wealthy landowners from Nottingham and those who knew him considered him an introverted figure who chose to avoid games and college activities. Chaworth-Musters and his good friend William Syer Bristowe had both arrived in Cambridge in 1920, and Chaworth-Musters looked to Bristowe and his friend Tom Lethbridge to join him on his adventure. The inexperienced expedition party was further enhanced by the inclusion of James Wordie, a don from St. John's College.

Wordie was an experienced geologist, climber and explorer and had previously been part of Shackleton's unsuccessful attempt to reach the South Pole during the years 1914-1916. He was of a slight build, but an enigmatic figure that loved to make jokes in his broad Scottish accent. He was renowned for telling stories laced with fact and fantasy and almost every utterance was greeted with amused scepticism. Wordie was 14 years senior to the under-graduates and provided the party not only with experience, but credibility.

By 1921, the heroic age of polar exploration, pioneered by the likes of Shackleton and Scott, had passed. With most of the Arctic and Antarctic now plotted, the notion of journeying purely for the sake of adventure had reached an end. The emphasis of future exploration had now become science-based rather than heroic, and expedition parties assembled from the great universities of Oxford, Cambridge and Scotland soon became the norm. Funding had also become an issue, for in those post-war years, the Government was reluctant to contribute, and reliance was placed upon individuals to self-fund, hence those involved were usually young men from wealthy or privileged backgrounds.

Wordie, however, was a valuable asset to the proposed Jan Mayen expedition party; although his credentials lay in the heroic age, he was a prominent geologist and an experienced climber to-boot. The objectives he set for the Jan Mayen expedition were to study the geology, make collections of the wildlife, flora and fauna and to ascertain whether the island was still volcanically active. This final objective could be achieved by climbing the 7,470-foot Mount Beerenberg, a peak that dominated the island's northern region. The volcano had been named after the Austro-Hungarian Lieutenant Beer, who made a previously unsuccessful attempt at the summit in 1911.

During the planning of the Arctic expedition, Chaworth-Musters received word of a Norwegian party that was intending to visit Jan Mayen that coming summer. Funded by the Norwegian Government, the party was being led by Hagbord Ekerold, whose mission was to establish a weather station and to build a radio-transmitter on the island. Ekerold was a tall, swarthy man over six feet in height, who Bristowe once described as being, 'Good-looking in a fierce way with aquiline features, a strong chin and penetrating brown eyes.'[11] When approached, Ekerold was quite happy for the Cambridge party to join them on his expedition, albeit for the payment of a modest fee. The English contingent met up with Ekerold in Bergen on 10 July, but news of the expedition had spread and eventually reached the ears of a Swiss mountaineer and glaciologist called Paul-Louis Mercanton, a professor at Lausanne University. Mercanton was a portly, middle-aged man with a bridged nose and limpid eyes whose cheerful disposition inspired him to sing patriotic songs whenever the sun shone. It had always been Mercanton's ambition to climb Mount Beerenberg and after an approach to Ekerold, he too was accepted on board the expedition.

Wordie was delighted to have Mercanton onboard and remarked: 'We were thus unexpectedly reinforced by an experienced climber, who was also prepared to undertake glaciological studies in a unique field.'[12] Wordie had been impressed with Shackleton's man-management skills during the 1914-1916 Antarctic Expedition and being the eldest of the English party, he naturally assumed responsibility of the younger men, but this position was possibly undermined by Mercanton's late inclusion. Because of his experience, it was inevitable that Wordie would take control of the expedition, even though the initiation and the bulk of the arrangements had been instigated by Chaworth-Musters.

The younger men appeared unconcerned by the inclusion of an outsider and Bristowe, appearing to speak on behalf of the younger members of the party, remarked: 'We could scarcely help liking him (Mercanton) although he was helpless and so aggravating that he became the constant butt for jokes and criticism, all of which he took cheerfully and without malice.'[13] He continued, by suggesting that Wordie, although a likeable man, was not a born leader, although he had observed that he did always seem to get his own way. This was cannily achieved by some circuitous route rather than by direct order. Bristowe added that Wordie's greatest asset was his shrewd common sense. Being of a similar age and a skilled climber and a professor to-boot, Mercanton's presence possibly undermined Wordie's role as leader of the party.

After lengthy administrative delays and reports of skulduggery, the expedition, comprising of two vessels, finally departed from Bratvaag at nine o'clock on the morning of 1 August 1921. Nine of the men, including Ekerold, sailed in the *Polarfront* – a 25 ton, 45 foot wooden sealer. A similar, but larger vessel the *Isflugen* – 70 feet in length and weighing 45 tons – contained the remaining 12 of the party, including the five-strong Cambridge men comprising of Wordie, Chaworth-Musters, Bristowe and Lethbridge. The Cambridge contingent also included Richmond-Brown who was commandeered as a 'campman' to the party. During the voyage, both vessels encountered engine trouble and after a rough passage, they arrived at Jan Mayen after eight days at sea. *Polarfront* and *Isfuglen* were anchored in Jameson Bay and the parties rowed ashore.

The Cambridge party erected their tents at Jameson Bay, not too far from where Ekerold and his men began assembling their wireless plant. It was too late in the summer for studying the nesting habits of the island's bird life and for gathering flowering plants. Undeterred, Musters and Bristowe began the task of gathering fauna, whilst the others commenced their preparations for the assault on Mount Beerenberg. It was decided that the summit party would comprise of Wordie, Mercanton and Lethbridge, who incidentally had no climbing experience, but was chosen by Mercanton who described him as having, 'Incredible fitness, politeness and unbelievable self-discipline.'[14]

On the first day that the whole island was completely free of fog, the climbing party set off on their ascent of Mount Beerenberg. On 9 August, an advanced camp was established on the upper front of the moraines, 2,770 feet above sea level. The following day, the ascent of the Beerenberg was made through a wide, dry valley, aptly called the *Ekerold Valley* in honour of the Norwegian's achievement with regard to the establishment of the wireless station in Jameson Bay. The climbing party crossed a series of frontal moraines that passed above, and about two miles to the east of Palffy Crater. The small cinder vent had been visited and named by the previous Austrian party in 1911. The party chose the highest of the frontal moraines to pitch their tent.

The next morning brought heavy rain which delayed their progress, but by 11.00am they were ready to commence their ascent. For 300 feet they toiled up a gentle un-crevassed slope to a prominent nunatak, 5,600 feet above sea level. Here they found a cairn, established by the Austrian party as part of their previous survey. Wordie requested that Mercanton lead the party to the summit. He was to be followed by Tom, the least experienced climber, whilst Wordie chose to bring up the rear. The party encountered no real problems until a large crevasse was encountered at 7,200 feet, but Mercanton utilised his experience to expertly navigate the chasm.

After a climb of a further 400 feet, the bergschund was reached after Mercanton had skilfully scaled a vertical ice-wall. The party ascended a further 150 feet to a ridge of steep snow and they found themselves on the edge of the great ice-filled crater. The void was estimated to be half-a-mile wide, with a depth of 500-800 feet. One of the Beerenberg's later eruptions had breached its northern side and through this gap poured the Weyrecht Glacier, which cascaded down to the coast 7,500 feet below. The party had finally made it to the summit after an eight-hour climb from their advance camp.

Although having initial reservations about Mercanton, Wordie had allowed him to lead the ascent party, although his diaries reveal that he was critical of Mercanton's choice of route and his behaviour on the climb. Mercanton had the privilege of being the first to reach the highest point of Beerenberg and it was possibly this honour that left a sour taste in Wordie's mouth. It was an act that resulted in the later criticisms recorded in his diary. Whilst at the summit, Mercanton marked the occasion by burying a cylinder containing souvenirs collected from the party. His contribution included the first tooth of his only child. Wordie was not impressed with this emotional gesture, especially after Mercanton had insisted on flying the Swiss flag above the Union Jack. Wordie's distaste was shared by Tom who demonstrated his aversion in a more light-hearted way by depositing a fly-button in the cylinder, a sarcastic gesture in opposition to Mercanton's sentimental act.[15] The party were, however, the first to reach the summit after two previous failed attempts.

Mercanton, Wordie and Lethbridge remained at the summit for two hours in the hope that the mist-obscured sun would reveal itself in all its glory to enable them to take a fitting photograph. The descent was further delayed due to Mercanton's dallying; his behaviour puzzled Tom, and he recorded the Swiss as being somewhat, 'Strange in his actions.'[16] During their vigil, Wordie made aneroid readings and gave the Beerenberg a reading of 8,090 feet. His analysis revealed a discrepancy from the previous Austrian party's theodolite measurement of 8,350 feet. Although it had taken then eight hours to reach the summit, they returned in half that time.

The evening was spent at the ascent camp and the following morning they were awoken by the high-spirited Mercanton:

'Woken up confoundedly early (8am) by Mercanton singing lewd French songs.'[17] Tom recorded his disdain in his diary: 'Cursed inwardly.'

Departing the ascent camp, they abandoned their camping equipment, for it was their intention to return to make a second ascent of the Beerenberg, but this ambition was never realised. On returning to the camp on 29 August, they discovered their tent had blown down and was filled with ice and the ensuing blizzard forced them to retreat to base camp.

After the encounter with Beerenberg, Tom and Wordie relieved Bristowe and Musters at the southern camp. During their stopover, the pair made a number of excursions out across the island; one included visiting Mercanton who was undertaking studies of the southern glacier. Tom tells of one particular sortie where he and Wordie climbed all of the southern peaks of Jan Mayen in a single day.[18] The pair had camped in a small, two-man tent on what Tom described as an ash-desert where they were visited by an unwelcome blue-fox cub that entered their tent. On one expedition, he explained how the pair where enveloped by a fog that disorientated them and hindered their return to camp. He insisted that he had had a good idea of which direction to proceed, but Wordie was resolute on using his compass and led them to a rocky headland overlooking bays they had never witnessed before. The compass appeared to be a complete half-circle wrong. Pragmatically, Tom stated that you must always trust your compass, or go by the light of nature. He had trusted Wordie, but admitted that he would have taken a different route himself. The pair arrived safely back at their tent at 10:30pm, after climbing another 1,500 feet to their camp.

It was during this excursion that Tom encountered the 'Brocken spectre' phenomenon that he was to frequently refer to in his later works.[19] He describes how a gleam of sunlight through the mist had thrown monstrous images of their dirty and unshaven figures on to the fog across the valley.[20] He concluded that this was most probably how stories of giants and supernatural beings had originated, an observation which led him to later proclaim:

> ...there is no such thing as supernatural. All phenomenon classed under the heading are natural phenomenon, governed by natural laws, but these laws have as yet to be worked out.

The party's mountaineering achievement was eventually recognised by *The Times* and heralded as the mountaineering event of the year. Wordie was given full credit for the achievement and there was no mention of Mercanton being the first to reach the summit. It was, however, Wordie who cannily cabled their achievements to Arthur Hinks back home at the Royal Geological Survey. The conquering of Beerenberg also realised one of the party's objectives by establishing that the volcano was no longer active. The expedition was also a success for the Norwegian contingent that had independently gone about their own business on the island by instituting their weather station and installing radio communication to the island. Their own government acknowledged their success when the island was eventually proclaimed part of Norway in 1929.

As Bristowe acknowledged: 'The younger members of the party had also gained something intangible which combined a feeling of self-reliance with a thirst for more adventure.'[21] Bristowe was indeed perceptive, for the Jan Mayen expedition of 1921 was just the start of a lifetime of adventure and discovery for Thomas Charles Lethbridge.

The 1921 expedition provided Tom with his first opportunity to undertake archaeological digs at abandoned Eskimo houses around Baffin Bay. On arriving back in Cambridge, he returned with a large collection of antiquities collected on his travels. One of his finds included a perfect little volcanic 'bomb' that he discovered beside a small crater on the island. The discovery, which was about the size of a golf ball with a tail upon it, was of obvious geological interest and captured James Wordie's imagination. On the journey home, Tom went to inspect his geological curiosity only to discover that it was missing from his luggage. It was immediately obvious that the 'bomb' had been filched and Tom suspected that the culprit was Wordie. When the opportunity arose, he made a search through the suspect's belongings and, sure enough, found the missing object. Retrieving it, he chose to lodge the 'bomb' in a more secure hiding place amongst his own belongings. By the time the party arrived back in Norway, this 'cat and mouse game' had been repeated several times with Wordie proving to be the eventual winner. The two men never discussed the incident and Tom philosophically conceded defeat, for he realised that the object would eventually end up in the Sedgwick Museum. He realised that Wordie's intentions were honourable and that the geological curiosity was deserving of a prestigious location in the museum and concluded: 'Never trust a curator, whose heart is in his job, with anything you value.'[22]

Two years after their successful trip to Jan Mayen, James Wordie embarked upon his fourth voyage in the northern oceans. The expedition was undertaken in the summer of 1923 and provided Tom with another Arctic adventure. This time, the seven-strong party was made up of six Cambridge men, many of whom, including Tom, had just completed their degrees. Accompanying Wordie and Lethbridge on the voyage were Lord Cawdor, C.C. Duchesne, R.H. (Bobby) McClaren and L.S. Mayne. The party was further enhanced by the inclusion of Tom's school friend, Humphrey David. The objective of the expedition was to explore the east coast of Greenland, conduct geological and archaeological investigations and repeat the pendulum gravity experiments that had been carried out by Edward Sabine between 1818 and 1820.

'In glorious weather,' the *Leda* departed Newcastle at 5.00pm on 7 July.[23] The party arrived at Bergen at 8.30am the following morning and the day was spent sightseeing. This included a visit to the local museum where they viewed a wonderful collection of Viking antiquities. The next day, they departed for Tromso onboard the *Haakon VII* and after making a number of ports of call, they arrived at their destination at 5.30am on 14 July. That evening was spent at the Grand Hotel where they ate dinner – a meal that upset the stomachs of both Tom and David. However, the pair had recovered sufficiently the following morning to visit the museum and to then take an afternoon stroll where they chanced upon some Lap tents that were made from sods of turf.

The party set sail from Tromso at 8.00pm, onboard the *Heimen,* captained by the experienced Norwegian Lars Jakobsen. The journey began well and their first port of call was to the previously established radio station on Jan Mayen. Their departure, however, was late in the season and encroaching ice hindered their progress. The party departed Jan Mayen on 21 July and two days later they had entered the pack ice in 74° 30′ N. By July 27, *Heimen* had reached within 30 miles of the coast and the land from Cape Broer Ruys and Sabine was clearly visible. The 72-ton sealer had passed from light open ice pack into a region of extremely heavy floes and within 24 hours, had become imprisoned by the encroaching pack ice. For James Wordie, the scenario would have bought back disturbing memories of his previous entrapment on board *Endurance* as part of Shackleton's failed attempt to reach the South Pole eight years previously.

The prolonged delay in the ice put a strain on the expedition's food supplies and the party were forced to supplement their diet with polar bear meat. Tom remarked that the shooting of the polar bears was far worse than shooting dogs, but realised that when needs must, beggars could not be choosers. On one occasion on 24 July, he recalled a bear that had been wounded and not killed outright. The animal roared in pain and attempted to escape from its hunters across the ice. Not wanting to see the animal suffer, Tom joined a party of men to pursue the beast to put it out of its misery. During the chase, he stepped upon a snow-covered crack in the floe and plummeted into the polar sea. After being rescued by David – who had previously suffered a similar fate – he nonchalantly shrugged off the incident, suggesting that his fall into the icy death trap had filled him with surprise rather than terror. It was, however, an experience that he would utilise as a unique metaphor for his later discoveries as a result of his own experimentations into 'the odd'.

Under the skilled seamanship of Jakobsen, *Heimen* was navigated eastwards into more open waters. Once the edge of the ice pack had been reached, it was apparent that the ice margin had been driven 30 miles to the west between 23 July and 4 August. A week of dense fog engulfed the party, but eventually cleared enabling Jakobsen to make another, but unsuccessful, effort to reach the Greenland coast. The party then attempted to access the mainland by following the ice edge south to Scoresby Sound, but once again any approach was deemed impossible.

During their time trapped in the pack ice, the party continued to supplement their diet by shooting polar bears and grey seals. The bearskins were salted and put into barrels and since the blubber had been taken off they were allowed to drag astern in the water. A layer of salt was then rubbed into the skin and then it was folded up and put into a barrel and a strong solution of brine poured in. To relieve the boredom, the party would regularly venture onto the floes and partake in games of golf and ice hockey. On the evening of 12 August, Tom, Cawdor and David took to sea on a sealing expedition onboard the ice-boat *Bismark*. The fog descended and the party soon became disorientated and it seemed likely that they would have to spend the night on the floe under their upturned vessel. However, after rowing for about half an hour, the *Heimen* was sighted and they returned to the ship just as she was about to sound her foghorn to attract them.

The *Heimen* had spent the best part of a month desperately doing battle with the ice, but by mid-August the expedition to reach Greenland was abandoned, much to Wordie's frustration. After a 'counsel of war', it was Jakobsen who finally made the decision to return home, for he no longer wished to risk his ship, or further endanger his crew. The decision to abort the expedition was a setback and as a result of their disappointment, many of the party felt that Jakobsen and his crew had abandoned the mission too easily and were critical of his approach. David noted in his log:[24]

> All they have done is go up and down in the loose pack ice and when a favourable day occurred steam west until they came to the heavy Polar ice and then go straight back again into the loose ice & then steaming in a SE or NE direction & again go in. It seems that they should have kept more to the edge of the heavy Polar ice so as to avail themselves of a possible opening. Any way they would be on the spot instead of being out away in the loose pack ice where they could not possibly see an opening in the Polar ice.

The comments, however, were born out of frustration and with hindsight Jakobsen's decision to abort was the only sensible option at such a late juncture of the season.

On 19 August, the dejected party made a brief stop at Alden – a town of about 1,000 inhabitants – at the head of Seydisfjord before arriving back in Aberdeen on 29 August. Here they took delight in shaving for the first time since leaving Tromso – 45 days previously. Jacobsen was quite emotional on their departure and seemed genuinely sorry that he had failed to get their party to Greenland. After saying their farewells, the party separated and Tom, Duchesne and David caught the 7.30pm train to

Euston. Fourteen years would pass before Tom would receive a further opportunity to return to Arctic waters.

As a consequence of the haul of Eskimo finds and curiosities that Tom had accumulated during his Arctic expeditions, he often found himself frequenting the University Museum of Archaeology and Ethnology back home in Cambridge. Here he would spend hours drawing specimens of various types of brooches and other archaeological finds. The drawings enabled him to assemble a personalised textbook of antiquities housed in the museum. His interest in archaeology and his induction to the Cambridge museum was to prove to be crucial to his career; it was here that he would encounter a body of men who would shape and influence his own thinking.

Chapter Three

Ghosts and Ghouls

Tom had been only 18 when he first experienced the 'ghoul' whilst out walking with his mother in the Golden Ball covert near Wokingham. However, this brush with 'the odd' appears not to have been an isolated incident. Whilst he was studying at Cambridge, his mother, Violet, moved into a rented a house in the Shropshire village of Little Ness. The house was situated near to a medieval church that had a large burial mound that Tom believed to be associated with the Roman, or Anglo-Saxon period. During university holidays, Tom would often visit his mother in her Shropshire home and during his stopovers, he claimed to have experienced an unpleasant feeling, similar to which he had previously experienced in the Golden Ball covert. The Little Ness 'ghoul' appeared to permeate his bedroom, a room darkened by the presence of a large cedar tree that grew outside the window. The tree had been planted too close to the window and blocked out the light making the room dark and dingy. He claimed that if his mother had actually owned the property, he would have encouraged her to have it chopped down.

The owner of the rented property had once lived in the house and his wife claimed that her young son, who had since died, had often enjoyed climbing the tree. The boy's mother had often demonstrated a desire to return to the house because of the happy memories associated with it. Tom deduced that the room was somehow haunted by the presence of the dead child and that the presence in his bedroom was possibly a projection from the boy's mother's mind. Although he was never able to see the dead boy, he believed that someone on the correct wavelength would be able to pick up the images that he believed were being projected by the dead boy's mother.

Two facts emerged from the Little Ness experience; the first was that Tom himself was the receiving set and, secondly, he knew the identity of the transmitter. He concluded that the ghoul in the bedroom had no connection with the spirit-world and that the sensation that he had experienced was simply a projection from the mind of another living person. Tom never mentioned the sensation that he had experienced in his bedroom to his mother, but her presence in this and the Golden Ball incident appeared to be a common factor, therefore suggesting that she too was possibly 'sensitive' and prone to such happenings. It is likely that Tom inherited his own faculty from his mother's side of the family. It is from these early experiences of 'the odd' that Tom began to formulate his theories on ghosts and ghouls.

Whilst studying at Cambridge, Tom would have been first to admit that he was far from being a model student, but he doesn't appear to have been alone in his indifference to further education. He was one of a group of privileged young men, whose thoughts were preoccupied by shooting, fishing and sailing rather than concentrating on their university studies. One such student who shared Tom's indifference to learning was Geoffrey Walford, who occupied a room in New Court at Trinity. Walford became friendly with Tom after the pair had undertaken a Hebridean voyage together in the summer of 1922. The expedition had been hastily arranged after plans for a second Arctic adventure with James Wordie had been shelved. Joining them on the adventure were Wordie, Tom's school friend William Syer Bristowe and the eminent Cambridge geologist Alfred Harker. The party sailed on a 16-ton yawl called the *Elspeth* hired from and captained by a gnarled old Highlander called John Robertson, a man who knew every treacherous tide and shoal in the western waters.

Elspeth departed Gourock in the Firth of Clyde and journeyed through the Kyles of Bute and along the Crinan Canal and the tide races in Scarba Sound to the Garvellachs , before crossing over to the Outer Hebrides.[25] The party enjoyed stops at Oban, Tobemorry, Eigg and Rum, also staying over at Loch Torridon, Gairloch, the Summer Isles and Lochniver. On Friday 21 July 1922, the party departed from Tarbert on Harris on their homeward journey to Skye. Whilst crossing The Minch, exceptionally calm weather impelled them to have a change of heart and it was decided that there would be an impromptu stop on Eilean Tighe, one of a group of islets that form the Shiant Islands.[26] The party's request to explore the island didn't go down too well with their skipper. Robertson was at first defensive of his desire not to land, but in a whispered voice he warned them: 'Yon island is nae place to visit. The wee green folk dinna like it.'[27] Robertson had grown up with the superstitions and folk-tales of the islands and it was left up to Wordie to pacify their skipper. It was decided that there was no need for Robertson to land and once reassured, he agreed to row the party ashore and then return to *Elspeth* and circumnavigate the island until his passengers were ready to return.

The landing party took with them their lunch, which consisted of a wicker basket containing sandwiches, five bottles of beer and a mackintosh to act as a groundsheet. To lighten their load, they deposited their lunch on the summit of a grassy bank and proceeded about their business on the island. Tom discovered the ruins of a shepherd's cottage and soon unearthed the remains of a much earlier kitchen midden. Bristowe stayed close to Tom and pursued his own investigation into the insects and spiders of the island. On reconvening, the party were astonished to discover that their lunch had vanished – wicker basket and all. The disappearance astounded both Tom and his friend, for both chose to comment on the unusual incident in their diaries. There seemed to be no possible explanation, for their landing party included the only visitors to the island. There had been no opportunity for Robertson to return to the island to snaffle their lunch; in any case, they trusted him implicitly. The notion that an animal or a bird had filched the heavy basket was considered to be out of the question. On hearing of the vanishing basket, Roberstson was keen to get the party away from the island, insisting that the disappearance was due to the little folk who it was told, didn't like intrusions on their island. 'Let us be away before worse befalls... I warned ye,' he prophetically remarked.[28] On the journey back to Skye, whilst Robertson was cooking the lythe he had caught earlier in the day, Bristowe discovered that a dozen glass tubes, stored in his waistcoat had also vanished. He was certain that he hadn't dropped these whilst on Eilean Tighe and once again, the disappearance was accredited to fairy folk activity. The missing test tubes and the vanishing lunch were indeed a mystery, but one can't help speculating that either Roberstson or one of the other members of the party took a less ethereal explanation of the mysterious events to their grave!

Tom was with Geoffrey Walford when he experienced his first sighting of a ghost later that same year. One evening, the two friends were sitting in Walford's room in New Court at Trinity College. It was approaching midnight when Tom, feeling weary, decided to retire to his bed. Rising to his feet, he said goodbye to his friend and turned towards the door. Just as he did so, a man wearing a top hat entered the room and rested his hands upon the table. Tom bade his friend and the stranger a 'good evening.' The stranger didn't reply and Tom left the room. The next day, he bumped into his friend on Trinity Street and enquired of the porter's business the previous evening. Walford seemed puzzled and replied that he hadn't received any visitors, apart from Tom, that evening. A short disagreement followed before Tom reached the conclusion that he had in fact witnessed a ghost.

The porters at Trinity were accustomed to wearing top hats, but only on Sundays. At the time of the sighting, Tom hadn't realised that it wasn't a Sunday and had ingenuously presumed that the man he had witnessed was indeed a concierge. After thinking long and hard about the man's appearance, he realised that the figure he had seen wasn't a porter after all, but a huntsman dressed in hunting kit. He concluded that the pale, slightly built man with the pointed face that he had seen in Walford's room was possibly a projection of one of the many Buxtons who had a history of occupation in the room now taken by his friend.

Tom believed that the projection – like the one he had experienced at Little Ness – was created subconsciously by the mind of a person still living, or the memories of someone long deceased. Initially, he had suggested that Walford had in some way been responsible for the 'projection' of the Trinity ghost, but later concluded that he did not know who was responsible, or who was transmitting. To simplify his theory, he was to later use BBC engineers as an example: the engineers were not responsible for the content of the programmes they transmitted and they were also not the power that actually broadcast them, yet their minds were necessary for the actual broadcasting to take place. He applied this analogy to a ghost, suggesting that some minds think up the ghostly projections, while others provide the force to actually project them. His scenario would also require a third 'responsive' party to actually witness or receive the images. It was this 'sensitive' role that Tom had once again fulfilled that night in Walford's room.

Throughout his later works, Tom would cite numerous tales of his encounters with 'the odd' and it is blatantly clear that he was sensitive to such occurrences. By reading through his works, we are able to construct in our mind's-eye a unique picture of his fascinating and intriguing world. He never deliberately set out to make a study of 'the odd'; in fact, the occurrences he experienced were simply by-products of his more formal investigations. However, the incidents became so frequent that they couldn't be ignored. It was always his remit to simply 'find things out' and he therefore saw no division between his historical studies and his investigations into the paranormal.

As we study his books, we are privy to an intellect that develops and advances before our very eyes. Tom's skill was that he was able to combine the 'far-out' and the mundane with such dexterity that the two become intrinsically linked. There were many strings to his proverbial bow and the reader is inclined to ponder on his influences and what made him tick. It is indeed a privilege to witness first-hand the workings of this imaginative and unravelling mind.

Chapter Four

The Magic Key

Throughout his work, Tom demonstrates startling clarity, but the inspirations behind his complex trains of thought remain intriguingly elusive. His ability to discuss such diverse subjects as the horned beetle known as 'bolboceras armiger' alongside the oscillation of a pendulum during the divination of truffles in his garden is truly remarkable.[29] His published works provide us with many clues, but notes compiled for his unfinished autobiography *The Ivory Tower* – written during his final years – reveal glimpses of those who influenced and shaped his thinking. The annotations are crucial to our understanding, for they provide us with an insight into his life at Cambridge. Tom also claimed his notes were an attempt to,

> Dispel the popular concept of dons as being a collection of quiet delicate-minded men in ivory towers, who have never seen the world and are hardly cognisant of the facts of life.[30]

Tom's private income provided a 'safety net' that facilitated a footloose and impetuous approach to life. His initial indifference to his studies and undertakings at Cambridge epitomise this stance. From his privileged position, he was able to view the world very differently from his peers. His friend William 'Whiskers' Bristowe's anecdotal references enable us to elucidate Tom's presence and it is clear from these citations that he initially arrived at Cambridge for the experience and not with any specific, or academic objective.

Whilst at university, he was privileged to rub shoulders with scholars from a wide variety of disciplines and he utilised these associations to his own advantage. Although initially unfocussed, he was no idler and he astutely embraced his opportunities, ensuring that he fully exploited his contacts with the great men with whom he had become associated at this great seat of learning. It is from these inadvertent beneficiaries that he compiled his wide-ranging database of wisdom. We know that he was a great believer in the power of general knowledge and although he respected the vocation of the specialist, he later realised that a universal perspective was required if the mysteries of our ancestors, or our universe for that matter, were to be unravelled.

Tom considered himself fortunate to have lived during the tail end of a golden age. He considered it an honour to have co-existed with men who had knowledge of 'the old ways' and were cautious of the mechanisation of their vocation. He considered the experience of associating with those who had once utilised ancient methods of agriculture and transport to be to his advantage. During his time at Cambridge, there were still men at Brandon who knapped flints for muzzle-loading guns and his observance of these skills enabled him to see how easily it could be done. He believed that this knowledge was advantageous in the interpretation of ancient things, often only perceived in a vestigial light. This insight and 'hands-on' approach enabled him to comprehend the detail and the intimacies of his vocation. He believed that those who grew up in the mechanised age would lack the benefit of first-hand experience; he therefore valued his privileged position during this unique watershed.

It is likely that one of the first men Tom encountered at Cambridge was Miles Burkitt – son of the distinguished divinity professor F.C. Burkitt. In 1913, Burkitt jnr had become the first to deliver public lecture sessions at Cambridge. As a consequence of these addresses, the Board of Anthropological Studies had recommended the establishment of an undergraduate BA Honours Degree in Anthropology at the university. When Tom started his own degree at Cambridge in 1919, Burkitt was earning a living from fee-paying students and perceived himself as a knowledgeable amateur. In her study of prehistory at Cambridge, Dr. Pamela Jane Smith describes Burkitt as a dilettante with a moral purpose and suggests that he 'Delighted in the avocation of prehistory.'[31]

Burkitt was no original thinker and his position was therefore at odds with Tom Lethbridge who simply wished to find things out. They were destined to be eternally at odds regarding procedure and protocol and their spats became legendary in the university corridors. In 1932, Tom became embroiled in a confrontation with Burkitt and Grahame Clark, for their failure to acknowledge investigations carried out at Shippy Hill by Tom's friend, Derek Leaf. In a letter to his good friend, Sir Cyril Fox, Tom wrote:

> Well to cut the thing short, he (Burkitt) took G. Clark down and sure enough there was a tiny sand island covered with implements and scraps of broken pottery. When they got back, Burkitt was so excited that he wetted himself three times and without a word of congratulation to Leaf or consulting anyone got G. Clark to dig the place.[32]

Disagreements between the pair were often prolonged and public affairs, but their relationship appears to have prevailed without any lasting animosity.[33] It is likely that Burkitt's theological views provided common ground for discussion, for he believed that the soul equated to conscious intelligence and was a trait developed in humans during the Upper Palaeolithic period. He had conceived this view from his study of the Old Testament and his European anthropological studies. Although Tom wouldn't have shared his religious beliefs, it is certain that the two would have enjoyed theological debates that would have provided Tom with trains of thought that would influence his later thinking.

It was during Tom's frequent visits to the University Museum of Archaeology and Ethnology that he encountered the curator, Louis Clarke. Clarke was an enigmatic character and made an immediate impression on Tom. Of slight build and short in height, Clarke stood out from the other dons with his laid-back sense of dress and long hair. Many likened him to a clean-shaven version of Charles I, although Tom considered him to be more of an Oliver Cromwell type figure. Clarke once explained to him that he dressed and wore his hair long so that people would think him eccentric, an impression that provided him with a carté-blanche to 'get away with murder'. It is likely that Tom found this edgy attitude appealing. Clarke, however, was not what he seemed. Although at Cambridge he was considered the height of respectability; in London, he was known to live 'the highlife'.

Clarke had been encouraged to take the post of curator at Cambridge museum by Sir William Ridgeway. He was a wealthy man who had a vast span of general knowledge, although he did confess to a profound disliking of the Romans and Ancient Egyptians. His vast knowledge, however, didn't stretch to music or motorcars, subjects that he professed to know next-to-nothing about. He was a good-natured soul who was able to see the funny side of most things and in his old age, developed a genius for finding and sending vulgar postcards to his friends at Christmas time.

Clarke took a liking to the new industrious and focussed Tom Lethbridge who had now become a frequent visitor to his museum: often spending hours sketching and drawing objects. Clarke encouraged his visitations and on one occasion, Tom reciprocated and invited Clarke over to Trinity to view some of the Viking objects that he had brought back from a recent expedition to Scotland. Tom had been warned about dons and their unique ability to filch objects for their own collections and Clarke was no exception and usually got what he wanted. He was even known to spend evenings playing bridge in order to win a single pot, or a relic for his collection. Tom also accompanied Clarke on numerous missions out into the Cambridgeshire countryside to buy and obtain objects for the museum. He soon realised that his mentor had an uncanny knack of obtaining items at knockdown prices. It was a gift, which, unfortunately, Tom did not share with his friend.

After obtaining his degree, Tom found himself at a loose end. He had decided not to go into business, for he believed that the government would only take away any money that he earned. His dilemma was eventually solved when Clarke made him an appealing offer:

> Wouldn't I like to come to Cambridge as a volunteer and dig for him? This was a great compliment for, as I had never entertained the thought of going into business, I accepted his offer and never regretted my decision.[34]

Tom's role as the Keeper of Anglo-Saxon Antiquities was purely an honorary position; however, he took his responsibility seriously. Coupled with his own private income, he was able to pursue his vocation without the pressures normally associated with employment. His work at the museum also brought him into contact with a host of people who brought with them their own unique skills and personalities.

On returning from the 1921 Jan Mayen expedition, Tom continued his friendship with James Wordie, often joining his friend on car journeys out into the Cambridgeshire countryside in search of geological formations, or flint implements. It was during these frequent fieldtrips that Tom's interest in archaeology was fuelled. He suspected that Wordie found archaeology more appealing than his own profession of geology. It was a hunch that was confounded when his friend eventually became Chairman of the Faculty Board of Archaeology and

Anthropology. On returning from Jan Mayen, Wordie was elected a Fellow of St. John's College and appointed a tutor there in 1923. Despite his position, Tom had always doubted his friend's commitment to his chosen vocation; not once during their trip to Jan Mayen had Wordie been spotted with a geological hammer in hand. In fact, Tom wondered if his friend knew anything about geology at all.

Wordie, however, was quite canny when it came to the rub and when once questioned about his geological knowledge he responded by stating: 'I can get £100 any time I like from some firm or other for what I have learnt.'[35] Tom claimed that although Wordie had his full share of Glaswegian shyness, he maintained a finger in many university pies.

Although not a demonstrative character, Wordie had returned from the First World War, where he had served as a gunnery officer, to discover that St. John's was full of conscientious objectors. It was rumoured that it was his clandestine skills that eventually led to them all eventually being removed. Tom knew that behind his broad grin and twinkling eyes was a man who, albeit in a round about fashion, always got his own way.

Wordie was blessed with a sense of humour and was more than happy to be the butt of Tom's japes and torments. On one occasion, whilst walking around Tom's garden, he asked the name of a plant. His host replied: 'That James is something you'll never have heard of. It's called Honesty.'[36] The comment tickled his friend. Tom was always one for inventing nicknames and often referred to his learned friend as 'the sea-green incorruptible'; however, Wordie answered to many names, including 'Lord Bergen of Zoom' and 'the stormy petrel'. It is clear that on his entry into Cambridge, Tom not only made an impression on his fellows, but also on the senior men of Cambridge. As well as being good company, Wordie was impressed with his young friend's ability to observe and his eye for detail.[37]

Another of Tom's fellows who boasted a nickname was Cyril Fox, who was known throughout the university as 'Samos'. The name was derived from a type of red, Roman pottery often found in the Cambridgeshire region. As well as lecturing, Fox also managed the field laboratories in Milton Road and had even found time to write a book entitled *The Archaeology of the Cambridge Region (Cambridge University Press, 1923)*. It was a publication that had advanced the whole outlook of British archaeology and had earned the author a Doctorate of Philosophy. It was a title that was to haunt Fox, for if his fellows ever had occasion to question him, they referred to him as the 'philosopher'. Tom greatly admired Fox, not just for his monumental literary achievement, but also for his aptitude and patience, for he had once observed Fox's dexterity as his two young children crawled all over him and his papers whilst he persevered with his work.

Cyril Fox arrived at Cambridge in October 1919 aged 37, but unlike Tom and the influx of privileged young men who enrolled as undergraduates, he entered the university as a *Fellow Commoner*. At the time, it was the practice of most universities to keep places open for older men to obtain their degrees, for the Great War had created a necessity to provide for those who had become embroiled in the conflict. The status of *Fellow Commoner* brought with it a certain eminence and many who entered on this standing were entitled to the same privileges as the dons. This elevated status resulted in them having limited contact with the undergraduates. It is therefore surprising that a great friendship developed between Tom and Cyril Fox – a Fellow Commoner who was nearly 20 years his senior.

During his early days at Cambridge, Tom became a prolific letter writer. Whenever away from the campus, he corresponded with Fox on a regular basis, usually with updates on his excavations, or queries regarding his discoveries. It is clear from their early letters that Fox derived a certain enjoyment from the amusing addresses he received from his young friend. It appears that Tom saw it as a challenge to cordially insult Fox at least once during his opening lines. Two such greetings – 'Dear Prickwilly...' and '...you're a damned lousy scab,'[38] – are typical of Tom's dispatches. The friendly insults demonstrate to us the trust that Tom had developed between himself and his learned friend.

In the spring of 1924, Fox, assisted by Mediaevalist Dr. W.M. Palmer, and later by Lethbridge, dug a section through the Devil's Dyke on the edge of the Fens. It had been suggested by Sir William Ridgeway that the great dykes had been inaugurated in the early Iron Age. This theory, however, didn't hold with Fox and he set out to disprove Ridgeway's conjecture. He quite logically believed that any objects found in undisturbed earth below the banks must be older than the banks themselves. As Fox had suspected, the dig did not reveal evidence to support Ridgeway's theory.

It was during the digging of the Devil's Dyke that Tom encountered the dangers associated with his profession. On one occasion, he and the site foreman, Shippea, had just vacated a trench in which they had been working. Louis Clarke, who had visited the site earlier in the day, had commented that the whole of the excavation was a potential death trap. As the pair sat eating their lunch, there was a tremendous roar as the supporting timbers buckled and the whole of the cut caved in, filling the trench with broken timbers, chalk and rubble.

Solving the riddle of the Cambridgeshire Dykes was one of Sir Cyril Fox's greatest achievements. Ridgeway's theory of a pre-Roman origin was there to be challenged and when 50 decapitated skeletons were discovered in the Bran Ditch, complete with Anglo-Saxon accoutrements, Tom suggested that they were attributable to the Wars of Heptarchy and most likely dated from the seventh century. From this conjecture, he initially surmised that the Dykes were East Anglian defences against the valiant old pagan, penda, but he realised that his notion was purely conjecture. Tom always kept his ear to the ground, for he realised the importance of local knowledge. A burial was uncovered by a Mr H. Pepper whilst digging out a rabbit, and an investigation into his discovery revealed further male skeletons. All appeared to have been mutilated by axes and one was found to have been buried with a pot dating to the British-Romano period.

Shortly after World War II, Fox's theory on the Dykes was further enhanced by the discovery of human bones in the Fleam Dyke near Mutlow Hill. Tom wrote to Fox explaining of the find uncovered in a rabbit hole by a schoolboy:

> He told his bumbrusher who passed the glad tidings on to us. I had a look yesterday there is a new rabbit burrow on north side of the northern one of the two holloways south of Mutlow Hill.'[39]

Tom also included a free-hand sketch in his correspondence of the locality and where the bones had been found.

It was now becoming apparent that the dykes had nothing to do with the Anglo-Saxon wars, for the dead had been found respectfully buried in the Fleam Dyke and was in stark contrast to the decapitated burials at the Bran Ditch. The discoveries suggested that the warriors at the Fleam Dyke had been successful in the defence, as opposed to their unsuccessful counterparts at the Bran Ditch. It was obvious that the dykes represented a violent phase in Cambridgeshire history associated with the late Roman period. The evidence suggested that the Fleam Dyke, Bran Ditch and the Devil's Dyke once formed defensive boundaries between forest and fen across the only access to East Anglia from the south/west.

Fox was prone to drop by on his workforce, often delivering a morale-boosting address that permeated an infectious enthusiasm amongst his workers. On one occasion, he flung his arm around Tom and remarked: 'My God, Tom, what wouldn't you give to have seen it manned and the cry to go up: There the Buggers are!'[40] It was these moments of inspiration that stayed with the young Tom Lethbridge, for it relieved him of the mundane drudgery associated with archaeology and brought to life the people and places they had chosen to investigate.

Fox wasn't alone in his ability to bring history to life. Dr. Palmer was also renowned for his ability to extract interesting information from his discoveries. The Cambridge fraternity knew him as 'Uncle Palmer', a name devised for him by Cyril Fox's young children. Palmer had the ability to illuminate history by reciting human tales associated with his findings. It is apparent that Tom observed Palmer's dexterity and made a mental note to apply the same technique to his own studies.

Many who came into contact with Tom during his time at Cambridge could not fail to be impressed with his enthusiastic reconnaissance and excavation skills. His stimulating, wide-ranging and often mind-blowing conversations in the field were a delight to behold. He was also renowned for his elaborate picnics, gargantuan high teas and hearty breakfasts that often included four fried eggs and six rashes of bacon... for the first course! This, coupled with Dr. Palmer's dangerous mix of homemade cider and beer, which more often than not shattered the bottles into which it was poured, made excursions out into the Fens memorable experiences for those that accompanied Tom and his associates.

Another figure to make an impression on Tom was Sir William Ridgeway, a giant of a man and a real 'old-timer'. He had a rugged face, boasted a heavy moustache and was renowned for a distinctive holler that preceded almost every utterance. He was also known to love a good row or spat and had once informed his good friend Jenkinson – the university librarian – that: 'If there's any damned swine in this college, Jenkinson, who you want a row with, I'm your man.'[41] Although a Professor of Classical Archaeology, he had an interest in genetics and had once written a book on the thoroughbred racehorse. Before he arrived at Cambridge, he had travelled the world and he carried with him an air of authority. It was, in fact, Ridgeway who had encouraged Louis Clarke to become the curator of the museum, much to the annoyance of Fox, who had fancied the job for himself; although Tom, like Ridgeway, believed that Clarke was the most suited for the post. He lived in nearby Fen Ditton, but originated from a West-Country family who had settled in Ireland before the Battle of the Boyne.

Tom had first met Ridgeway one dark winter's evening whilst digging out Anglo-Saxon graves at the cemetery at Little Wilbraham. Ridgeway had little time for the older men at the university, but got on better with the younger, more enthusiastic ones. He was prone to wearing a white bowtie and a dark suit and Tom likened him to a West-Country Elizabethan. He remarked that if only he had had a pointed beard on his chin and ruff around his neck, he would have certainly looked the part.

Ridgeway was an illustrious teller of Irish stories and Tom considered him a real bard. So adept was he that, 'You could see happenings in imagination as he recounted them.'[42] One story in particular amused him and concerned a dinner party that Ridgeway had once attended:

> In the middle of the meal Ridgeway happened to peer down at his lap and to his great alarm saw a large expanse of white. Thinking that the worst had happened and that his buttons had somehow failed in their duty, he hastily stuffed the offending object into his trousers and made sure that he was securely buttoned up. Later on he looked down again. There was the white thing still in view. With growing horror he pushed it in and waited anxiously for the end of dinner. When the ladies rose to leave the men to their port, Ridgeway was securely fastened to the skirt of his next-door neighbour.[43]

Tom considered Ridgeway's unique ability to bring his own tales to life, most appealing.

If Tom ever unearthed anything unusual, Ridgeway was always his first port of call. His house in nearby Fen Ditton was old and had a large study situated on the first floor. Tom often wondered how the timbers stood the weight of all the paraphernalia that was housed there. The tables were piled high with books and in some places the dust was at least an inch thick. Although his eyesight was failing, Ridgeway found his way around his study with a reliance on an unerring memory. On one occasion, Tom had offered to retrieve a book for him from upstairs, but Ridgeway was the only one accustomed to his own unique filing 'system' and replied: 'Ach no, me bhoy... every rat knows his hole.'[44]

When he died in 1926, he left his entire collection to the museum.

Ridgeway was indeed from the old school and some of his views and opinions were not conducive to the changing times at Cambridge. Miss Maureen O'Reilly had been appointed as Sub-Curator to Louis Clarke at the museum and not approving of seeing women in such positions, he encouraged Tom to supplant her. For once, Tom had a difference of opinion from his mentor and chose not to heed his words. He realised that O'Reilly was well suited for the job and her need for employment was far greater than his. He was quite happy to continue his work at the museum as a volunteer.

During the early part of the twentieth century, Cambridge appears to have been a male dominated institution and often Tom's recollections and anecdotes are certainly indicative of the time. Reading through notes compiled for *The Ivory Tower*, one might easily be led to believe that his life at Cambridge was one long jape. However, this does not do justice to the serious investigation undertaken by him and his fellows. Even during their adventures, it is clear that they always remained focused upon their undertakings, although Tom was always quick to deliver ironic, or sardonic humour at any given opportunity.[45] The male dominated culture to which Tom was party did not, however, prejudice his involvement and respect for female academics. On the contrary, his support for Maureen O'Reilly evidences this.

Maureen O'Reilly was married to Alfred Haddon, an anthropologist who had written an important book called the *Races of Man and their Distribution (MacMillan & Co. 1925).* Haddon had a particular interest in sheila-na-gigs – rude carvings often found in Norman churches. It was an interest that would be pertinent to Tom's later studies. On one occasion whilst visiting churches to the north of Wisbech, Haddon became bored and asked if they could go outside and search for gollywogs. Of course he meant sheila-na-gigs, but as Tom would later define, the mistake was not too way off the mark. In Tom's *Gogmagog – The Buried Gods,* he would suggest that a sheila-na-gig was simply a god with ogling or rolling eyes that had survived in the grotesque child's toy known as a gollywog. With this in mind, Haddon's statement appears not to have been a mistake, but an insightful piece of observation.

Tom was later to develop a notion that folklore, once stripped of the barnacles of time, would often contain elements of truth. This theory is likely to have originated from his associations with Manny Forbes – a Cambridge don who taught English Literature. Forbes was indeed a 'character' and once accompanied Tom on a Hebridean cruise with Sir Cyril Fox and Sir James Wordie. It was, in fact, Forbes who suggested that place names in England and Scotland that made reference to 'Nine Maidens' were, in fact, allied to the nine phases of the great Earth Goddess Danu, Annis, or Diana. He even suggested that this association could be linked to the dance known as the 'Nine Men's Morris'. Through these experiences and associations, we witness the sparks that ignited Tom's imagination.

Tom's ability to draw on local knowledge is exemplified in his associations with William Cushi Frost. Frost was a first-rate foreman who had been trained and employed by Cyril Fox. His father had been a farmer in the same village as Dr. Palmer's father and both men had had an equal start in life. Palmer, however, had gone on to become a respected Medievalist, but Frost still continued to live in a mud-floored cottage in Balsham. Frost was a reliable man and Tom knew that he could leave him unsupervised whilst undertaking the cutting of a section through a dyke and still return to find him hard at work on his return. Frost was a local fellow and an inveterate poacher, but Tom recognised a man whose local knowledge was invaluable to his own researches.

Tom learnt many priceless nuggets of information about local fenland traditions from Frost. One amusing custom in particular he found most intriguing. Frost once explained that a broom left leaning against a wall, or a cottage door, meant that the mistress' husband was away and that it was safe for her lover to call. Always one to look for parallels, Tom likened this to a custom observed in the Arabian Knights where a walking stick was utilised in a similar fashion. He remarked that after gaining knowledge of this local idiosyncrasy, he often kept an eye out for prominent brooms in the fenland villages. He pondered on the misfortune of local parsons who inadvertently made daytime house calls to homes with brooms leaning outside.

Gordon Fowler was also a local man who ran the water transport system for the beet factory at Ely. He was a collector of both objects and information and knew everyone in the vicinity. Fowler was prone to ringing at all hours to share his newly acquired knowledge and discoveries. He had shown Tom how it was possible to locate all of the old courses of the Fenland rivers by means of the raised banks of silt which were left standing when the peat dried and shrank through drainage. He restored their old name of 'roddam' to them and plotted all the main courses on to maps. It was this study that was to earn him an honorary Master of Arts.

Although he did not set out to be a radical thinker, Tom's ambition from the outset was purely to rely on his own instinct and commonsense. He was unconcerned with protocol and was never restricted by the boundaries of his vocation. He soon realised that his profession was hindered by dogma and it worried him that 'facts' took so long to be accepted. He was even more concerned at the amount of time it took information to filter down to students and scholars. Throughout his career in Cambridge, he witnessed untold injustices, where commonsense 'discoveries' were often ignored by the academics, only for them to re-surface years later with the original initiate unrecognised or unreferenced.[46] He once remarked how his friend, Sir William Ridgeway, once proved beyond all reasonable doubt that the people of Mycenae were Greeks and spoke Greek. It took 30 years before this fact became universally recognised with Ridgeway receiving no credit for his informed proclamation.

Tom's financial independence provided him with the freedom to pursue his role as the maverick. However, his 'unconventional' approach to his vocation often left him exposed to criticism from those who trod a more traditional path. The Cambridge history don Charles W. Phillips was one of many who criticised Tom's approach, accusing him of being, '...able to do rather second-rate work and get away with it.' Phillips also suggested: 'Though very able and producing interesting ideas, had no real conscience in his work in the last analysis.'[47] Phillips' view of Tom's activities were tainted by the fact that whilst writing up the Cambridgeshire earthworks for the Victoria County History, his site visits revealed many instances of unfilled trenches and test holes attributable to Tom. In Phillips' eyes this could only be considered shoddy workmanship and it led him to accuse Tom of treating his fieldwork as a mere pastime.

It is unlikely that Tom would have agreed with Phillips conjecture. His independence created a freedom that he chose to exploit and he perceived his role more as an initiator and instigator. His shoddy workmanship experienced by Phillips would have been considered by many of his fellows as a sign of arrogance; as if he considered it below him to finish off an excavation once he had achieved his own objectives. Tom, however, was not consciously being arrogant; his motivation was to simply find things out. His failure to follow protocol was more likely due to the impatience of an inquisitive mind. He considered the more mundane tasks of his undertaking were best suited for less imaginative minds.

Not all of Tom's influences and stimuli originated from his associations with his fellows at Cambridge; we know that even as a youth he had an enquiring mind. It is apparent that throughout his life, Tom was able to absorb and draw upon the influences and skills of those with whom he associated. His scope of learning had no boundaries and, indeed, exhibited no prejudice. He was equally able to perceive conundrums through the eyes of a digger on an archaeological site as through those of a Cambridge don.

By observing his fellows, it enabled him to understand what made the people around him tick. He realised that if he understood their skills, then surely he should be able to apply this understanding to ancient lives. Through this inspired application, he was able to fathom and provide answers that would, to the scientific mind, always remain beyond reach. Sir Cyril Fox once suggested to him that 'controlled imagination' was the magic key that was required to unlock the door of the past and those without the key, however knowledgeable, were always destined to remain on the wrong side of the door.

Chapter Five

In Search of a Goddess

On his 32nd birthday – 18 June 1900 – the Reverend Canon Arthur Gordon Robertson was appointed Headmaster of the Chorister's School and a Vicar Choral of Salisbury Cathedral. He was an athletic young man who brought energy and enthusiasm to the posts. The Reverend Robertson soon asserted his authority on the school, instigating the tightening of both physical and intellectual discipline. His charming wife, Frances May, also threw herself unsparingly into the task of running the domestic side of the school. She became a delightful hostess and her wit and humour soon became renowned throughout the seat of learning. The couple's enthusiasm and dedication was soon reciprocated and it wasn't long before *The Close* took the new Head and his wife to its heart. Shortly after taking charge, the couple gave birth to a daughter, Sylvia Frances.

To assist her with her duties, Frances May employed a matron to help, not only with Sylvia's care, but to lend a hand with the boys at the school.

During her formative years, Sylvia assisted her parents at the school and on reaching her 18th birthday – just after the end of the World War I – she even took a class of young boys of her own. Growing up in *The Close,* Sylvia became friends with Jane Fisher, whose family lived nearby at *Mompesson,* 35 *The Close.* Family affiliations with Cambridge bought Jane and Sylvia into contact with a group of friends – undergraduates that included Richard Bott, Scroope Egerton, Chetwynd Tolbart, Geoffrey Walford and Tom Lethbridge. It wasn't long before Sylvia and her friend became romantically linked with Tom and Walford respectively.

Romance blossomed and Tom and Sylvia became engaged in March 1922; the couple eventually married on 6 February 1924. Their wedding took place in Salisbury and was solemnised at the cathedral church in *The Close*. To mark the occasion, the Choristers from the school harnessed and pulled the newly married couple's motorcar from the West Front of the cathedral to the school. The union was witnessed in the presence of Sylvia's father and Tom's mother, Violet. At the time of his marriage, Tom was registered as still living with her in the rented house at Little Ness.

After the death of Tom's father, Ambrose, in 1909, Violet Lethbridge had eventually found a new love interest in Brigadier General Laurence George Frank Gordon, who Tom – always one for nicknames – sardonically referred to as *Sugar Gordon*. The couple were eventually to marry on 6 January 1926, but Tom was not overly keen on his mother's new flame and referred sarcastically to his new stepfather as, 'a Brigadier of Social Viceroy ADC'.[48]

Shortly after their marriage in the autumn of 1924, Tom and Sylvia moved into The Lodge at Waterbeach on the main Cambridge to Ely road. Sylvia's mother, Frances May, travelled up from her home in Salisbury to assist her daughter with the move into her new matrimonial home. The visit, however, was marred by tragedy; on the day of the relocation, Frances experienced an apoplectic fit and died before doctors could reach her. Tom, always the one for the understatement, suggested: 'This was a pretty devastating thing to happen in the middle of a move.'[49] Sylvia's father, Canon Arthur Robertson, was informed of the tragedy by telephone and immediately made arrangements to be driven over to Cambridge. Two days later, after plans for the funeral had been made, Tom drove his father-in-law back to Salisbury.

On arriving back at the Robertson home, Tom and his father-in-law were greeted by the Canon's sister and after washing and changing, the three sat down to dinner. The Canon sat at one end of the table with his sister to his right, whilst Tom was given his dead mother-in-law's chair at the opposite end of the table. During the meal, Tom described a feeling of being enclosed by someone he could not see. Not wanting to alarm his father-in-law, he remained discreet, but he was not able to hide his anxiety from the Canon's sister, who noticed that Tom had become distressed and agitated during the meal.

Tom was aware of the notion that recently departed spirits remain, momentarily tied to their earthly surroundings until their bodies are buried. It was a belief that was as old as Homer's *Odyssey*. Although Tom considered this belief plausible, he understood that there was an alternative explanation for the presence he had experienced at the dinner table. He suggested that Canon Robertson, still suffering from great shock and bemusement at the sudden death of his wife, was still thinking, either consciously or subconsciously, about her. Tom believed that during his musings, he had unconsciously projected an image of his spouse into her seat – the one that he had occupied during dinner. He believed that his presence had acted as a kind of receiving set for Arthur's unconscious projections. It was a similar sensation to the feeling he had experienced in his room at Little Ness. As a postscript to this unusual story, Tom remarked that previous to his mother-in-law's death, he had accompanied her on a visit to a cousin renowned for her foresight. On leaving, Frances had asked her relative to tell her fortune. The cousin showed a reluctance to indulge, but after persuasion she took Frances' hand and explained that she would be shortly taking a long, unexpected journey. Tom believed that his mother-in-law's cousin had somehow accessed a future memory and he concluded that her prophecy demonstrated a flaw in our preconceived concept of time.

After Frances funeral on 11 October 1924, Tom and Sylvia returned to Waterbeach to begin their married life. Tom believed

The Lodge to be of considerable significance, for he believed that it had been built upon the site of a Toot Hill – a synod site or a place of general administrative assembly. It was also situated upon a section of the Car Dyke and its position provided Tom with an opportunity to conduct an archaeological investigation into the remains of an Anglo-Saxon hut in the relative comfort of his own backyard.[50] His excavation, in June 1926, was instigated after workmen, whilst previously undertaking the sinking of a well, had discovered a boat buried in the grounds of *The Lodge*. Tom reasoned that the boat must have been a relic from the days when the dyke was navigable and full of water and may well have been moored at a creek, or dock near to a settlement site. On moving into his Waterbeach home, friends had suggested to him that if he got drunk one night and sat on the bank of the old Roman canal in the moonlight, he would witness the ghostly old barges passing by.

He never did indulge in his friends' whimsy, but once he and Sylvia had settled into their new residence he set about cutting a section through the silted up dyke. His excavations happened upon the remains of a dwelling and from the contents of the midden that formed the floor of the hut, he deduced that the site could be dated to the pagan Saxon period. He concluded his investigation by suggesting that the ditch itself was most probably silted-up by the time the Saxon hut was constructed. From this evidence, he figured that the ditch had fallen into disuse some considerable time before the Anglo-Saxon settlement was established. Tom's excavation provided further evidence to the theory now embraced by Sir Cyril Fox that the Car Dyke was indeed attributable to the Romans.[51]

Whilst living at *The Lodge*, Sylvia gave birth to their first child, a son, on 19 March 1925. While undecided upon a name for his new infant, Tom took it upon himself to refer to his offspring as *Gunnar*, a name he had lifted from the Viking Sagas.[52] Young *Gunnar* soon became Christopher John and was eventually baptised at Salisbury Cathedral. In attendance were his Godparents, Humphrey David, Geoffrey Walford and Sylvia's friend, Jane Fisher. The following year, Tom and Sylvia became parents again when their second son, Hugh Periam, was born on 21 July 1926.

By the summer of 1927, Tom had reached the ripe old age of 26 and had been in possession of his father's inheritance for five years. With a wife and young family to support, he decided to invest his money in real estate. In 1904, Henry Boyd had begun building up the Middlefield estate south of Cambridge through the purchase of parcels of college land and in 1911 he had commissioned Luytens to build a property on the estate. Tom purchased the land from Mrs Mirrelees for the princely sum of £6,200.00 (approx £138,446 today). In the summer of 1927, he moved his family from Waterbeach into *Mount Blow*, the Luyten's house situated in Shelford, a small village to the south of Cambridge.

Tom's relocation was coincidental with Sir Cyril Fox's move to Cardiff, where he had secured the post as the Director of the National Museum of Wales. As a consequence of his departure from Cambridge, Fox's employee, William Frost, found himself redundant. Realising Frost's predicament and the esteem held for him by his previous employer, Tom offered Frost the annex of his new residence and employment as an excavator and general gardener and handyman at his new home. Frost was excited at the prospect and accepted Tom's offer. His eagerness, however, got the better of him and he handed in his 'notification to quit' at his old lodgings long before Tom had secured the deeds on the property. Tom wrote to Cyril Fox explaining his desire to employ and re-house Frost, but referred to his new employee's moving arrangements as a complete, 'balls up!'[53]

On 12 June 1928, Tom and Sylvia attended the wedding of their friends, Jane Fisher and Geoffrey Walford, at Salisbury Cathedral. The following year, the newlyweds became parents and Tom was honoured by being chosen as Godfather to their son, Mark. By now, Tom and Sylvia had settled into *Mount Blow* and later that year, Sylvia once again became pregnant, eventually giving birth to their third child, a daughter, Belinda Mary, who was born on 13 April 1930. Tom chose his good friend 'Whiskers' Bristowe to be her Godfather. Things, however, did not run smoothly for his new family; during the subsequent years, Sylvia was beset by mental health problems, a condition that had troubled her even before she had married. Tom became concerned about Sylvia's wellbeing and made constant reference to his wife's illness in his correspondence to his friend Sir Cyril Fox.[54] Like most men of the time, Tom simply presumed it was the woman's job to look after the children and continued to live the lifestyle that he had been accustomed before he married. By providing a roof over their heads and money in their pockets, it is quite likely that Tom considered his support adequate provision for his wife and young family, and the birth of his children didn't appear to deter him from pursuing a bachelor's lifestyle. In the same year of Hugh's birth, he was to be found plotting middens on South Uist, the following year sketching the reef at Benbecula and in the summer of 1929 undertaking a trip out to the Skelligs with his good friend 'Whiskers' Bristowe. Tom was indeed in a privileged position. His post at the Cambridge museum was purely honorary and coupled with his private income, it enabled him to do pretty much as he pleased. He therefore took every opportunity to adventure. His Arctic trips had been punctuated by annual expeditions exploring the Western Isles and their associated archaeological sites.

During their journey to the Skelligs in 1929, the Irish people and their culture beguiled both Tom and his friend. On a drive from Cork to Kerry, Bristowe observed: '...the most beautiful girl I have ever seen.'[55] It is clear that both men had an eye for the ladies; however, the delights of Ireland were tempered with a necessity to fully embrace the culture of the island. On one occasion, the friends were preparing to leave a pub in Fenit to head for Candiha to catch a boat they had commissioned, when two strangers invited the pair to drink with them. As they were in a hurry, they politely declined, but were given a stark ultimatum by the two men: drink or 'you must fight with us...'[56] Tom and Bristowe chose the more conducive option and became instant friends with the two protagonists. On their drive to the boat, the pair picked up a young 14-year-old hitchhiker, who had bade a farewell to his friends and family and was heading, ticket in hand, to America to meet up with his uncle who had preceded him. Tom and Bristowe felt glad that they had been able to assist him on his adventure.

Their destination was the Skelligs, a grouping of islands that lay 10 miles out into the Atlantic from the south/west corner of Kerry. The pair had a notion of stopping off on Little Skellig, for it was renowned for its colony of gannets, but their boatman advised against such a visit, citing the threat of attack from the nesting birds. Like many of the offshore islands, the Skelligs are renowned for their tales of hauntings and the presence of supernatural beings.

Arriving on Skellig Michael, the two friends landed at a small quay beside a spacious cave. An ascent was made up 600 ancient stone steps to some fairly level ground below the ultimate pinnacle. On the platform, they discovered a grouping of unoccupied sixth-century, monastic dwellings, which had been established not long after St. Patrick had introduced Christianity to the islands. The site was also littered with old tombstones and an old cross indicating the burial sites of the occupying monks. The remains of a small oratory and five perfectly preserved beehive cells intrigued Tom and while he conducted an archaeological investigation of the site, Bristowe wandered off to visit a nearby lighthouse to investigate the possibility of seeking overnight accommodation.

The lighthouse keepers informed Bristowe that there was no possibility of them staying on the island, as permission would have to be sought from Trinity House in Dublin. They also added that no one in their right state of mind would want to stay there anyway, as the island was haunted by 'invisible men'. They told of 'things' that bumped against their bolted door at night and of banshees wailing from the graveyard. Bristowe reasoned with the lighthouse men that surely the bumping had a logical explanation and the wailing was almost certainly due to the circling shearwaters. The keepers were unconvinced by Bristowe's reasoning; they believed that the strange occurrences were due to the uneasy consciences of the dead monks, or the poor souls whose lives they had been unable to save after a shipwreck a few years before. It is clear that the stories were originally intended as a deterrent to ward visitors off the island, but through their constant telling and retelling, the spectres had become a 'reality' for the cocooned lighthouse keepers.

When Bristowe returned, he found Tom looking pale and shaken. Before he could ask what was wrong, Tom replied, 'For God's sake let's get off this island at once.'[57] He explained that whilst climbing through some nettles below the oratory in search of ancient rubbish heaps, he had experienced a sensation, as if he was being willed to fall over the cliff upon which he had been climbing. The feeling became so strong that he was forced to concede defeat and return to the safety of the cliff top.

When Tom returned to Christ's Saddle, a plateau of land about the size of a tennis court, the force struck again and he was thrown flat on his face. Bristowe found his friend's story extraordinary, especially coming from a man as powerful and fearless as Tom Lethbridge. Coupled with the stories told to him by the lighthouse keepers, it all began to sound extremely sinister. Their descent to the boat was made with backward glances, but their spirits were elevated by their reminiscences of 'the most beautiful girl in the world' sighted by Bristowe earlier on their adventure.

Under the mentorship of John Robertson, Tom had become an able seaman and his passion prompted him to obtain his own vessel, *Polly,* purchased from Cockeral Grieve, a man who had fallen on hard times. In September 1931, he had sailed the vessel around the coast to over-winter her in Chichester Harbour. The journey turned out to be a nightmare and Tom had to draw on all his experiences gained in the Minch to successfully steer her home. The journey involved sailing at night and Tom found it challenging and misread a number of lights. The daylight also proved to be problematic and in his logbook he noted a near miss in the Channel: 'Europa or Bremmen (sic) passed close, coming out of the murk at great speed.'[58]

Two years later, Tom's seamanship was also tested during a Scottish cruise with his good friend, Geoffrey Walford. The idyllic trip around the lochs and harbours was shattered when *Elspeth's* motor caught fire and they were forced to berth at Tobermory under sail alone; a skilful manoeuvre was required in the crowded harbour:

> ...we managed however to skull her with the tiller between two swell motor yachts who gaped with fear, and came to an anchor in a very good berth. 'Glory be to God' said John (Robertson) 'that you have such lovely patience with the tiller'. There's many a one would have thrown it from him in disgust! Got the sail off her in a flash and fairly wiped the eyes of the motorboat men.'[59]

During Tom's frequent absences, Sylvia dutifully continued to bring up their young family back home in Cambridge. Sometimes, however, she felt duty-bound to accompany her husband on his frequent sailing adventures. This often entailed leaving their young family behind with their nanny, Miss Linford. Although she was happy to accompany her husband, it was clear that her heart lay with her children back home in

Cambridge. During their frequent excursions, often as far afield as the Outer Hebrides, she demonstrated an eagerness to return home to her brood, but as the children got older, Tom considered it appropriate for them to accompany them on their summer excursions north.

It was during the 1930s that Tom embarked on the production of a series of privately printed books that documented his love of the sea. The publications were quite exclusive and were intended as Christmas gifts to his relatives, close friends and colleagues. He saw this annual undertaking as an opportunity to document and portray his love of the ocean. Each publication – printed by W. Heffer and Sons Ltd. of Cambridge – contained reproductions of his own sketches and engravings depicting maritime scenes and illustrations of sailing vessels he had encountered upon his travels. Tom's boyhood pastime of observing boats in Falmouth Harbour inspired him to compile a couple of small pamphlet of his own illustrations.

In 1932, he produced a short eight-page compilation of his work. The unbound assemblage was hand-stitched and contained six pen and ink illustrations of vessels he had sketched that year. The front page featured a sea-shanty that was replicated and illustrated throughout the short volume. The following year, he produced *Some West-Country Coasters,* a short tome that contained six of Tom's delightful drawings, accompanied by a short introduction.

In the autumn of 1934, he produced *From Dublin to Elsinore in a Sailing Ship,* a slender volume that documented his summer's voyage from Ireland to Denmark on board the *Passat* – a four-masted barque. The journey had taken the *Passat* south along the Welsh coast and then west through the English Channel, before eventually crossing the North Sea, from north of Yarmouth. His attention to detail was exquisite as he described the changing weather conditions, the landmarks around Britain, including the winking light off Lizard Point, and the numerous ships they encountered on-route. Details of his trip were documented in a 92-page logbook[60] that records his arrival in Elsinore (Denmark) as 23rd July 1934:

> We anchored at Elsinore and left the ship in great sorrow. We had no time to make the rest of the passage to Mariehamn, but perhaps the 'tall ships' will survive a few more years yet.[61]

This quote suggests that Tom was in a hurry to return home. The reason for this haste was that he had planned a summer cruise to the Western Isles with his family. He wrote excitedly to Fox explaining: 'Well, we're off now for the Western Isles to break in my spawn to the sea.'[62]

It appears, however, that having his wife and children in tow was usually the exception rather than the rule. The party sailed onboard 'Elspeth' – a 16 ton Yawl – skippered by his sailing mentor, Robertson. Also onboard 'Elspeth' was a guest of Tom's, the 'sensitive' Elizabeth Gimson.[63]

Gimson claimed to have an ability to foresee the future. Throughout the voyage, she compiled an assemblage of scribbled notes and line drawings of her premonitions and intuitions. Tom commenced his logbook in a somewhat disbelieving manner, but as the voyage progressed, his views on his guest's ability began to change. Whilst moored at Loch Creran, Tom recorded her 'observations':

> Ashore to the Cailleach and on to the sithean (Gaelic for a fairy mound or castle). Elizabeth said she saw six men and a black flat-bottomed boat at the Cailleach. They were carrying a corpse, several with a plaid. She said she saw men carrying kegs up it. Also wilder men crawling through the undergrowth with knives in their teeth.

Also that there was a girl dressed in white buried nearby, who she thought had been sacrificed long ago. Also some vessels going up the loch. One which she drew was high stemmed and would have passed for any poor attempt to draw a Viking or mediaeval galley. She said it had blue painted topsides and was unpainted below and that there were a lot of ornaments up the high stem.[64]

Tom remained level-headed throughout, but became intrigued by Gimson's visions:

> I do not set much store by this from the point of view of an experiment. It is the sort of stuff that might be in anyone's head. However the corpse and the men with the black boat was borne out in a remarkable manner...

Shortly after the statement had been transcribed and witnessed, just such a boat, as described by the sensitive, came into the anchorage from around the headland. It was a funeral party adorned in black, which rather shook Tom and encouraged him to carry out further experiments.

Gimson also claimed that by simply holding an object she could gain knowledge of its history and perceive the time from which it came. At Loch Corrie, Tom brought back a number of items he had retrieved from a nearby cave for Gimson to hold:

> She then held a bone and said she thought it belonged to a stag. She said she could see with the stag's eyes and that everything looked quite different to her own vision, distant things were vague and indistinct. She could see more like a panorama with very sharp focussing up to a point. Trees and grass were quite unlike what they appear to us and she was aware of all sorts of things moving.
>
> She was very sensitive in her feet and could notice all things moving in the grass. It will be very interesting to see what the bone is. At any rate this seems a most startling piece of evidence, for of course an animal would see things in a

> different manner to a human being owing to the position in which the eyes are set in the head. I do not know if this has ever been discussed or whether she might have read anything about it... but I fancy not her knowledge of zoology is limited, as far as I can see, to the simplest facts of natural history.[65]

Always the pragmatist, Tom carried out a whole variety of tests as the opportunities arose, commenting:

> As the experiment goes on I am becoming sensible that she must either have the knowledge of an encyclopaedia or else the information she gives comes from nothing in her ordinary conversation to suggest that she has very much varied learning. It is becoming evident that the second alternative is now the more probable....'

Gimson left the cruise, along with Sylvia and the family, on 25 August and Tom was joined by his 16 year-old first-cousin, David Greenhill-Gardyne, also known as 'Bonny Danny', referred to in Tom's books as 'D.G.' and reported as wearing a 'Glenforsa Bonnet'.[66]

Having never met his cousin before, Tom asked Gimson before she disembarked what he would be like. Gimson created a picture of him in her mind's eye and replied:

> ...not very tall, darkish with peculiar eyebrows and a nice grin. He would have some tuslan [I couldn't make out this word – maybe tartan?] and something given to him especially for the trip. He would be shy at first but suddenly confide his ambition to me.[67]

On greeting David on the pier he was astonished to find that his cousin matched Gimson's description exactly. Tom noted that he

> ...had his father's peculiar eyebrows, a low voice and a peculiar habit of looking in the opposite way. He also noted that he was a bit of a know-all – like his father – but not a bad chap. A nice grin.

After David's eventual departure, Tom was left alone with Robertson to reflect on his experiences with the sensitive. Before leaving the party, Gimson had been asked a number of questions relating to what would happen to Tom after she had departed. Her forecasts were recorded, but Tom's subsequent entries in his log suggest that they were mostly incorrect in their omissions rather than their forecasts.

Returning from the cruise to the realities of Cambridge, Sylvia became increasingly unstable and unable to cope. With sickly children and Tom's continual forays away from Cambridge, she found herself hospitalised on numerous occasions. The consequences of this internment resulted in Tom being responsible for his young family. I'm 'up shit creek again,' he once remarked to Fox, a reference to him being left literally holding the baby.[68] Once again, he looked to his nanny and family to bail him out of his predicament. He would often make the long journey south to leave his children with one or the other of their grandparents, the respite providing him with the time and space to continue his vocation and to pursue his numerous hobbies and indulgencies.

The following year (1935), his close friends and relatives were treated to another of his privately printed tomes: *North About – Notes on a Passage from the Clyde to the Åland Islands*. Once again, the discourse documents a voyage undertaken during the summer months of the corresponding year. The book details how the party, once again onboard *Passat*, departed Greenock Pier on 3 July. Wind conditions were not conducive and the vessel had to be aided by a tug; it was an assistance that would be repeated over the next three days until conditions became favourable to enable their progression. Eventually, on 6 July, the party set sail from their anchorage in Kilchattan Bay and clearing the Mull of Kintyre; they journeyed north, passing South Ronaldsay and Orkney on 10 July. Six days later, the Danish coast was in sight and they passed through the narrow channel outside Copenhagen and on into the Baltic Sea.

On 18 July, the *Passat* passed through a magnificent storm off the coast of Gotland and Tom commented on the great banks of shining cloud over Sweden and remarked on how the Swedish coast appeared similar to that of Essex. At the entrance to Mariehamn, he was overwhelmed by the boats in the harbour and remarked that the *L'Avenir* – a local fore-and-aft schooner – looked 'As if she had slipped by mistake out of some print of the early nineteenth century.'[69]

The following Christmas (1936), he delighted his associates with a short volume entitled *Short Splices – Some Notes on Ships and Boats*. Here he took the opportunity to report what a disastrous year it had been for older sea-going vessels. He reported the loss of *Parma* to the breakers yard and the grounding of the *Herzogin Cecile,* who had come ashore in Sewer Mill Cove near Salcombe, a notorious black spot for sea-going vessels. Clearly Tom was witnessing the end of a maritime era and was astute enough to realise the value of his own observations and documentation. His pessimistic prologue was rectified by the inclusion of a number of sightings of sea-borne vessels he had spotted from the lighthouse at Bull Point.[70] In this short volume, he paints an idyllic picture of a sunny April day spent with field glasses and a cine camera watching the ships navigate the Bristol Channel.

The work is concluded by some thoughts on cobles and currachs, spotted off the Northumbrian coast. Here he dismissed the notion that cobles were of a Viking derivation and suggested that they may have had a Celtic origin and that their true ancestor was the currach. He commented upon the remarkable coincidence of cobles on the Northumbrian coast with that of the abundance of monasteries in the vicinity. He cited the Northumbrian monastic sites of Coldingham, Lindisfarne, Jarrow, Wearmouth, Hartlepool and Whitby as examples, suggesting that it was Irish priests who first introduced the currach to the area.

Tom's maritime indulgencies in the West Country were a direct result of his frequent trips to visit Stubbington Preparatory School in Fareham-on-Solent where his two young sons, Christopher and Hugh, were boarders.[71] Whilst driving home to Cambridge, Tom often took the opportunity to visit his mother who was then living at *High Elms* in Bracknell. On one such occasion, he witnessed an unidentified flying object whilst driving down a lane towards Alton. Through the windscreen of his car, he witnessed a green globe that descended down to the road. He described the object as being approximately three feet across with indistinct edges. The object's rate of descent indicated that it would have hit the road only seconds after Tom had passed under it in his car. The object made no impact sound and with hindsight, he realised that he should have stopped his vehicle to inspect the scene. However, the night was wet and Tom was without his coat and he chose to drive on rather than stop to investigate further. On reaching his mother's house, his story was met with disbelief as it was by his fellows back home in Cambridge. Many suggested that the object witnessed by Tom was most likely to have been ball lightning. A Later experience of tracking balloons whilst studying cosmic rays whilst on the west coast of Greenland, led him to conclude that the object he had witnessed in the lane near Alton must have been of a considerable size.

Throughout his career, Tom would be responsible for over 60 archaeological reports, each demonstrating his unconventional approach to report writing. In 1936, the Cambridge Antiquarian Society had published a report on the excavations of a Christian,

Anglo-Saxon cemetery at Shudy Camps in Cambridgeshire. The report was compiled and illustrated by Tom and is typical of his innovative approach. It is difficult to imagine what his peers and the academics of the day thought of him – this young upstart, who presented his reports as if conducting a briefing in a local hostelry whilst presiding over a pint of ale. Tom's unique approach is apparent in his preface to the Shudy Camps report; his wit, informality and observation to detail are evident within the first paragraph. It was an approach that led a former Cambridge pupil to remark: 'he brought the 'archaeology of death' to life.'[72]

Tom was conscious that he had a task to fulfil, but from the outset it was always his intention to broaden his brief and extend his assignment far beyond the reporting of the mere facts in hand. He commenced the Shudy Camp report by first apologising to his reader, explaining that the report had indeed been, 'An onerous business to compile,'[73] and therefore must, out of all necessity, be a tedious read. He used his casual introduction as a manoeuvre to entice and captivate his readers. The mundane report is transformed by the inclusion of a tale of a bleak midwinter's day, when a snow squall at a graveside turned his colleague, Dr. Palmer, into a 'snowman'. Here we see the arch storyteller at work and this poetic approach must have sent reverberations through the Cambridge academia. In his dialogue, he incorporates a remark made by Joe Hall – one of the workmen on the dig – regarding the discovery of a female skeleton in one of the graves. 'Would that be woman?' queried Hall. Tom replied that it was. 'Well,' he responded, 'I reckon that they must have been about the same then as now, small as mice and spiteful as devils.'[74] The remark may seem out of place in today's politically correct world. It was, however, not Tom's intention to offend, but to paint a picture of the camaraderie of the workforce, and the remark must be perceived in the context of the time.

Tom was keen to demonstrate to the reader the jovial air that presided over the Shudy Camp excavations. He describes how one of his volunteer helpers, when clearing grave number 85, discovered a fragmentary male skeleton that had been laid to rest on its back, with its legs straight and arms placed across its pelvis. During the course of the burial, a pot had been placed on the right-hand side of skull and 56 disc-shaped bone playing-pieces and a decayed bone object that resembled a die had been placed to the left of the corpse's feet. The volunteer happened to remark upon the handful of bone objects, which Tom described as looking like, 'ratafia biscuits'. The digger aggressively demanded: 'Ought a man's ankles to look like that?' It was a comment that inspired him to question whether he was being held personally responsible for an Anglo-Saxon bodily malfunction.

Nearly 150 graves were discovered at Shudy Camps and Tom's report details the contents of each individual burial. In the report, grave-objects and finds are beautifully illustrated in Tom's unique style. His artwork alone demonstrates a thoroughness of mind and provides the report with authority.

It was Tom's colleague, Dr. W.M. Palmer, who had been responsible for the discovery of this second cemetery at White Hills Field situated at the juncture of the roads from Shudy and Castle Camps leading to the village of Bartlow. At the time of the dig, O.S. Crawford was in the process of compiling a map of the distribution of Anglo-Saxon sites, so it was considered appropriate to discover a few of the burials merely for the purpose of identification.

The Shudy Camps excavations revealed two types of burial, those with the heads facing south/west and the others, which faced north/west. The orientation of the burials and many of the objects exhumed were also found to be similar to those discovered at nearby Burwell. However, environmental conditions at Shudy Camps were not conducive to the preservation of bone and many of the skeletons had almost disappeared and, consequently, relatively few bone objects were unearthed.

Tom remarked that the nearby Burwell site had revealed long, bone combs that resembled those associated with the Viking period. However, the normal comb of the pagan period was double-sided or, if single-sided, was normally short in length. The excavations also revealed an absence of pagan Anglo-Saxon brooches and only six weapons were found on the site. Few of the graves had associated objects and it was these cumulative observations that led him to conclude that the cemetery was of the later Christian Anglo-Saxon period. Graves with associated ornaments were considered closer to the pagan Anglo-Saxon era. It was therefore apparent that the cemeteries at Shudy Camps differed widely from the normal pagan Anglo-Saxon cemeteries of the district and the finds also revealed little of British-Romano influence. There was however, plenty of evidence to make connections with the pagan Anglo-Saxons and this substantiated the claims that the Shudy Camps cemeteries were of the later period.

Although Tom had become quite the expert in the Anglo-Saxon archaeology of the fens, his adventurous heart raced when opportunities arose to take to the sea and explore the Hebridean islands. He still nursed a desire to return to Arctic waters, for it had been 14 years since he had returned from the aborted trip to East Greenland with James Wordie in 1923. Since his return, he had bided his time and cursed the circumstances that had led him to miss out on Wordie's 1929 expedition to East Greenland and his consequent visit to West Greenland and Baffin Bay in 1934.

Chapter Six

The Big Freeze

In 1937, James Wordie began assembling a party to visit North-West Greenland, with the objective of undertaking an investigation into cosmic radiation at great altitudes and high latitudes. To achieve their intention, it was the party's aim to launch a series of pilot balloon flights carrying cosmic-ray apparatus from different locations along their route. At the time of the expedition, aerological observations in the polar-regions were somewhat scanty and the conditions, particularly in the stratosphere, were practically unknown. De Quervain, Mercanton and Jost had made previous attempts in 1920 and Hobbs had made similar extensive balloon flights in West Greenland in 1931, but although Wordie's experiments were to be more limited than their predecessors' efforts, it was planned that they would extend 10° further north to latitude 79°. It was also the expedition's intention to carry out their experiments at far greater altitudes.

The assembled company consisted of 10 men, nine of which were picked from Cambridge. Those chosen to accompany Wordie were Dr. Hugh Carmichael from St. John's College and Dr. E.G. Dymond, a Lecturer from Edinburgh University. Both men had scientific backgrounds and were to be responsible for the study of the cosmic radiation. I.M. Hunter was also enrolled with a view to his expertise regarding radio-communications with the balloons. Lethbridge, T.T. Paterson and R.W. Feachem were chosen with a view to them undertaking archaeological investigations on-route, although Dick Feachem's remit as a botanist was extended to incorporate a study of plant life encountered during the expedition. Harald Drever, Angus Robin and Derek Leaf were, like Wordie, geologists and would be responsible for geological and topographical surveying. Robin was also President of the Cambridge Mountaineering Club, a standing that would provide the party with a valuable asset regarding the inhospitable terrain that awaited them in North-West Greenland. Funding for the expedition was obtained from the Cambridge and Edinburgh Universities and the Royal Society also made a further contribution. However, the bulk of the expenditure was contrived from the participants and once again exemplifies that scientific exploration was indeed the vocation of the privileged classes.

The party sailed from Leith on 27 June 1937 onboard the *Isbjorn,* captained by the Norwegian Albert Bergerson and his dog *Bjorn.* The party arrived in Godhavn on 15 July and here they conducted their first balloon flights from Disko Island. The *Isbjorn* continued around Baffin Bay and further balloon flights were conducted at Nugssuak, Upernivik and Ryder Island. Whilst on Rhyder Island, Tom was able to investigate a rectangular house site on the edge of a small bay on the eastern side of the Island, which was threatened by the encroaching sea. It was a site familiar to Paterson who had previously undertaken a dig there in 1934. Excavations at the house revealed a large quantity of objects that predated the trading activities of the whalers that had once frequented this coast. Tom suggested that many of the finds were almost 500 years old.

After crossing Melville Bay, the company arrived at Thule on 7 August. Whilst the party carried out further balloon experiments, Paterson and Drever were left at the Thule Trading Post and Paterson utilised his time by learning how to make string figures from the local Innuit. It was this insight into indigenous culture that later inspired him to produce his study *Eskimo String Figures and their Origin.* Further balloon flights were undertaken on Wolstenholme and Cary Islands; during the undertaking of these experiments, Tom was able to conduct three examinations of village sites, two on Cary Island and another on North West Island. His investigations revealed that all three sites were positioned on raised beaches, below precipitous cliffs and had all had southerly aspects. Each site consisted of five long houses, each with umiak stands beside convenient bays.

As part of his enquiry, Tom and his party excavated one of the smaller huts on Isbjörn Island and removed turf from another to enable them to make a plan of its construction. The absence of middens outside of the huts indicated that they were not occupied for long durations, therefore suggesting that the dwellings were never intended as permanent structures. After finishing the excavations and experimentations on the Cary Islands, the party departed on 12 August and after proceeding north across Smith Sound, they rounded Cape Sabine to arrive at Turnstone Beach on 17 August.

Turnstone Beach was a name contrived by Wordie's party, but they had no doubt that it was the place fancifully referred to as *Eskimopolis* by the Norwegian Arctic explorer, Otto Neumann Sverdrup, who attempted to circumnavigate Greenland, via Baffin Bay, between 1898 and 1902. Their arrival on Turnstone Beach provided Tom with an opportunity to excavate the remains of further Innuit winter houses and, aided by Paterson, Feachem and Leaf, they continued to dig for three days whilst further balloon experiments were carried out by the rest of the party. The weather during the dig was not favourable and a cold north/east wind not only made conditions chilly, it also presented the possibility of ice-flows being blown from Kane Basin into Buchanan Bay. However, good fortune and congenial tides prevented this happening and the bay never became completely filled with ice.

After three days of digging, Wordie decided that conditions had improved sufficiently to justify leaving Tom and his three companions to conduct their enquiry on Turnstone Beach, whilst the *Isbjorn* and the rest of the party proceeded north to the Bache

Peninsula. After further digging, Tom and his cohorts completed their excavation, but at the lower levels they discovered, not surprisingly, that much of the ground was frozen. The expedition party encountered around 13 hut sites in all on the gently sloping beach. Their investigations revealed that several of the huts had been previously dug out, possibly by Sverdrup's party. Further excavations at the dwellings revealed numerous objects and provided them with evidence that many of the huts were of great antiquity. One in particular had part of its whale shoulder blade and rib roofing still in place. Tom concluded that the economy of the Innuit must have been considerably affected by the whaling industry.

On 20 August, the party moved away from Buchanan Bay and began their journey south along the coast of Ellesmere Island. The north/easterly winds that had prevailed during their stay in Buchanan Bay were replaced by more hostile conditions as they proceeded south across Smith Sound. The party arrived in Jones Sound on 22 August and conducted a further balloon flight at Craig Harbour. Here they encountered the post of Corporal Hamilton and Private McWhirter of the Royal Canadian Mounted Police. Staying with them for the winter was Robert Bentham, who was undertaking geological and topographical maps of southern Ellesmere Land. Once again, Paterson took the opportunity to study two local Innuit families, whilst McWhirter and Bentham joined the expedition party on board the *Isbjorn* in the crossing to Cape Hardy.

The *Isbjorn* anchored half a mile east of the cape and Tom disembarked and almost immediately located a compact village of old winter houses. During the two-day dig, Tom verified the location of one of Dr Frederick Cook's winter camps. On finding the site, he mockingly stated: 'We can therefore claim to have trodden in the footsteps of the master.'[75] In 1808, the American Cook had made a false claim to have arrived at the North Pole, a year ahead of Robert Peary. Cook's camp appeared to have formerly been an Eskimo winter house that had been renovated by Cook to form a comfortable shelter that he had occupied on his return from Axel Island. From his excavations, Tom deduced that the early occupiers of the Cape Hardy camp appeared to have been less nautical than those who utilised the huts on the Cary Islands, Turnstone Beach and South Ryder Island.

Tom and his fellow archaeologists made further important discoveries including the unearthing of a cartridge case, two buttons and a piece of oak timber that revealed traces of one of the missions that had endeavoured to seek the lost Franklin expedition that went in search of the north/west passage the previous century. Returning to Craig Harbour on the evening of 25 August to deposit McWhirter and Bentham and collect Paterson, the party began their journey back to Godhavn the following day to conduct their final balloon flight.

On their return journey, the party sailed to Cape McCulloch on 27 August and steamed up Coutts Inlet on Baffin Island where they passed through a narrow fjord with steep sides. The fjord ended after 42 miles and the scenery became gentler. They witnessed marine terraces and beyond a glacier, a lake that appeared to be about two miles in length. Here they went ashore and Tom discovered three old Eskimo winter houses and some tent rings that appeared to have been occupied comparatively recently, certainly within the past couple of years. After completing their successful circumnavigation of Baffin Bay, Wordie's party returned to Goodhavn on 10 September. After conducting their final balloon flight, they set sail for home, passing Cape Farewell on 15 September. The *Isbjorn* arrived back in Leith on 1 October 1937.

In his report in the Geological Journal, Wordie found it necessary to propose new names for his sketch map of the expedition. The Committee on Names in Greenland accepted his suggestions and as was the custom in the early days of Arctic exploration, the crew chose to name unchartered topographical features after members of the expedition party. As a consequence of this practice, the two lakes on Baffin Island hence became known as Lethbridge Lakes.

Before Tom had embarked upon his passage to Baffin Bay, he had decided to split his Middlefield estate and had arranged for a new property to be built in nearby Stapleford. On returning from his Arctic adventure, the discovery of finding the property still incomplete was to be the least of his worries. Whilst he had been away, Sylvia had suffered a nervous breakdown and had been admitted to a nearby nursing home. In a letter to Cyril Fox, he wrote:

> Life here is pretty lousy. I returned from mapping huts and villages all around the Arctic to find Sylvia in a nursing home with a nervous breakdown and half-witted nurses in charge. The new Mount Blow was half built and the flat half arranged and my papers were all endwise. Very jolly all round. I hated the home she was in and disliked and distrusted the doctor. Having the devil of a time trying to get her charged over into a more congenial place.[76]

As a consequence of his Arctic adventures, Tom became increasingly convinced of the prowess and aptitude of ancient mariners. Knowledge gained from his excavation at Eskimo camps on Jan Mayen and his most recent investigations on Turnstone Beach led him to compile a short volume entitled *Umiak – the European Ancestry of the 'Women's Boat'*. Privately published during the Christmas period of 1937, the modest publication was only 14 pages in length, yet it provided a snapshot of one of his obsessions: the relationship between the Innuit skin-covered boat known as the umiak and the curraghs and cobles found in the northern waters of Britain. Tom surmised that ancient people – strand lopers – had camped along the northern beaches of Scotland and had created temporary, domed shelters. Due to the absence of forest and tree-cover in the northern lands, they had fashioned tents constructed by stretching animal skins over a woven framework of Arctic birch or willow. The skin was then laced together and smeared with animal fat for preservation and weatherproofing. The lightweight structure would have resembled an upturned bowl. Here, Tom's imagination really has its head, and he suggested that during high winds, the structure was perhaps blown from its beachside mooring and flipped on its back onto the sea, where it floated, lightly on the water. Here we are privy to the birth of a commodity that doubled as a method of transport and a shelter.

Umiak contained a number of line drawings that illustrated the construction and anatomy of the umiak. Photographs were also included that depict examples of the vessels that Tom had encountered on his travels. They exemplified not only his observational skills, but also his ability to accumulate a sound understanding of the workings and construction of each vessel. The slim volume was only a taster of what lay in store, for many of the ideas featured here were later expanded and developed 11 years later in his first major publication *Merlin's Island – Essays on Britain in the Dark Ages (Methuen & Co. Ltd.1948).*

One particular illustration, dated 1929, depicts two men from Kerry carrying a curragh on their heads. It is likely that this observation led him to conceive and illustrate *The Highly Conjectural Table to Show Some Possible Lines of Evolution From the Primitive Skin Tent* that was to feature in *Merlin's Island.* By constructing this speculative table, Tom was able to suggest that a skin-covered tent or shelter was an inverted prototype for all skin-covered vessels. This remarkable assemblage defines his approach and illustrates a prowess of ingenious thought.

Even at this stage of his career, Tom was not afraid to deviate from the narrow path walked by academics. It is apparent from his writings that he was quite comfortable presenting his ideas and theories as suggestions and possibilities, when factual information was found to be wanting. He was convinced that his conclusions were equally, if not more, imposing, having been gleaned not solely from archaeology, but from history, mythology and first-hand experiences. On first reading, *Umiak* seems little more than an extract from a notebook of a seasoned traveller, but a further glance reveals evidence of an enquiring mind. It contains wit, humour, enthusiasm and all of the elements that were to fuel and illuminate his future works.

By 1938, Tom's new property was finally completed and soon after he moved into the new Stapleford house taking *Mount Blow* – the name of his previous property – with him. That Christmas, he still found time to produce the next in his series of small annual publications. *The Fishermen of Durness* was a short study of a unique fishing community. He commenced his investigation by articulating that there were two types of enquiry: one that concentrated upon the spectacular and another that choose to focus on the more routine aspects of existence. He believed that it was the observance of the latter that revealed the most about the lives of the ancients. From the examination of everyday objects, the investigator was able to piece together the communities and trade-roots of the ancient mariners. He realised that the fisherman's life was reliant upon supply and demand, for he had witnessed first-hand, the transient nature of the industry. He was able to equate this with the disappearance of a fishing community on Piper's Island in Loch Hourn, for this was a change that had occurred within living memory. Tom only knew of its existence from a tale told to him by an old man from Skye. Once abandoned, the sea had soon overwhelmed the once busy harbour and now nothing physically remained of the once thriving community. He astutely realised how important it was to document and record a vocation that was vulnerable and prone to the whims of nature.

He continued his study with a brief discussion on the men who worked the salmon nets and suggested that their boats were a survival of something far more ancient than the scaffie. He pinpointed a likeness between the Norwegian pram and the British coble and suggested that its origin was a fusion between the pram and the long Norse cod-boat. It had come to his notice, while observing the lobster fishermen of Faraid Head – a promontory facing Cape Wrath across from Balnakeil Bay – that local inhabitants used upturned Scaffies as cottage roofs. This observation led him to suggest that the rounded end of the Hebridean Blackhouse was not simply a device for lessening the windage on the corners of the building, but a legacy from the days when long houses evolved from circular dwellings through the convenience of using old, upturned boats as roofs. He humbly concluded his enquiry by remarking:

> Here, as with the expert on classical sculpture, I am trusting to my eye and to my intuition alone. Still, where a boat is concerned, I feel I have as much right to my opinions as any art critic has to his.[77]

Within months of settling into his new home, Tom received a requisition from the Admiralty. He was requested to undertake a secret reconnaissance mission in northern waters. With the rumblings of war in the air, his involvement in the scientific expeditions in the Arctic the previous decade had made him a prime candidate to search out German bases in Iceland. Tom immediately realised the futility of the expedition and remarked: 'One might as well look for Christmas trees in a dung hill I should aspire.'[78] However, he was quick to seize the opportunity, for he realised that the operation would provide him with a fully paid passage to a region that continued to intrigue him. It appears that the briefing that Tom received from the Admiralty's didn't include the importance of confidentiality. Within days of his notification, he was writing to his friends not only informing them of his 'secret' mission, but also places and time of rendezvous with individuals from the ministry. His contempt for the charge was illustrated in a letter sent to Sir Cyril Fox prior to his departure: 'Don't spread it about but I am just off on a ridiculous expedition to look for German bases in Iceland.' He continued: 'I have to stop as I have to execute a Power of Attorney in the public lavatory at Liverpool Street Station at 10 o'clock.' His contempt for the operation was confounded by his closing remark: 'Well I must go and glue on my false beard.'[79]

In the summer of 1939, at the expense of the Admiralty, Tom, accompanied by his good friend, C.F. 'Fred' Tebbutt, travelled once again to the frozen north. The friends departed from the UK on the morning of 18 July onboard *Vega,* arriving in Stavanger at lunchtime the next day. The following morning, they departed for Reyjavik from the port of Bergen onboard *Lyra,* whose captain Tom referred to as 'King Arthur' for his custom of inviting guests to sit with him at a round table.

Lyra arrived in Reyjavik on 21 July 1939 and Tom recorded the scene on their arrival:

> The first thing we saw being two U boats tied up to a quay (26 and 27). They left at 2pm, but they were so obviously there waiting for trouble that it gave one quite a nasty feeling.[80]

Tebbutt remarked that they were suspicious of any German 'tourists' they encountered as no German was allowed currency in travelling abroad at the time.[81] Both he and Tom recorded how a young Scot from Glasgow called Jack (surname) was introduced to them by the Consul, but was under suspicion; the previous year, he had taken the Mayor's son from the Westmann Islands to Germany for education. Tebbutt also explained that there were a number of Irish anti-British who were stirring up hostility among any German tourists they encountered. It is clear that Iceland was a very nervy place in the days preceding World War II.

Tom had visited Iceland once before, after escaping the Greenland pack ice in the summer of 1923. The pair journeyed north with the objective of visiting sites mentioned in the Sagas and to study the birdlife and the inhabitants of the island. Tom was particularly interested in their boat building culture and their relationship with the sea. On his previous visit, he had been particularly impressed with the ingenuity of the inhabitants of Seydisfjord, who he had witnessed walking around on stilts made from Bath Oliver biscuit tins. It appears from his own schedule that the mission set for him by the Admiralty had become secondary to his own information gathering objectives.

Whilst at the harbours of Reykjavik, Keflavik and Grindavik, he witnessed fine flotillas of open fishing boats, which he described as being worthy of attention. With great raking stem posts and crews of 10 or 11 men, he likened them to the one in which Thoro – he of the Viking Sagas – was lost whilst out fishing and from which his ghost crew returned to Frodiswater. The ghost story was familiar to Tom, for he likened it to the 'invisible men' of Skellig Michael that had plagued the lighthouse keepers back in 1929. Here at the Icelandic ports, Tom saw evidence of Celtic influence all around him and poured scorn on the history books that suggested the Icelandic race was of pure Norwegian extraction. To prove his conjecture, he went looking for evidence of the *Papar*, the Irish saints who, according to the Landnamabrok, had lived in Iceland before the arrival of the Vikings.

During their quest, they were twice provided with hospitality at farms of the local *squiresons of provsts*. Their first host was a Norseman through and through, but the second resembled a Kerry man that Tom had encountered on his Irish adventure with Bristowe in 1929. On meeting their guests, their host was convinced that they had been sent by God to prove that the *Papar* had carved out the neighbouring caves. Tom believed that his host may have been perfectly correct in his assumption, but voiced no strong feelings on the matter. The caves in question, however, were quite remarkable and resembled the Hebridean mound known locally as a *Sithean,* or *fairy hill.* Tom believed that the *Papar,* or possibly the Irish and Scottish Thralls, might well have bought the culture over to Iceland with them, for the mounds were indeed similar to earth-houses found in their homelands. Their host was enthralled by his visitors' knowledge and interest, but Tom informed him that nothing could be proven unless a full excavation was carried out on the mounds.

That evening, they stayed overnight in the local vicarage, but their stop-over was marred by Tebbutt's reaction to a local delicacy he had eaten, which contained last year's suet, blood and oatmeal. Tom declared that such Icelandic dishes didn't always sit too well with the British palate, further remarking: 'Last year's fish is all very well but last year's blood is a bit thick.'[82] After Tebbutt had recovered from his bout of sickness, they retired to their beds. Tom was to sleep in the library and was shown to his room by the *provst* who pointed out a book on a shelf written by Bishop Gore. It was a book that he considered to be the finest written in the English Language. When Tom happened to remark that he not only knew Gore, but had also been confirmed by him, his host appeared humbled as if Tom had, through his association, somehow acquired the mantle of his hero. Tom later remarked that the reverence of the moment was marred by an unpleasant snort of amusement from his friend and the entry of the lady of the house, who proceeded to distribute chamber pots to them without a hint of embarrassment.

Lethbridge and Tebbutt stayed at *Hotel Borg* in Reykjavík where Tom wrote to Fox explaining his discoveries on the island. The letter is full of references to places they had visited that were mentioned in the Sagas and of observations of boats, stunning scenery and of their intention to visit the islands of Vestmannaeyjar. The letter reveals that the two friends had made an extensive tour of the island, but it contains no mention of

German bases and one wonders if the confidential nature of Tom's mission had finally sunk home. It is more likely, however, that he had realised the futility of his operation and had turned the expedition into a glorified sightseeing tour.

During their visit, they encountered the excavations in Thjorsadale that were being conducted by a joint Icelandic, Scandinavian and Finnish party. Tom witnessed the ancient farms that had been covered by ash from Heckla being beautifully excavated. He considered it most instructive to have witnessed the humble ruins of these old halls and noted that the small and inconvenient nature of the dwellings of the exiled Norsemen was in distinct contrast to the images conjured up in the Sagas. However, he compared this tumbling down imagery of palaces to the slumping of the Irish Saga-stock when the hill of Uiseneach was excavated and the pictured luxury was reduced to pits full of animal bones and a single Roman brooch.

The next port of call on the Icelandic expedition was the Vestmannaeyjar, or the West Man's Islands, as the Vikings knew them. They are famous for their puffins and this was the most likely motivation for their visitation. The mail packet from Reykjavík to Bergen was known to stop off at the islands, but Tom and Tebbutt arrived there on a fishing boat that had departed from the lowland town of Stokkseyri south of Reykjavík. The story of how the islands got their name is told in a book entitled *The Settlements of Iceland* that was published in a translation from the Icelandic of 'Ari the Learned' by the Reverend T. Ellwood in 1908. The story concerns two friends, Ingolfr and Hjorleif, who chose to settle on the islands with their families. By visiting places described in the Saga, Tom was able to pour doubt on the legitimacy of the story due to inaccuracies he had encountered with the topography described in the tale. The experience provided him with an insightful lesson regarding the authenticity of second-hand knowledge. During his expedition, Tom discovered a fine example of an anchor known as a killick and on returning to Cambridge, he contrived a model of his discovery, which he duly presented to his friend, H.H. Brindley. The model eventually ended up in the National Maritime Museum where its presence was regarded as being most pertinent.

The two friends returned to Bergen and sailed home onboard *Vega,* which they managed to catch with only an hour to spare. On the homeward journey, Tom was obliged to share a cabin with two Icelanders who appeared to be taking advantage of the free-flowing, tax free alcohol onboard ship:

> Just nicely asleep when our bedmate brought in another sod called Marcus Einarsson, his son called Anus Marcusson (or something like it) and a red-headed woman. They drank a bottle of whiskey with much tumult and noise. I got fed up and went out scowling which rather spoilt the party.
>
> During the next day he gradually continued to soak and so did Marcus. At dinner our chum went to the table in the middle of the dining room and started talking to himself about his wife and his mistress while Marcus was busy raising his arm in salute and then fell into the table of cold food on the table. The captain had him removed to the cabin but not before he had kissed the stewardess who had her hands full of dishes. I think she kicked him in the proper place to judge by his squawk...

After the shenanigans onboard *Vega,* Tom was no doubt relieved to finally arrive back in Britain. On 15 August, Tom expressed his heartfelt feelings at returning home to a country on the brink of war: 'Hot in England – but thank God it's here. So ends this log.'[83]

Chapter Seven

The Rumblings of War

Tom returned to a Britain under the shadow of war. As the eventful year of 1939 drew to a close, he became increasingly concerned for the safety and security of the University Museum of Archaeology and Ethnology in Cambridge. With the curator away in Norway, Tom took it upon himself to secure the contents of the Downing Street site. With the aid of Clarke's assistant, Maureen O'Reilly; his wife Sylvia; her cousin, Mina; and technician Len Morley, he set about dismantling the museum collection. Objects were packed in boxes, which in turn were protected with asbestos sheeting, trestle tables, crates, boxes and tons of sand. Many of the university staff were shocked by Tom's destruction of the museum, none more so than Professor Minns who found the sight of a shirtless Tom Lethbridge toiling away in the street quite distressing. Many objects were removed from the building for safekeeping and Tom even persuaded Louis Clarke to stash items from his own collection in the Balsham Caves that were consequently duckboarded and sealed with bricks and mortar. Despite the evacuation of many valuable exhibits, the museum remained open for business during the war years.[84]

As the museum prepared for war, Tom was once again called upon by the Admiralty to undertake another Arctic reconnaissance. He was presented with the plans for his latest mission and was stunned by his commissioners' lack of general knowledge and what was expected of him from the mission. On receiving instructions, he had become worried about his own wellbeing; he considered the mission to be suicide. However, his fears were eventually allayed; on arriving at the Polar Institute with his kit, he was relieved to discover that the mission had been aborted. The Admiralty's plan to send an unarmed trawler into Arctic waters had been replaced with a notion to utilise two cruise ships to fulfill the mission.

Even with the eventual outbreak of war, Tom still managed to find the time to produce his annual Christmas tome. Entitled *News from Tili*, the small volume contained a discourse of his summer trip to Iceland with Tebbutt and was illustrated, in his own inimitable style, with photographs and sketches rendered on his expedition.

The Hitler War brought new challenges for Tom and as part of the war effort he became an ARP warden responsible for the Downing Street site and was given overriding powers by the Senate. He considered his responsibility like: 'Suddenly being put in charge of a beleaguered city which you have only seen from the gatehouse.'[85] He also became responsible for the Home Guard and commandeered a room in the museum, utilising it as a company office for a 1,800 strong unit. Tom was never one to do things by halves and he even obtained a catering licence to provide for his troops. The task bestowed was not taken lightly and realising the importance of local knowledge in the event of a German invasion, Tom placed a reliance on his friend and tenant, William Frost, whose local knowledge was unrivalled.

In spite of Tom's wartime responsibilities, his commitment to archaeology wasn't impeded and consequences in the field imposed their own unique demands. During the Second World War, it was found necessary to level the Snailwell barrows for the construction of the Snailwell Airfield.[86] Before the railway was established, the grouping of ten barrows stood on open heathland and lay close to the line of the Ickneild Way. Unlike the nearby barrows on Royston Heath or Upper Hare Park, the Snailwell barrows stood in a hollow between two downs and Tom concluded that they were never intended to form a prominent addition to the landscape. He considered that their positioning was most likely due to the positioning of a nomadic encampment located along the fen margins and sandy islands where their herds would have found good grazing.

The excavations were carried out with the Cambridge Society's funds, and Tom was fortunate to work alongside Dr. Mortimer Wheeler's foreman, W. J. Wedlake, along with Dr, Grahame Clark and Mr. C.W. Phillips. Dr. G. Bushnell was responsible for surveying the sections and Tom took responsibility for photographing their activity. In his report, he concluded that the barrows were indeed attributable to a nomadic group, for there was not a great range in time from the construction of the first barrow, attributable to the Beaker Period, and the final phase, attributable to the collared urns. At Snailwell, he found no evidence of the elaborate rituals, first recognised by Sir Cyril Fox at similar barrows in south Wales.

Back in Cambridge, Sylvia's young cousin, Mina, who had assisted Tom during the dismantling of the museum, had moved from her Devonshire home in 1938 to take up the post as the first paid secretary at the University Museum of Archaeology and Ethnology, Cambridge. Mina Elizabeth Leadbitter was the daughter of Mathew Graham and Violet Eirene Ricketts Leadbitter[87] (she was known as Eirene), a family that hailed from Northumberland, where Mathew's father, Joseph, had worked in the shipbuilding industry.[88] The Leadbitters were living at 60 Percy Street in Oxford when Mina was born on 13th April 1919,[89] but moved to Devon in 1927. On 24 August of the same year, Mathew was ordained as the rector of the Church of St. Andrew in the Dartmoor village of Moretonhampstead.[90]

In 1938, a nineteen-year-old Mina moved to Cambridge where she became a frequent visitor to her cousin's home in Stapleford. Mina was a distinguished and slender girl who bore a striking resemblance to the actress Celia Johnson. Her diminutive stature made her appear somewhat fragile, but her deceptive, ethereal presence concealed a strong-minded young woman. Her determined self-assurance was in stark contrast to her cousin's calculating and more demanding nature.

Throughout the war, Sylvia's health continued to be problematic and her continued periods of hospitalisation resulted in Tom and Mina spending more and more time in each other's company. This was not just at the Cambridge Museum, but also at Mount Blow, where Mina would often visit to assist Tom with the children.

The eventual outbreak of war, however, brought many challenges and placed demands, not only upon Tom but those around him. Mina found herself back in the West Country where she was seconded to work as an assistant to the head mistress at Croft House School in Shillingstone. Sylvia, during her intermittent periods of good health, was commandeered to work on a mobile ambulance; a set-up described by Tom as, 'A proper Irish Parliament.'[91] However, her long-standing mental frailty had put considerable strain on the marriage and tales of her associations with other men during Tom's frequent expeditions away from the family home were renowned. Tom was, however, aware of his wife's numerous liaisons and once remarked to Sir Cyril Fox that it was, 'no fun sharing life with a nymphomaniac.'[92] It is clear that whilst Tom's mind was preoccupied with Eskimo houses on Turnstone Beach, his wife had sought solace in the arms of men who were more eager to satisfy her unquenchable desires. Back in the West Country, Mina was not happy with her position at the boarding school and she eventually absconded. It is likely that she had already grown attached to Tom and the enforced separation from him only exacerbated her desire to return to Cambridge.

At the beginning of 1940, Tom was beset by a family tragedy. His sister, Jacintha, had married Thomas Rogers on 29 March 1928 at the Cathedral in Mombassa in East Africa. Four years later, the couple had been blessed with a daughter, Mary Rose. The birth of their daughter followed two years after the tragic loss of their son who had died shortly after birth in 1930. On 6

February, Jacintha and her husband were found dead in a tragic shooting incident at Sheldon in Devon. Tom's niece, Mary Rose, aged only seven, was left orphaned and was taken under the wing of her grandmother, Violet, and her husband, Brigadier Gordon. Mary Rose was only two years younger than Tom's own daughter, Belinda, and she often found herself visiting Cambridge to stay with her Uncle Tom and Aunt Sylvia.

Later that same year, Sylvia's father died at his home at *Rowdens*, Netherhampton in Salisbury and was buried on 7 August 1940.

After the death of Sylvia's mother, Frances May, the Reverend Arthur Robertson had met and remarried his new matron, Dora Butterworth in October 1925. The couple had continued to live at *The Close* up until his retirement in August 1929. The grief and worry of the year's tragedies put enormous strain on both Tom and Sylvia. Their marriage was becoming unsustainable and the couple mutually agreed to separate and were eventually divorced on 6 June 1943. It is apparent that the marriage had been under considerable strain for quite some time and it is likely that the death of Sylvia's father provided the couple with an opportunity to end their marriage without disgracing the Robertson family name. In a letter to Sir Cyril Fox, Tom remarked that he had just experienced, 'a domestic earthquake,' but he didn't provide his friend with the brutal details.[93]

After his divorce, Tom and Mina became inseparable and the friendship eventually became more intimate. It is likely that the Leadbitter family back in Moretonhampstead were none too pleased to hear news of the developing relationship between their daughter and an older, married man. But it was not the 18 year age difference between Tom and Mina that caused fractions in the Leadbitter household, or the fact that Sylvia and Mina had been cousins. What most concerned Mina's mother, Eirene, was the insanity that ran in the Lethbridge family.[94] The criticism was unjustified, for although the Lethbridge family were renowned for their odd behaviour, madness was not one of their failings. It is likely that the tales of the eccentric Lethbridges were renowned in the West Country and it was these that caused Mathew and Eirene cause for concern.

As a result of his divorce, Tom was obliged to make provision for his ex-wife and children and with the breakup of the marriage he put the recently built *Mount Blow* up for sale. The property was eventually sold to Major French in November 1943 and after providing for Sylvia he began to think to the future. With monies from her settlement, Sylvia bought *South Farm House* in the village of Upper Lovell near Warminster and moved there with her daughter, 'Binny', who still remained living in the family home. With the sale of *Mount Blow,* Tom moved into lodgings at Grange Road in Cambridge, where he became a tenant of Mrs. Lock and Miss Graves. He also rented *Church Farm* in Little Evesden and during his tenure he experienced another occurrence of 'the odd' that initially troubled him. Usually, Tom would retire to bed at about 10 o'clock, but was often awoken two hours later by footsteps outside his room. On several occasions, he had ventured onto the landing, but there was no sign of the perpetrator. He therefore assumed that the footsteps he heard were not connected with this world and commented that: 'Nobody living had passed.'[95] He deduced that they were most likely due to the nervous anticipation of somebody in a past or future time that dreaded the approach of some other person. As a consequence of this apprehension, they had somehow forced the frightening sound onto 'the field' of *Church Farm*.

As World War II neared its end, Tom was becoming tired of Cambridge. His role as a volunteer had become irksome and he sensed a change of culture that was not to his liking. For once, he found himself at odds with the world; the war was getting him down and even the cheap toilet paper supplied by the museum was not to his liking. However, one aspect of his life was blooming and that was his love for Mina.

The couple's relationship flourished and the pair eventually married in Oban on 18th July 1944. Unlike Sylvia, Mina was footloose and fancy free and it was likely that this aspect appealed to the adventurer in Tom. As secretary at the University Museum of Archaeology and Anthropology, Mina had also developed her own interest in archaeology and was a willing accomplice on Tom's many jaunts around Britain. The newlyweds decided to make a break from Cambridge, for Tom had become tired of what he later described as the 'whispering campaign' that prevailed at the university. There had always been differences of opinions between the dons, but previous conflicts were always conducted in an orderly and open manner. The backbiting and skulduggery that was now ubiquitous and infuriated a man who revelled in open debate. As a result of this culture change, Tom and Mina bought a farm on the Scottish Island of Kerrera with the proceeds from the sale of *Mount Blow* and moved north.

Tom's break from Cambridge was, on paper, a fairytale ending to many years of personal disquiet and upheaval in war-torn Cambridge. In a letter to Cyril Fox he voiced his ambition to use the peace and quiet of Kerrera to catch up on his writing, for it was an aspect of his life that had been neglected due to his recent matrimonial problems with Sylvia. Tom and Mina's farm, *Ardantrive,* was situated on the north end of the small island and although Tom had gone there primarily to farm, his enthusiasm for archaeology had not waned. Around the corner from his farm, he found two caves worthy of his attentions. In one, he found the remains of Bronze Age flints and pottery and in the other a midden that contained an abundance of animal bones and shells. He also uncovered a number of bone pins and an iron knife that he dated to the Viking or Medieval period. One of the bone pins was carved into a dragon's head that he concluded must have been copied from a ship carving.

On one occasion, Tom thought that *Ardantrive* was haunted, after hearing strange noises at the farm, but a thorough investi-

gation revealed a young man hidden in the loft. It transpired that the clandestine lodger was the brother of their two Hebridean maids, Flora and Mary, who had been concealing their sibling in the attic.[96]

Tom and Mina worked hard at *Ardantrive*, but it appears that they had underestimated the demands of a pastoral lifestyle. Although not work-shy, Tom began to realise that the effort involved was not paying off and the enormous energy required to keep the farm ticking over distracted him from the main objective: catching up on his writing. The relative isolation of Kerrera was not quite the idyll the couple had sought and they soon began to miss Cambridge and their friends. Tom kept in touch with his fellows back home through his frequent correspondence and was, on occasion, visited by many of his friends, including Miles Burkitt and his family.

With the sale of his property in Cambridge and Sylvia's settlement, Tom had placed a reliance on the productivity of the farm. However, the couple's 'Robinson Crusoe'[97] existence proved to be challenging, for it was a vocation undertaken during difficult times and conditions. Due to the war, rationing was still in place on the mainland and Tom and Mina soon found that islanders were frequently stealing their farm animals for their own subsistence. It became apparent that their pastoral dream was unsustainable and a decision was made to cut their losses and return home.

Back in Cambridge, a decision had been made to save an Anglo Saxon cemetery at Lackford on Cavenham Heath from obliteration. Tom was seen as 'the man for the job' and was contacted with a view to him returning to conduct the excavation. In view of the situation at the farm, the couple required no further encouragement. With their Scottish island dream in tatters, they upped sticks, sold *Ardantrive* and returned to Cambridge,

On returning, Tom and Mina took up another short-gap residency at *Church Farm* in the village of Little Evesden before

moving to their new home, *Treverbyn,* at 12 Sedley Taylor Road, Cambridge on 18 March 1946. Incidentally, three days before their relocation, the couple were burgled. Tom referred to the intruders as 'sods', for they stole what he considered to be his best suit and tidy trousers.[98] Tom's daughter, Belinda, now a teenager, often visited from her home in Upton Lovell and assisted her father in the repairing and conservation of his pots and relics.[99] Tom was also kept busy at the Cambridge museum and once admitted that he did not have time to read newspapers; although he did confess to buying the *Daily Mirror,* as it contained Hugh McClelland's cartoon strip, *Beelzebub Jones,* which was adored by his daughter. Tom used to cut out the strips and paste them in a scrapbook for her to read during her frequent visits.[100]

Treverbyn was situated near to the curiously named Gogmagog Hills: a place that would eventually prove pivotal to Tom's future relationship with Cambridge academia.

Chapter Eight

Treasure Trove

Within three months of moving into *Treverbyn,* Tom found himself involved in a real archaeological whodunit. One June evening in 1946, Tom's friend, Gordon Fowler, rang him to enquire if he had seen the evening papers. Tom was oblivious to the headlines and it was left to Fowler to explain about a recent discovery of a magnificent hoard of treasure. The find, according to Fowler, included, 'A great dish with gods and goddesses rolling all over it.'[101] The hoard was being held at a police station in Newmarket and Fowler suggested that Tom first go over to view it and then proceed to Bury St. Edmunds to convince the coroner to pronounce a verdict of 'Treasure Trove', thus preventing the haul being sold and possibly shipped to America.

Tom and Mina arrived at the police station to discover the magnificent silver hoard spread over a billiard table. On closer inspection of the treasure, he was able to pick out the dish that Fowler had described and a myriad of silver items including cups, salvers and two long-tailed silver spoons that he understood to be christening gifts. One of the spoons was engraved with the words PASCENTIA VIVAS and the other with PAPITTEDO VITAS. Tom was just spelling out the inscriptions when a constable approached him and enquired if he had discovered names written on the items. He replied that he had and that the writing denoted two girls' names. The constable then asked him to read them out and duly recorded the names in his notebook. Tom found the incident highly amusing due to the fact that the girls in question had been dead for at least 1500 years!

On seeing the hoard, Tom knew immediately that it was the most important discovery of Roman treasure ever recovered in

England and probably Europe. He realised it was now time to act on Fowler's advice and establish the haul as Treasure Trove. The following day, he drove over to Bury St. Edmunds with the Cambridge don, C.W. Phillips, to meet with the coroner. During their meeting, Phillips, not realising that the coroner represented the Crown, managed to rile the official by informing him of his duty to the nation. The coroner responded to Phillips' impudence by enlightening his two visitors that he had been a captain in the Home Guard and didn't need reminding of his duty. Realising that Phillips had jeopardised their mission, Tom let it be known that he too had been in the Home Guard and had served as a major. Instantly, the coroner's attitude to them changed and a more convivial atmosphere prevailed. It was not long before the coroner had agreed to their request and assured them that an intelligent jury would be chosen with a view to delivering the verdict of Treasure Trove on the hoard.

Whilst awaiting the inquest, the story of how the silver haul came to end up on the billiard table at the Newmarket police station came to light. It appears that four years earlier, in 1942, a man named Butcher was ploughing a field for a landowner called Rolfe at a place called West Row. Butcher had been using ploughing equipment supplied by his employer, Sid Ford, a friend of Rolfe's for over 40 years. The field in question was familiar to Tom; he had excavated a rather uninteresting Roman villa there back in 1923. At the time of his excavation, locals had informed him that a treasure lay buried in the field. Tom considered the tales odd and was suspicious of the fact that this knowledge had survived in the locality since Roman times.

During the ploughing of the field, Butcher had hit upon the big silver dish, the item later described to Tom by Fowler and although he hadn't informed the landowner of his finding, he did report his discovery to his employer, Sid Ford. Butcher and Ford returned to the field and amidst a snowstorm, unearthed the rest of what was later to be known as the Mildenhall

Treasure. After retrieving the hoard, they carried their booty from the field and took it back to Ford's nearby workshop. It was told that Butcher received no recompense from Ford for his discovery, but many considered it more than a coincidence when, shortly after the find, Butcher set himself up as a smallholder. Ford was an expert metal worker and was known to Tom; he had been responsible for making him a stainless steel rod that he often used for probing in the earth. Once Ford had completed the task of cleaning the treasure in his workshop, he took it over the road to his house, where it took pride of place on his dresser.

Here the treasure remained for four years until Dr. H.A. Fawcett, a collector of antiquities – especially worked flints – from Buckinghamshire, paid a visit to Ford's home. Ford was renowned for his trading of metal objects unearthed in fields during the course of his work. Tom and his colleagues frowned on this cottage industry; although the objects bought by the likes of Fawcett often ended up in museums, their history and archaeological background were never recorded. From an academic perspective, their value was therefore strictly limited. When Fawcett encountered the silver items on Ford's dresser, he immediately informed him that he was concealing Treasure Trove and consequently threatened to report Sid and his haul to the British Museum. Although it was never stated, it is quite likely that Fawcett had offered to buy the treasure from Ford, but when a mutual price could not be agreed, the pair had quarrelled. As a result of their fallout, Fawcett had taken his subsequent stance of reporting Ford to the authorities.

On hearing of Fawcett's threat to inform the British Museum of his stash, Ford took fright and confessed to the local constabulary about his illegal effects. As a consequence of this confession, the police duly impounded the haul and hence, it was at this stage of the proceedings that Tom entered the fray when confronted by the treasure spread out on the billiard table at the Newmarket police station. After the haul had been impounded,

Fowler paid Ford a visit and asked to be shown exactly where the treasure had been discovered. Ford obligingly divulged the spot, but Fowler was aware that he had informed other interested parties of different localities. It was clear that Sid Ford still had something to hide.

The inquest was held at Mildenhall and Tom was called as an expert witness to represent the British Museum. After the background of the case had been delivered, Dr. Fawcett was called upon and asked whether the silver hoard on display in the court was all that he had seen when visiting Sid Ford's home. He responded by stating that he thought some of the items were absent. His reply confirmed Tom's suspicion that much of the treasure was missing, although the court appeared to take little notice of Fawcett's observation.

Next in the witness box was Sid Ford, and Tom admitted that it was difficult not to like him, but it was obvious that some scam was taking place. Ford was asked how he encountered the treasure and he explained the story of how he and Butcher had unearthed the hoard. When asked what he thought the treasure was made of, he replied, 'Pewter'. His response was met with incredulity by the court, as everyone present knew that Sid Ford was an expert in metals and was unlikely to have made this error of judgement. The judge asked Ford to mark an 'X' on a map to indicate the place where he had found the treasure. Fowler noted that the spot identified by Ford did not tally with any of his previous indications.

When Tom was called to the witness box, he was asked to consider the possibility of whether the treasure could have been lost in that particular field. The question was pertinent to whether the silver haul should be considered Treasure Trove, a definition that, at the time, related to a hoard that had been deliberately concealed and remained unclaimed by people or peoples unknown. Tom insisted that this scenario was impossible. He was then rigorously questioned by a KC from London, employed by Frost, to dispute the Crown's right to the treasure. The man tried desperately hard to get Tom to admit that the hoard could have been lost and suggested that many finds of pewter had been made close at hand in the fen. Unfortunately, the KC had been inadequately briefed regarding Tom's knowledge of the region and was left floundering by Tom's response. He explained that indeed, many things could be lost in fen peats, but certainly not on skirtland fields that consisted of sand on top of chalk rock and had never, at any time in their history, had peat on them. Tom later remarked that it was the first time he had been questioned by a barrister and considered it lucky to have come out of the encounter unscathed; yet he recognised that however skilled his opponent might have been, he knew he could not deny the truth when it confronted him.

The hoard was eventually declared Treasure Trove and transported to the British Museum. In such cases, the finder would usually be entitled to compensation equal to the value of the treasure. However, in this case, it was decided that as Ford had deliberately concealed the treasure for four years, his right to recompense was considered void. In response to the verdict, Ford attempted to sue the coroner for wrongful detention of his property. His case, however, was thrown out of court; the coroner, as a representative of the Crown, could not be prosecuted. Many believed that Sid Ford had got his just rewards, but Tom and his friend, Sir Thomas Kendrick from the British Museum, were none too sure. They believed that if finders of treasure, whatever their circumstances, were not compensated for their discoveries, there was a danger that future hoards may never be reported to the authorities. In turn, many objects could be passed on to private collectors of antiquities or even sold abroad, therefore depriving the nation of its heritage. After lobbying the Treasury, there was a change of heart and Ford and Butcher were awarded £1,000 each, although this was scant reward for a treasure that at the time was estimated to be worth in the region of £60,000. With the compensation paid to Ford and Butcher, many thought that this was the end of the Mildenhall Treasure mystery, but they were wrong. Tom was still not convinced by Sid Ford's story of how the treasure had come to be in his possession and he was also certain that the treasure, now housed in the British Museum, did not represented the entirety of the hoard.

Tom decided that it was time for Ford to come clean and divulge the true site of where the Mildenhall Treasure had been unearthed. After scrounging a couple of mine detectors from Bruce Milford at the British Museum, it was Tom's intention to find the hole from which the treasure had been exhumed and then recover the rest of hoard. There was, however, one small problem; although Ford and Butcher had found the treasure, the field in which it had been unearthed did not belong to them. Rolfe, the owner of the field, knew nothing about the discovery of the treasure until he read the headlines one day in a local newspaper. He was therefore very angry at his neighbour's attempt to deceive him and forbade Ford from entering upon his land. Tom, however, realised that he required Ford to pinpoint the spot in the field where he had first found the treasure. With Fowler's assistance, Rolfe was persuaded to allow Ford back on to his land, after Fowler had convinced him that treasure may still lay buried in his field. Fowler had explained to Rolfe that if further treasure was unearthed, he might well be eligible for compensation should the discovery be classed, once again, as Treasure Trove.

Carefully avoiding Rolfe's house, Tom, Fowler and Ford returned to the field that now contained a crop. After making a number of paces from the gate, Ford pinpointed the spot where he had discovered the treasure. Tom and Fowler made their own cross-bearings so that they could return to the exact spot at a future date. When the crop had been harvested, the pair returned to the field with mine detectors and digging tools and relying upon their previous calculations, they were able to pinpoint the exact spot identified to them by Ford. Their initial task was to visually scan the field for pertinent surface objects. Their survey revealed an abundance of silver items, including part of a Georgian silver teapot, a lid of a claret jug and the handle of a silver plated soup tureen. It was clear that the field had been mischievously primed, not necessarily to fool trained archaeologists, but to deceive local treasure hunters into believing that this was indeed the treasure field.

Tom and Fowler continued their search of the field using their mine detectors, devices that delivered a high-pitched scream into their headphones each time they encountered a metal object. They discovered an abundance of Roman iron nails, thrown up from Tom's previous excavations in the field 24 years earlier. However, their sweep of the field revealed no buried silver and Tom returned home with a headache. Convinced that Sid Ford was not telling the truth, Gordon Fowler continued his detective work away from the field and stumbled upon an intriguing story.

In 1922, a firm of solicitors from Bury St. Edmunds had approached Sid Ford's father and offered him £20 for the right to dig in his field – the one adjacent to Rolfe's where it was alleged that the Mildenhall Treasure had been found. The solicitors had received a letter from a man overseas, who in turn had received notification from a woman from West Row who it was inferred once lived in the house now occupied by Rolfe. She had informed him that 'the treasure' was buried so many paces from the meadow gate. When notified of this latest development, Tom realised that his initial suspicions regarding stories of buried treasure were indeed justified. When Tom had been with Sid Ford in the field, he had noticed an old pintle for hanging a gate hammered into a tree that grew on Ford's land. During their conversations, Ford had mentioned that an old footpath had once crossed and passed over Rolfe's field. Tom had not made much of this at the time, but in view of Fowler's latest discovery, alarm bells were set ringing.

Sid Ford's father had given the solicitors the right to dig on his land and Sid himself had taken an interest in the excavations beside the field gate. Tom and Fowler were unable to find any information regarding the man who wrote the letter from overseas, or find any living representative of the solicitors involved. However, they did find a man living in West Row who, when travelling to work one Monday morning many years before, had encountered a number of men putting a sack into a hole and then filling it in. He had not reported the incident, for fear that it was a body the men were burying and he didn't want to become embroiled with the police. Tom began to think about the woman who had instigated the mystery, the one who had once lived in Rolfe's house. He believed that maybe the solicitors' men had been digging at the wrong gate, for if she was responsible for burying the treasure, it was more likely to have been interred on her own land and not in the field owned by Sid Ford's father.

Tom's mind immediately sprang back to the gate pintle he had seen in the tree when walking with Ford in the field. Returning to the field, he found that the pintle was no longer there, but was able to identify the tree to which it had previously been attached. He realised that this must surely be the gate to the old footpath previously mentioned by Ford. An exploratory trench was dug on the boundary fence on Rolfe's side and although it had been over four years since the unearthing of the Mildenhall Treasure, Tom found evidence that roots had been cut and re-grown. The remains of a yellow enamel tin box were also unearthed. Tom realised that Sid Ford had waited to dig Rolfe's field in bad weather and had already known that the solicitors had dug by the wrong gate. With this knowledge, all he had to do was dig in the right place to find the buried treasure. If this was the scenario, the mystery still remained of where the treasure originally came from.

It transpired that the woman who had lived in Rolfe's house was the widow of a celebrated character called Black Jack

Seaber, who had featured in a book by Baring Gould, a relative of the Cole Ambrose family of Stuntney near Ely. The family were great collectors of antiquities, many of which had found their way into the Cambridge museum. Black Jack was a wealthy landowner and his wife was known to walk around with gold sovereigns sewn into the hems of her petticoat. Tom deduced that it was likely that Black Jack had acquired the Mildenhall Treasure locally and after she was widowed, his wife, with her own health failing, had written to a favoured next of kin overseas, informing him of the hidden treasure. It was known that she despised her relatives and that by burying the family wealth into the yellow tin trunk she would deny them of any inheritance.

The remaining mystery was; how did Black Jack come to acquire the treasure in the first place? Tom believed that it most likely came from the Roman house that he had excavated in Rolfe's field in 1923, although he was quite aware that the Lark Valley, upstream from Mildenhall, had produced hoards of pewter, silver and even gold objects. However, in his own account of the proceedings, he suggested that his friend, Gordon Fowler, in his untiring quest to unearth the truth, came closest to solving the mystery. During the course of his investigations, Fowler had discovered someone who had in their possession a bible that had once belonged to their grandfather who was once a shepherd. Tucked inside the pages was a note, dated 1860, explaining how the owner had once discovered 'the silver bells' on Cavenham Heath. The bells were renowned in local folklore and were, according to Tom, in all probability, the missing bowls from the Mildenhall Treasure. The village of Cavenham is approximately seven miles from Rolfe's field and therefore only a short pony cart, or horse ride away.

At the end of World War I, three remarkable silver objects had been discovered by Miss Nina Layard in a small area above the skirtland on Cavenham Heath. The items were identified as 'crowns', but Tom believed that they were most probably female diadems made of thin silver bands around the head, adorned with silver feathers. Further excavations at the site of the finds near the Lark river, resulted in the discovery of part of a bronze feather that had once belonged to a fourth headdress. The site of the discovery was on the edge of an Anglo-Saxon cemetery, which Tom had previously been called upon to save from destruction. During his investigations, he found the remains of two ransacked Roman brick-built tombs, as well as at least 500 Anglo-Saxon burials, a figure that probably represented a third of the overall number. As a result of his study, Tom came to the conclusion that a large Roman house had once stood not too far from the foot of the bluff and this is where he believed the Mildenhall Treasure had originally been found.

Tom's detective work in attempting to solve the mystery of the Mildenhall Treasure is typical of his approach and demonstrates the workings of an enquiring mind. His ability to spot detail (for example, the gate pintle in the tree on Ford's land) and his ability to link all of the information gathered together, enabled him to assemble informed explanations based upon the evidence available. The effort he put into his research and his analysis is breathtaking and presented anyone wishing to challenge his ideas with a daunting task. However, it was always his desire to get to the heart of the matter, so he welcomed any constructive criticism that would further enhance the quest for the truth. It is clear that Sid Ford had made a habit of trading in objects and antiquities, and Tom's investigations revealed that his story of the discovery of the treasure in Rolfe's field was a fabrication to cover his own back.

It was suggested that the Mildenhall Treasure would be best housed in the Cambridge museum, but Tom realised the impractical nature of such a notion. Due to the enormous value of the treasure, the museum would not have been able to guarantee its safekeeping and even the police, when arranging transportation of the hoard to the British Museum, had been concerned about its security. Tom agreed that the British Museum was indeed the most secure and appropriate environment to display the treasure, therefore providing access for the greatest number of people. A complete facsimile of the treasure is now displayed at the Mildenhall Museum.

Although there was always plenty to occupy Tom in Cambridge, he was still not entirely happy. The change in culture at the university that had influenced his decision to leave two years earlier was still prevalent. A change in staff had resulted in a major culture shift and he found himself at odds with the 'nit-wits', now in positions of authority.[102] For the first time in his life, money was now an issue and he began to question his unwaged role at the museum. It was a position that did not even grant him expenses and he believed that this unwaged status was detrimental to his position and standing. He even considered taking a job elsewhere, but even with things as bad as they were at Cambridge, he believed it was a far better place to be than Oxford. His main gripe was with the intimidating culture that now prevailed. He believed that the fear of overstepping the restrictive defined boundaries of the archaeological profession inhibited the advancement of knowledge. In 1952, he aired his concerns to Sir Cyril Fox:

> You can never get people to say anything these days. Now that archaeology is a profession none of the younger men dare to open their mouths.

He continued:

> I am terribly tempted to leave this place to die of constipation and come down to the west to encourage lawlessness amongst the young gentlemen.[103]

Having spent a year on Kerrera, with a climate that benefited from the effects of the Gulf Stream, Cambridge now felt decidedly cold.

Chapter Nine

Damnable Heresies

Although Tom found himself ostracised on his return to Cambridge from Kerrera, it would be another 12 years before he felt compelled to finally disassociate himself from the 'whispering campaign' that continued to prevail at the university. By 1948, he had experienced nearly three decades in the field and the results of his experiences were encapsulated in his first major publication, *Merlin's Island – Essays on Britain in the Dark Ages.* The publication of his first major work marked an upturn in his fortunes, for the year began with yet another family tragedy.

Tom and Sylvia's second son, Hugh Periam, had become a Lieutenant in the Gordon Highlanders and during a posting in the Second World War, was stationed at the King David Hotel in Cairo. Although he was not present when Irgun fighters bombed the Jewish-owned establishment on July 22 1946, he did, however, witness the appalling aftermath and carnage and as a result of this exposure, he was admitted to a military hospital with symptoms akin to post-traumatic stress disorder. On discharge, Hugh returned home and as part of his convalescence he travelled north to stay at Finavon Castle, home of his great aunt Rachel Greenhill-Gardyne (nee Lethbridge).

During his stay in Scotland, Christopher Lethbridge, who had become concerned about his brothers wellbeing, visited him at Finavon. Christopher's visit was fleeting, for he was embroiled in the finals of his medical degree and as a consequence of this commitment, he returned to Cambridge to complete his studies. On the morning of January 7 1948, Hugh borrowed a gun with the intention of hunting rabbits, but later that day he was found dead in the castle grounds, having turned the weapon upon himself. He was aged only 20 years. The shock of hearing of his brother's death left Christopher blaming himself for having abandoned his brother in Scotland. The feelings of guilt were to trigger Christopher's own, lifelong battle with mental illness.

Hugh's death impacted heavily upon Tom, but he threw himself into his work and later that same year his efforts were rewarded with the publication of *Merlin's Island*. Published by Methuen & Co. it is difficult to imagine the impression that this radical view of British history had on a post-war Britain. Throughout the war, Tom had continued to live a relatively privileged existence and his cosy position at the museum would, for most, have been sufficient, but for Tom, the proverbial boat was always there to be rocked. *Merlin's Island* was a book written during his short tenure on Kerrera, by a man who appeared to care little for the rules laid down by his profession. It portrayed a maverick that detested the orthodoxy and dogma that surrounded him. It also perpetuated the quirky approach demonstrated in his report writing and in his lectures. On completion of his first major work, he remarked to Cyril Fox: 'It isn't a respectable text book so I thought I'd give it a fanciful title.'[104]

The provocative stance is continued throughout the volume, as Tom Challenges a remark made by his friend, the Cambridge medievalist, Dr. W.M. Palmer:

> Who is this young man who has just written a book? No man ought to write a book until he has studied a subject for at least twenty years.[105]

Tom's response was unequivocal; he believed that lengthy studies often created 'information overload' – a condition that often resulted in a mass of detail and triviality, which often clouded and silted the mind. Tom considered himself a protagonist of what he called 'the commonsense' attitude to archaeology. He described his book as a collection of 'damnable-heresies' that blew like a breath of fresh air through a room, musty with the smell of textbooks and museum exhibits.

Tom was astutely aware of his place in history. In a changing world, on the cusp of the mechanical age, he realised that his adventuring and fieldwork were being carried out during a unique epoch. He feared that although future generations would have superior techniques for archaeological analysis and research, they would not be conversant with what he considered to be the last stages in the evolution of civilisation. The development that had been growing steadily since the arrival of the earliest cultivators and boat-builders was now on the verge of accelerating beyond comprehension. He therefore believed that his own 'commonsense' approach to his vocation was as (if not more) important than the technician's, or the academic's view. It was this philosophy that fired him to kick against the dogma that prevailed amongst his peers and his profession.

Merlin's Island was published in the same year as Robert Graves' *The White Goddess* and in these post-war years of caution, it was Tom's publication that was considered the most favourable in academia. His level-headed, although at times controversial, approach was perceived to be the least radical of the two works. It was therefore inevitable that his book would draw more favourable reviews when compared with Graves' contentious study. Edward Hodgkin from *The Spectator* was one of many who had waited eagerly for Tom's first publication:

> It will be especially welcome to those who have for years hoped that Mr. Lethbridge would set down in book form the stimulating ideas he has developed in a quarter of a century of excavation and field-work and which has for so long infused his lectures and learned articles.[106]

Hodgkin continued, suggesting that Tom's ideas were 'Less exotic than Graves'.

Before the publication of *Merlin's Island,* Tom had a growing reputation in archaeological circles, acquired partly through his stimulating articles and lectures. His first published work was therefore long awaited and acclaimed by both his peers and the media.

The book contained six connected essays that dealt with various aspects of Britain in the Dark Ages. They are all likeable for their originality and coherency. They are written freshly with a wealth of discursive anecdote and with many a tilt at orthodox scholarship. He provided a brilliant sketch of the change from Roman Britain to Saxon England and stressed the devastating results of the freeing of the slaves as a consequence of the great Pict War of 367AD. He also attempted to illuminate the exaggerated chapter of the Anglo-Saxon and Viking invaders in Dark Age Britain. Dismissing the British contribution to English history, as would most of us, conscious of our Romano-British ancestry, he stated that Britain was as much the island of Merlin, as it was the land of the barbarian Angles.

He urged that fresh research be conducted into the Western and Atlantic aspects of early British history in the Dark Ages. He even suggested that the Celtic inhabitants of Western Britain, Ireland and Scotland had, in pre-Viking and perhaps even in Roman times, not only travelled to Iceland, but also to Greenland and had possibly 'discovered' America. He supported these informed 'possibilities' with a comparative analysis of Eskimo archaeology, suggesting that it was the Celtic influence on the Vikings that led them to Iceland and to Greenland. As a result of his own research, he believed that the Welsh tales of the discovery of America were not myths, but legends containing historical facts.

The opportunity was also taken to remind us that the scapular and the plaid were symbols of Roman culture and can still be found in areas that fell beyond the recognised borders of the Roman Empire. This observation exemplified the fact that the

Roman influence stretched way beyond the boundaries of her empire. He also observed that relics of the Dark Ages still survived in the thatched East Anglian barns and cottages, many of which are still ornamented with carved, wooden finials, or heads of dragons. He had witnessed these designs perpetuated on the wooden, Norwegian 'Stave Churches' and he further suggested that our turned-up thatch really is a shaft; the neck of the Saxon or Viking dragon, there to deter evil spirits from sitting on the roof.

Inspired by observing Kerry men in 1929, carrying their upturned curragh on their heads, he traced the history of boats in North West Europe back to the primitive coracle and suggested that they were, in fact, prototypes of boat and house types. He believed that they were all derived from the primitive skin tent and further suggested that the longhouse was imitative of an upturned boat. Here he sets the reader's mind racing at the possibility; was the long-barrow a form derived from the upturned boat? Its resemblance to a curragh is certainly very striking. In fact, the Balkan long barrows are even called 'navetas' locally and may be preserving an awareness of this affinity. It is worth noting that even certain Menorcan tombs are also named *navetas* by J. Ramis, who may also have been aware of this parallel. *Merlin's Island* was a myriad of informed possibilities and presented a challenge to those with less imaginative minds to prove to the contrary.

From his base at *Treverbyn,* he persevered with his vocation undertaking further investigations at the War Ditches an inappropriate term associated with an Iron Age structure excavated by Professor McKenny Hughes in 1939. In his report, written in 1949, Tom acknowledges the great men of Cambridge for succeeding in '...placing much knowledge of the early conditions of life in this part of the world at the disposal of those who wish to who about it.' However, he conceded that at the same time, they had, '...occasionally been responsible for drawing red herrings across our path,' concluding that, '...it has not been too easy to remove the scent.'[107] The remarks were directed at McKenny Hughes; although he was not entirely responsible for the term 'War Ditches', Tom considered him guilty of perpetuating the inappropriate name and falsely formulating a picture of an almost circular hill fort.

In his report, Tom was quick to heap praise on his digger, William Frost, whose industry at this and many other digs helped ascertain that the War Ditches were not the completely symmetrical fort placed on the map by McKenny Hughes. Tom admitted that he found it a pity to find fault with the work of a man, '...whose industry, ingenuity and original ideas did so very much to encourage the study of archaeology in our district.' It is clear that Tom was playing the diplomat even though he considered McKenny Hughes' original 'discoveries' responsible for the dogma that prevailed over the site.

During the 1950s, Tom's investigations in the Cambridge area led him to produce a report on the Byzantine influence in late Saxon England.[108] He began his report in his own unequivocal style by reiterating his mantra that archaeological dogma could retard the advancement of knowledge by many years. His opening gambit was typically provocative, but in view of his own discoveries, he deemed it important to reiterate his belief that dogma was the curse of all learning.

Tom had first encountered glaze whilst undertaking a dig at a moated site known as Flambard's Manor at Meldreth. He had been assisting Dr. W.M. Palmer to investigate a late Saxon site located below the floor of a building that had been destroyed by fire around 1070. Amongst the late Saxon pot-sherds, they had been surprised to discover fragments that were covered in a green glaze. Tom immediately deduced that the pots must have been imported from a distant land; at the time, no comparable pottery had ever been discovered in England or Western Europe. The find was contrary to the accepted belief that this glazed type of pot was first introduced to England by the Normans. Experts reacted in disbelief when the suggestion was made that this type of pot could have existed in Saxon times. In view of this reaction, it is clear why he commenced his report in such a challenging style.

As a consequence of this and other reported finds, Tom made a search of pot sherds in the museum and he found further examples of the unusual glaze. The pots upon which the glaze was present were easily identifiable; they were usually globular with flattish rims and had short spouts below the rim and little 'strap' handles. The knowledge of this unique type of pot was further enhanced in 1947, when a number of skeletons were uncovered at the site of a housing development at Thetford. Tom took it upon himself to investigate the discovery and deduced that the building work had cut into the site of the late Saxon town. Amongst the graves, he discovered a fragment of pot featuring the unusual spotted green glaze. Group Captain G. Knocker, who undertook a rescue excavation at the Thetford site, later verified Tom's discovery.

The origin of the green glaze pottery still remained a mystery until Mr. K.B.K. Stevenson – an expert on Byzantine pottery – visited the Cambridge museum. Stevenson revealed to Tom that the yellowy green glaze was a characteristic of Byzantine pottery and that the evidence pointed to a close connection between the potters' technique at Thetford and those in Byzantinium. The only anomaly was the difference in shape of the two types of pot. The Thetford pot shapes were derivative from the sub-Roman forms of Frisia and the Rhineland and the Byzantinium, from the late Roman forms of Byzantinium itself. Tom concluded his report by observing that Norman castles, or manors, were often built on pre-existing Saxon sites and therefore the traditional view (that glazed pottery was associated with the Normans) was understandable, but, in view of recent discoveries, open to question.

Chapter Ten

Facing the Ocean

After gaining his sea legs at a relatively early age, Tom was astutely aware of the superstitions and rituals associated with this passage. An uncle of his had once told him a story of how he had taken a ride on a MacBrayne mail packet and had become alarmed when he discovered that there were two priests travelling onboard the ship. It is common knowledge amongst mariners that having a man of the cloth onboard will tempt the fates of the ocean. His uncle's trepidation was confirmed; whilst during the crossing, the boat's engines failed and the party found themselves adrift amongst the reefs in the Sound of Gunns. It is therefore understandable that Tom feared for his own salvation when he found himself being driven around Cambridgeshire by Father Brown, accompanied by two priests. Once again, the fates were tempted as the car inadvertently cut across the path of an oncoming lorry, which narrowly missed the party by a whisker. Tom believed that their narrow escape was due, more likely, to a divine intervention, rather than the skill of the driver.

Father Brown, or Martin Charlesworth as he was more formerly known, was an authority on the Roman army. He would often stop Tom in the street to ask, 'What's new Tom, so that I can put it in my lectures?'[109] He was a round, jolly man and it was rumoured that he had entered the church in the hope of being made Bishop of Ely. His weight was a constant bugbear to him and on a vacation to Crete it was rumoured that he ate a slimming pill containing the head of a tapeworm. Tom commented that on his return from vacation he was a walking skeleton; he died shortly afterwards.

As a child, from the family home of *Trevissome,* Tom had often visited Falmouth Harbour and observed Brixham trawlers and topsail schooners and ketches as they prepared to set sail. He astutely commented that the picture that he had observed was none too different to what Nelson might have once perceived in his own day. These 'timeless' scenes were to arouse in him a lifelong fascination with the sea and the men and vessels that sailed upon it.

During his time at Cambridge, Tom came into contact with the zoologist, H.H. Brindley. The association provided him with yet another example of the value of indigenous knowledge. Brindley was a continual source of yarns and scandals and it was his stories of life at sea that had most intrigued the young Tom Lethbridge. He was a large man, 'with a head that seemed to grow out of his chest,'[110] and he had an appearance that overwhelmed many of his students. He was once known to have thrown an argumentative student out of a lecture room window! However, his appearance was deceptive; Tom saw the real man through his kind and twinkly eyes.

Brindley was a good friend of the author and politician Erskine Childers, who had also studied at Cambridge. Childers was also fascinated by the ocean and he spent many of his holidays sailing the North Sea, the English Channel and exploring the German, Dutch and Danish coasts. Tom never met Childers, but once heard what he believed to be a dubious rumour, that Brindley had been the inspiration behind 'Davies', Childers' hero in his only novel *The Riddle of the Sands* (Smith, Elder and Co. 1903).

Brindley had a fascination with anchors, especially ones of the ancient stone variety, known as 'killicks', that were used by fishermen throughout the world. He had developed a typological evolutionary system of the anchors that was demonstrated by a series of small models made for him by Moreton Nance, another anchor enthusiast. It is clear that Brindley's study of a specific aspect of a mariner's trade inspired Tom, and provided him with the understanding that the study of everyday objects was crucial to comprehending the evolutionary aspects of those that chose to make their subsistence from the ocean.

Tom was following in the footsteps of many great adventurers spurned from the Lethbridge clan, but it was his own travels and experiences that provided him with a wealth of first-hand knowledge that he drew upon for his literary work. Since his Arctic inauguration onboard *Isflugen* in 1921, Tom took every opportunity to take to the ocean. The long summer breaks at Cambridge provided ideal opportunities to explore the archaeology and natural history of the Western Isles. The vacations meant so much to him and it was from these experiences that he gained a wealth of indigenous knowledge that was crucial to his investigations.

During the 1920s and 1930s, Tom's mentor was the experienced seaman John Robertson, skipper of *Elspeth*, a 16-ton yawl. It was onboard *Elspeth* that Tom gained his sea legs under the mentorship of her skipper. As well as being a skilful sailor navigating the notoriously difficult waters of the Minch, Robertson also worked hard cooking and catching fish and rowing back and forth to collect supplies and mail for Tom and his companions. Familiar to all the local fishermen, he was a godsend to Tom, introducing him to many of the local inhabitants who were able to assist him with his research into the history and legends of the islands.

Tom held Robertson in high esteem, not just for his sailing prowess, but also for his vast general knowledge and skills as an orator:

> John talked of the (1914-1918) War and how he lost his 'Diette box' (sic) when torpedoed and how a shipmate had broken his pipe stem. John had said 'Och, it's all right, I'll soon sort it – there's lots of fine pipestems in ma Diettie box.' Then he said

> 'I thought that there was no Diettie box anymore and there were lots of little useful things in it.' Most pathetic. The treasures of twenty years and more in sail and steam all gone, with a beautiful blue blanket his mother had woven him. I should have loved to see the contents of that Diette box. There must have been some interesting things in it after all his 'sailorising and buggarising' as he calls it.[111]

Friends, family and colleagues from Cambridge often accompanied Tom on his annual summer cruises around the Hebrides. It is, however, the camaraderie that he shared with his fellows that provided him with the opportunities to revel in the often lewd and bawdy behaviour that prevails in his logbooks, diaries and letters. His early journals consist mainly of times, weather conditions, observations on flora and fauna and details of routes rather than descriptive narrative, but it was not long before he began to record the human side to his adventures.

During the summer of 1925, on the return leg of his Hebridean adventure, Tom's logbook bears witness to the high jinks that took place on their travels:

> On return journey had tea at Temperance Hotel. Somewhat audacious wench giggled at F's (Cyril Fox's) and Pistol's beards and winked at us all. On leaving she asked F. in a plaintive manner if he was soon returning, to which he replied that he was not returning soon and hoped he never would![112]

Further shenanigans were encountered 18 months later at Loch Maddy:

> For the last two hours the junior officers of the Plover had been ammusing (sic) themselves by pulling down the hair of the stewardess, filling her shoes with things, rolling her on the

deck and chasing her about to the accompaniment of many giggles.'[113]

The islands Tom encountered during this early period of the twentieth century were little explored and intriguing places that provided fine opportunities for him to pursue his many interests, including botany, ornithology and shooting. His logbook on his summer vacation to South Uist in 1929 details the birds – snipe, cock, geese, duck, plover and redshank – he bagged at Loch Maddy.

Many of the archaeological sites he encountered had remained undisturbed for millennia, buried beneath the shifting sand and heavy peat, their presence oblivious even to the local inhabitants:

> On the way back, met the factor and his wife resplendent in an orange jumper who related that Mr. Thom of Canna, who took no interest in antiquities, had been visited by the Ancient Monuments Commission. He had told them that there were no antiquities on the island, whereupon they produced my paper ['Exploration of a Cairn on Canna' PSAS XI pp238-239] which stirred his bile.[114]

The annual cruises also provided Tom with an opportunity to paint, and his dedication to his hobby was quite remarkable. His watercolours and sketches provide a unique insight into the maritime history of the islands (see Appendix 3). Often he would create pencil sketches on site, making detailed references of the colours and hues that he would recreate on his pallet when back on board ship, or in his lodgings. The notes he chose to make in his daily journals and logbooks also aided his recreation of the spectacular scenes to which he bore witness. Travelling to Loch Maddy onboard *Plover* during a rare winter excursion to the Hebrides, he noted:

> Incredibly calm crossing with quite perfect views of hills and islands. Cuillins pure white down to about 1000 feet level then shading into pinky brown... Moon came up over Blaven, slightly hazy. Lovely effects of moonbeams on the swell.[115]

Tom's experience of the ocean and his acute eye for detail provided a platform for his historical studies. In his introduction to his 1952 publication, *Herdsmen and Hermits – Celtic Seafarers in the Northern Sea,* he stated: '(I am) not like Strabo, who criticised Pytheas from the security of his library. I have crossed all of the seas mentioned...'[116] Tom's friend, Sir Thomas Kendrick, a historian of Anglo-Saxon art and the Keeper and (later in his career) Director of the British Museum (1950-59), wrote the foreword to the study.

The interchange of letters between Tom and his learned friend was intellectually stimulating, but often lewd and bawdy. They would write to each other professing to be spurned lovers, or homosexuals. They would often swap stories of outrageous happenings and occurrences witnessed in the field. On one occasion, whilst conducting a dig in Ireland, Kendrick directed his second in command to open his mail during his absence. The first letter opened by the subordinate was from Tom, but written under the pretext of being Kendrick's spurned lover. On his return, Kendrick was left to explain that his 'lover' was none other than his good friend Tom Lethbridge playing the fool! Kendrick found this incident to be highly amusing and as a consequence, relayed the details to Tom in Cambridge:

> Dearest boy, Your lovely letter was opened in my absence and nearly knocked out my second in command, who came in with a very red face to King and said 'Kendrick told me to deal with his correspondence, but it is most upsetting as the first letter I've opened is very private. It is from a woman and contains some very questionable remarks.' So dear even in my

drab life there is fun and games. Never fail to write to me beloved. It does my department good! T.[117]

Kendrick's responses to Tom's many letters were always equal in wit and wisdom, even if the subject matter was work related. Often he would write under the pretence of being his friend's maiden aunt, effectuating that he and Tom were cousins:

> Your aunt is always pleased to hear from you, dear boy, and sends you her fond love. She asks me to say that she knows that 'pectoral' is a disgusting word. It is only too obvious that her other nephew Tom Kenterchick delights in such filth. She has given him a piece of her mind. Every indication is that he is getting worse and worse. Your aunt wants you to help your cousin and stick by him. She is particularly anxious that you should advise him about the repulsive carving he has got hold of. He has had advice from some ship experts, and is in great distress because dear, he cannot believe that Viking ships put to sea with rude things sticking out of their arses... Your aunt must not be worried, dear. Her rupture worries her and she is afraid that something a young officer once did to her is now having its effects...[118]

On more serious matters, Kendrick's foreword to *Herdsmen and Hermits* affirms how his friend offers his reader a personal interpretation that he knows will bring them closer to the people he is studying.

The book provided Tom with the opportunity to further investigate the possibility that ancient mariners had embarked upon voyages of discovery in the northern oceans. The subject was close to his heart and was a theory that he had been mulling over in his mind for many years. He had first raised the subject 13 years earlier in *Umiak*. In his introduction, he described the sea-voyage on his return from his final Arctic adventure with

James Wordie in 1937. Travelling from Cape Wrath to Cape Farewell, he remarked on how he had witnessed the first Sunderland flying boat on her journey to America. He concluded that, with the arrival of the aeroplane, he had probably just experienced one of the last great voyages of discovery. The time-gap between Tom and the ancient mariners, upon which he had based his studies, was enormous, but the cultural gulf between his world in 1937 and that of the present day is even greater. It is difficult to imagine living in an unchartered world, where the little-explored northern lands presented a challenge and an opportunity to adventure. He realised, however, that for the ancient mariners, every journey beyond the sight of land would have been a perilous voyage into the unknown.

The book provided Tom with the opportunity to put in to context the northern fringes of Britain with lands to the far north. The Romans perceived Caledonia as a northern outpost, the fringe of their empire – the edge of the civilised world – but to the mariner, this northern outpost was just a mere stepping stone to a far greater 'empire' that lay in the northern waters beyond Britain. His study focused on the voyages of Pytheas, the Celtic monks and the Vikings and placed into context a breed of sea-going people whose lives were not restricted by petty and administrative barriers contrived by their land-locked counterparts. His often-controversial investigation demonstrated his unique ability to humanise his subject and thus, enabled us to perceive events through the eyes of the common-man and not through those of an academic or scholar. The book was to prove an inspiration for many, including the Arctic adventurer and writer Farley Mowat, who would take the study to a natural conclusion, further acknowledging Tom's insight and scholarship.

There are also many passages in *Herdsmen and Hermits* that indicate Tom's growing interest in witchcraft and its link to ancient fertility cults, an interest that would later be developed in *Witches – Investigating an Ancient Religion* (1962). He observed that the existence and persecution of witches in eastern Scotland in the Middle Ages may have stemmed back to the matrilineal Pictish tribes and that witches were perpetuating an ancient religion that had endured since pre-Belgic times. However, the essence of this work is encapsulated in the closing paragraph, a passage that reveals the humility and endeavour of a lone mariner adrift on an uncompromising ocean. The full force of man versus nature is encapsulated in these last few beautiful words that expose Tom as the arch-storyteller.

> I will leave this study with the picture of a great, grey sky, waste of tumbled seas. One tiny black dot is skimming over its surface. Day after day this dot flies northward. No friendly plume of smoke trails across the sky. Nothing is seen but the fulmars and shearwaters incessantly gliding over the wave tops, the tiny stormy petrels paddling on the water, or the occasional blow of the whale. Bearded, dirty, salt-caked men sit gazing out at the ever changing ocean. At night strange lights flicker in the sky, like a car's headlights seen over the top of a hill. Then one day the scream of terns is heard and soon high, jagged, blue mountains streaked with white, appear on the horizon. The 'desert' has been reached.[119]

1952 saw the publication of *Coast Wise Craft*. Contrived for the more general reader, this short book continued to provide the student with a snapshot of his passion and a glimpse of his unique observational skills. His perceptive words were beautifully illustrated with a number of his exquisite watercolours and line drawings. Tom used the book as an opportunity to perpetuate his belief that something of the individual was embedded into every object made by man. It was a conjecture that also applied to ship building throughout history. The concept of the instilling of the 'self' into inanimate objects was to be a key feature of his later work. Unlike the mass-produced items of modern times, he considered a ship to be as unique and as individual as its creator. He therefore understood that to fully comprehend the boat, one first had to study the men who sailed and built them.

He perceived the sea as the 'great highway' that created an international culture of trade and exchange of ideas. He had observed how the simplest of boats had developed from the skin-covered coracles and umiaks to the trawlers, schooners and ketches that he had observed as a youth at Falmouth Harbour. He believed that the hull of a ship was the single most important and significant step in the history of mankind – greater even than the invention of the wheel, or the control of fire – for it enabled mankind to cross boundaries set by the great waters that covered the globe. It not only enabled them to transport themselves, but also their ideas to the four corners of the earth.

The boat as a living, female entity had been a belief since the time of the first boat builders. 'Ships are like women... expensive to rig, and difficult to steer,' are the words that begin *Coast Wise Craft* and were once uttered to Tom by the captain of a barque. Today, these words may sound antiquated, sexist even, but their sentiment embraces the fickle wily goddesses know throughout history. He described how the stern of a vessel was often built to accommodate the shrine of a protective female deity and how an oculus was initially painted on the hulls of early vessels to act as a guardian. This eye goddess eventually evolved into the carved, often voluptuous figureheads, which we are all familiar with today. The protectoress existed to ward off the invisible demons that were known to besiege the seafarer and which in turn gave birth to countless superstitions that are renowned by those who sail the oceans.

Because of the physical restrictions imposed by this *Field Study* book, Tom hardly had time to 'break sweat' in the limited number of pages allocated to this publication. However, the reader is left with an abundance of information to mull over and ponder upon, including the curious use of the words 'Brig' and 'Ponto', Caesar's observations of the boats of the Veneti of Brittany and the brief inclusion of primitive stone anchors discovered in Iceland. All are subjects worthy of a chapter in their own right. Anyone unfamiliar with his previous works would have been intrigued to discover more of this enquiring mind.

Published as part of Thames and Hudson's *The Past in the Present* series and edited by Jacquetta Hawkes, *Boats and Boatmen* (1952) continued and expanded Tom's passion for the sea, first initiated in *Coastwise Craft*. He perceived the boat-builder as a crucial cog in the evolution of mankind, and he understood that from the earliest of beginnings, it had always been man's ambition to free himself from the tyranny of his environment. Unlike the farmer, who perceived the seaman as a poor cousin, Tom understood that the boatman's wealth and motivation was more ethereal. From his own experiences, he realised that the mariner was exposed to a far more malignant aspect of nature than that of the farmer, as he had no protective hedges and fences to bind his world. He understood that the seaman's reward for his daily perilous challenges were manifold, for his vocation exposed him to a wealth of culture that made him a true cosmopolitan, a stance that pitched him in sharp contrast to his land-locked neighbour.

Boats and Boatmen commenced with a humble claim: the author considered himself not suitably qualified to write such a book. Tom understood that the literate seaman was a dying breed. However, he was astutely aware of his position and responsibility as an historian. The work primarily concerned itself with the evolution of the boat and of the men that built them. Tom's passion for the subject is infectious and in his own unique style, he presented us with a compelling discourse. We are enthralled by his study of ritual and superstition at sea and his discussion on the meaning and origin of the oculus and the evolving nature and custom of the boat's protectoress, a train of thought first initiated in *Coastwise Craft*. This intriguing insight revealed that many of the customs familiar to us today have ancient origins. By suggesting that the broken bottle on the side of a newly launched ship was a substitute for an ancient sacrifice, he discloses that the launching ceremony was never originally intended to appease a god in heaven. Tom's fascination with the sea is encapsulated in this single volume and we should be grateful that he embraced the challenge to write this book. It is difficult to imagine anyone today having the enthusiasm and wealth of knowledge to be able to embark on a similar project. His endeavour has left us with a national treasure that is crucial to understanding what he believed to be the cornerstone of all British history – the sea.

In the autumn of 1952, Donald Boyd – Chief Assistant in the BBC's Talks Department – had a notion to assemble a series of broadcasts in which various speakers would scrutinise well-known stories and then pose the question, Myth or Legend? The idea was to examine ancient tales in the light of modern historical and archaeological evidence and then decide whether they were either fact or fiction. The series eventually materialised and an inaugural run of six broadcasts was aired in the spring of 1953.[120]

Produced by Michael Stephens, the series was considered a success and a second run of a further six discussions was commissioned by the BBC and broadcast during the winter of 1953/54.[121] In his notes, Stephens provided a brief explanation of the series:

> The talks are not designed to be sheerly, historical or archaeological and I am anxious that the sense of wonder in the original folk tale should not be lost in the re-telling of the story (sic).

Donald Boyd set out the theme of the twelve talks in *The Radio Times*:

> It makes a good story – but is it true? For anyone who wants a good story and an answer to that tiresome little question which threatens to spoil the whole effect... this... is exactly the right prescription... The difference between myth and legend, between invention and fancy on one hand and some kind of history on the other, is the theme of this new series of talks.

Tom was asked to contribute to the third talk in the second series of *Myth or Legend?* And his contribution was a 15-minute address entitled *The Isles of the Bless'd*. The Home Service programme was pre-recorded in a London studio between 1.15 and 2.00pm on 26 November 1953 and was broadcast on 11 December 1953, after initially being postponed from its planned airing on 6 December. In 1950, Bowes and Bowes had published *Herdsmen and Hermits – Celtic Seafarers in the Northern Oceans* in which Tom had explored the notion that pre-Columbian seamen had navigated their vessels, not only to Iceland and Greenland, but beyond to the Americas. He therefore embraced the opportunity to further investigate this theme when he accepted Boyd's invitation.

Tom understood that the quest to unravel the mystery of the 'Happy Isles' – a place of myth and legend – would require investigations into three distinct phases: the Greek, the Celtic and the Norse. The poems of the Greek poet Hesiod made reference to the Isles of the Bless'd – a place of luxury and contentment that that was said to exist beyond the Pillars of Hercules – generally accepted to be the Straits of Gibraltar.[122] Tom deemed it unlikely that the Greeks ever ventured further west than Gibraltar and he therefore considered their knowledge of the Isles of the Bless'd to be based upon second-hand knowledge.

In Ireland during the Dark Ages, folktales were abundant and spoke of a happy, or pleasant, land that lay to the west, beyond the sunset. These Celtic tales included the 'Land of Youth', the

'Land of Women' and the 'Plains of Pleasure', all of which bore a remarkable similarity to the tales told by the Greek poets. Many who ventured there were known to have travelled in glass-bottomed boats. Tom astutely identified these vessels as being skin-covered crafts, which when polished and greased were almost as clear as glass. It was told that men travelled for many weeks across the western ocean and often vanished forever, but if they did ever reappear, they returned as old men. It is from these adventurers that the stories of the charmed land beyond the sunset arose.

Tom was particularly intrigued by the tales associated with St. Brendan – a Celtic saint who was born in the west of Ireland in about A.D. 484. Tales of his adventures were later transcribed in the eleventh century and these tell of two prestigious sea voyages he undertook in a westerly direction. His first journey involved a passage in a skin-boat round by way of Iceland, Greenland and Newfoundland, but it was his subsequent journey that intrigued Tom. Accompanied by a number of companions, St. Brendan is known to have sailed due west in a wooden boat for 40 days, before eventually arriving in a land of fog and shoals. From further descriptions of the terrain, Tom surmised that his party had come to ground somewhere on the Ground Banks of Newfoundland. The accounts of the expedition relate how St. Brendan then proceeded south, where he encountered a land of hostile, dark savages. He is also known to have happened upon a single Irish monk – a survivor of an earlier mission. On his return to Ireland, St. Brendan recounted his stories of the happy land beyond the sunset.

From studying eleventh century accounts of St. Brendan's voyage, Tom was certain that many of the transcriptions were based upon historical fact, even though many of the tales had become embellished and exaggerated with medieval embroidery. Many contained Norse references that may well have been familiar to St. Brendan, as well as to those who eventually collated and transcribed the tales. The Norse tales, or sagas, are histories of important families primarily from Norway and Iceland. The recording of their adventures makes up the sagas, but this of course is not a definitive record of historical events. Tom was astutely aware that many far-reaching expeditions may well have taken place, but due to the prosaic nature of those involved, their endeavours were never recorded for posterity.

The stories of Eric the Red (the first settler in Greenland) and Leif the Lucky (an adventurer who visited him) highlight the apparent frequency of those that chose to venture into the northern waters beyond Britain.[123] After visiting Eric, Leif made his way to a place on the coast of North America. On his return, he revisited Eric the Red who was annoyed that his visitor demonstrated little interest in the fact that he had 'discovered' America. As a result of this nonchalance, members of Eric the Red's household decided upon their own initiative to revisit the land encountered by their dispassionate visitor.

Thorfinn Karlsefni was another explorer of North America, and Tom was certain that his accounts were entirely factual; they were entirely banal in form and contained little of the drama and sensationalism desired by those back home who craved the outlandish and the unusual. He considered it pertinent to comment upon the unostentatious nature of Karlsefini's observations.

> The main story, as far as it goes, is absolutely straight; but mixed up in it are little bits of descriptions which look as if they had been taken out of some earlier tales like that of St. Brendan. For instance, there is much talk of grapes growing wild, which gave the country its name of Vineland, of self-sown fields of wheat and other marvels, which sound very much as if they belonged to the older stories and not to the very prosaic expedition story of the Norsemen.

Tom suggested that sailors, especially traders of Tartesso, may well have been accidentally blown off-course and reached America by the winds known as the North-East Trades. He pointed out that Carthaginian coins had been discovered on the Azores. This suggested that this 'halfway house' had been visited in classical times and if this was the case, there was no reason why intrepid sailors could not have ventured further west and beyond to America. He reminded his listeners that stone axes, female figurines and certain kinds of painted pottery associated with European Stone Age culture had been discovered in Central America. He believed that far from being make-believe, the Greek tales of the Happy Isles were based upon much earlier sailor's tales from other countries. The later Irish stories appeared less make-believe than the Greek renditions and the later Norse stories appeared even more authentic in their style and attention to detail. The comprehensive nature of these later renditions reveals that they were indeed first-hand accounts and observations of actual voyages.[124]

Tom concluded his broadcast by remarking:

> ...the Isles of the Bless'd have shrunk, or grown, from some nebulous, unattainable, wonderful land beyond the sunset, to a thing we now know very well as the United States of America.

In 1953, Tom's interest in Celtic seafarers led him to pursue a historical conundrum across the Irish Sea. Following the critical acclaim of the *Axe Age* (Methuen, 1925), T.D. Kendrick's second major study, *The Druids* (Methuen, 1927), was a work that had influenced Tom during his first decade at Cambridge. Tom had become intrigued by his friend's theories on stone circles,[125] in particular, a quote Kendrick had taken from the *Tripartite Life of St. Patrick*.[126] Kendrick describes an event that is alleged to have taken place in the year 435(CE), when St. Patrick arrived in the

Plain of Slecht, near the modern Ballymagauran in County Cavan. It is understood that the site was once the residence of the chief idol of Ireland known as Cromm Cruaich. The statue was adorned with gold and silver and surrounded by a ring of 12 smaller idols covered in bronze.

Kendrick ascertained that what was being described on the Plain of Slecht was a stone circle with a centre stone, not dissimilar to the Boscawen-un ring in Cornwall. It appeared that the later Druids had modified, or 'customised', a Bronze Age stone ring for their own purposes. In early mediaeval times, this site was known as a place of pagan worship and also the scene of a mighty conflict between St. Patrick and the heathendom. It is told that Patrick struck and marked the main idol with his stave and caused the 12 lesser idols to be swallowed up in the earth as far as their heads.

What appears to have happened on the Plain of Slecht is a similar occurrence to the fate of the sarsen stones at Avebury in Wiltshire. The missionaries of the new religion considered the complete destruction of the stones far too dangerous; therefore, by burying the stones in the earth, a subduing effect was achieved.

In 1953, Mrs E. Ettlinger published a new theory on the Lough Erne Figures, suggesting that they did not represent the Seven Deadly Sins as originally suggested, but represented St. Patrick and some of his early converts.[127] It was this alternative theory that provoked Tom to contribute an even more radical response in the *Royal Anthropological Institute Journal* later that same year.

In his own inimical style, Tom set about deconstructing the Christian interpretations credited to the stones by submitting alternative explanations for each of the figures. The bell and the short sword, known as a 'crozier', in the hand of the statue accredited to St. Patrick were reinterpreted by Tom as an Irish short-sword and a sceptre, respectively. He suggested that there was nothing to imply the figure was a saint, but concluded that the statue may well have been a king, or chieftain meditating before giving judgement. Because of the apparent uniqueness of the carvings, Tom didn't believe that they stood alone in the archaeological field and began suggesting parallels for the figures.

Tom likened a cloaked female carving that accompanied the 'St. Patrick' statue with the Sheila-na-gig carvings of the eleventh to sixteenth centuries, even though the Lough Erne figure was not so aggressively indecent. However, he likened her to the Baubo figures described by Dr Margaret Murray[128] and further suggested that, although well know in the mediaeval period, these figures may have evolved from earlier roots, progressing from the suggestive to the emphatic.

Tom analysed the figures and concluded that they were 'stand alone' statues and were never intended as part of a building, or structure. Their weathering suggested that their position appears to have been out-of-doors and not within a roofed building, such as a church or chapel. Although incomplete, he believed that the existing set of statues were part of a larger group. No comparisons could be made, but he believed that the stones once formed part of some kind of 'modified' stone ring, or enclosure.

He suggested that a stone circle once stood on White Island and it was this enclosure that was, at some point in history, transformed into the statues we now know as the Lough Erne Figures. St. Patrick had already destroyed the most famous circle of Cromm Cruaich, an incident that took place in the year 435(CE) in County Cavan; the location being the adjacent county to where the Lough Erne Figures were discovered. Tom further suggested that it was these stones that replaced the idols destroyed by St. Patrick. Therefore, the intriguing likelihood remained that further stones awaited discovery.

Tom posed another possibility that he described as being, 'altogether too fantastic'[129]: could the Lough Erne Figures be the actual deities cursed by St. Patrick? He suggested that they could have been dug up from their distressful position on the Plain of Slecht and moved to a safer position some distance away. At first glance, the Lough Erne figures appear rudimentary when observed through Greek or Roman eyes, but through their primitiveness, they are masterpieces of expression. Tom believed that no Christian craftsman could have carved them. He suggested that the figures were probably hewn, perhaps 200 years before the arrival of St. Patrick, and although they could have been copies, he truly believed that the Lough Erne Figures were the originals claiming:

> Even St. Patrick couldn't destroy them and no one else ever dared to make the attempt. The most that could be done, as with the giant at Cerne, was to build a church close to them and hope that their influence would slowly decline. It needed a man with the fervour of St. Patrick or St. Coloma to dare to destroy such potent figures.[130]

Tom's focus on the Celtic seafarers appears not to have distracted him from his studies on matters terra firma. During the 1950s, Tom produced reports on his findings at the cemetery at Lackford in Suffolk and pewter dredged from the Old Croft River at Welney. However, not all of his studies were focussed on the Cambridgeshire region; his local research was often punctuated by his frequent trips to the Western Isles. In 1951, he undertook an investigation into the brochs and wheelhouses at Kilpheder and South Uist. Tom had first visited Kilpheder in 1925 when he had attempted to search for earth houses, but with little success.[131]

On 11 September 1950, Tom had purchased his own boat, a ketch, known as *Zoraida II*. The vessel was purchased for £1,000.00 (today's money: £20,000: Munby, 1996) from two partners – D.B. Scampton and J.W. Trebble of Rhy – who were planning to emigrate to New Zealand.[132] The capital was raised from the proceeds of the sale of jewellery items – heirlooms of the Lethbridge family.

Onboard *Zoraida II*, Tom sailed across the Minch to the Outer Hebrides. After dropping anchor at Lochboisdale harbour, it was his intention to visit the middens of the wheelhouses at Daliburgh and Kilpheder.

Earlier in the year, Dr. Werner Kissling had contacted him with a request to undertake investigations at brochs and wheelhouses on South Uist. For many years, Kissling had been studying and collecting examples of folk culture from the Outer Hebrides and Tom's curiosity for such matters had resulted in him agreeing to make the northern voyage. South Uist was not unfamiliar to Tom; over the past quarter of a century, he had made numerous visits to sites on the island. However, he utilised his 1951 visit as a reconnaissance mission for a future, more thorough excavation.

That particular summer had been very dry and Tom was able to distinguish the presence of the buildings by the discoloured grass that grew over them.

Assisted by local volunteers, Tom spent the next two weeks excavating the site and his investigations revealed that at least one of the dwellings consisted of a well-preserved wheelhouse with a large number of corbelled cells surrounding a central court or room. The discovery of a Romano-British type enamel brooch on a ledge in one of the chambers signified that the discovery was contemporary with similar buildings found by Captain Thomas and Erskine Beveridge at Uisnish and Machair Leathann, respectively. Once the interior of the wheelhouse had been recorded, it was considered necessary to take the protective measure of turfing over the excavation in the anticipation that they would return the following year. This second season's work was, of course, reliant upon the securing of sufficient monetary backing.

Tom was successful in his quest to seek further funding for a more comprehensive investigation on South Uist and returned to

Kilpheder the following year. He identified the wheelhouse as being called *Bruthach a Sithean*, or *Brutach Sitheanac*, which translated, simply meant *Brae of the Fairy Hill*. On one occasion whilst excavating in the depths of the wheelhouse, Tom and Mina took a break from their labours to meet their good friend, 'Whiskers' Bristowe, who had travelled to the island on a MacBrayne boat. On greeting their good friend, they were introduced to a gentleman who Bristowe had become acquainted on the crossing. 'May I introduce to you to the archaeologist friends of whom I spoke, Sir Hereward Wake? Tom and Mina Lethbridge.' Before Sir Hereward could reply, Tom, quick as lightening, replied, 'I am really delighted to meet you, Sir Hereward, because I have lately been trying to find your splendid ancestor in East Anglia.'[133]

As a result of his undertaking at the Pictish wheelhouse, Tom was invited back to the site four years later to present his discovery to H.M. the Queen. As part of her regular summer holiday cruise of the Western Isles, she was scheduled to visit South Uist on Wednesday 15 August 1956. After visiting a local seaweed factory at 11.48am, the Queen, accompanied by the Duke of Edinburgh, was introduced to Tom at the wheelhouse by the Lord Lieutenant. The visit was only fleeting, but Tom still had time to remark to her that she was probably the first monarch ever to see inside a fairy hill. She departed the wheelhouse at noon and Tom later remarked that she had shown considerable interest in his finding. He was also impressed and somewhat surprised at the Duke of Edinburgh's intimate knowledge of his enquiry, a discovery that prompted the retort: 'He's got brains.'[134]

On returning from his Royal encounter, Tom oversaw the publication of his next major historical study. Published by Andrew Melrose, *The Painted Men – A History of the Picts* (1954) is another insightful study undertaken in his own inimitable style. Once again, he set out his stall early by denouncing the use of references in his work and sidesteps the cry of, 'lazy swine!' with a shrug of his broad shoulders. After all, 'This is a story for general consumption, not a handbook or a report,' he contentiously retorted.[135]

It is clear that he shared an affiliation with his publishers, for the letters that exist between Tom and James Whittaker, Melrose's Editor and Managing Director, are quite extraordinary. They demonstrate remarkable scholarship, are filled with social comments, and exchange views on a myriad of historical matters, many of which later featured in the book. However, they also exhibit the lewd humour that was prevalent in much of Tom's correspondences. In one particular letter entitled, 'Bring your problems to us!'[136] Whittaker sets out his epistle such that it resembles a communiqué from a long-established family firm specialising in the treatment and care of bowel disorders. Having got wind of Tom's predicament, Whittaker ribbed:

> Poor sufferer! May we bring our lightning services to your attention, soliciting your custom in the humblest manner and assuring you that our only desire is to please, to allay your anguish, to alleviate your abraded bowels.

He continued:

> What is up with you all in Cambridge? I know lots down here have had 'flu and general collywobbles, but I haven't heard of such shitey aftermaths as seems to fall upon you Academics and grave-robbers.

After the jovial opening salvo, matters of a more serious nature resume, including the triumvirate nature of three-leafed clovers, chuckies, knuckle-bones and long-dead Hebridean shamen.

Tom commenced *The Painted Men* by dispelling the Victorian misconception that we must not fall into the Roman error of thinking that everyone who was not educated up to their own particular standard was a hopeless barbarian, lacking in knowledge, or intelligence. It was apparent that Tom felt an affiliation with the Picts, for his study revealed them to be a highly ordered and enterprising race and the story that emerges is quite illuminating.

The Roman occupation of Britain is placed into context and the occupiers are depicted, not as a static force, but as an evolving, integrating presence; it was never simply a 'them' and 'us' situation as is often portrayed in the history books. He demonstrates the needs and relationships that occurred between the British and their occupiers, an interaction that he conveyed in a very reasoned and plausible manner. The social implications of inter-breeding and the importance of preserving the empire are analysed and presented in a typical 'Lethbridgian' fashion. Whilst describing the Roman 'Push for Scotland', he revealed that there would have been no survivors in the Roman army from the original British invasion. His ability to expose human facets of history is to be admired, for one can only imagine the mindset of a group of young men, many of whom had been born and bred in Britain, who were being ordered to attack a race of people that many would have considered kin. He contemplated what would have been required to motivate them on this pointless, northern operation.

Much of *The Painted Men* was written from first-hand knowledge of the coastal geography of northern Scotland. Writing one particular passage in swirling fog whilst at anchor in the harbour of Eriskay, it is quite understandable how Tom was able to evoke the spirit of those that had inhabited the very same lands of which he wrote about, nearly 2,000 years before. He was not content to rely solely on archaeological evidence, even if this was to later put him at odds with his profession. To comprehend the bigger picture, he knew that all data had to be absorbed. He realised that even fairy stories, like *The Children of*

Lir, when deconstructed, revealed elements of long-forgotten truths.

In chapter four, he described the finds of the abandoned Kilpheder wheelhouse, revealing to us the swept floor, the ashes in the hearth and the possessions of the occupants abandoned in lockers in the walls. It is likely that the owners had probably gone off to their southern camp, but had never returned. One's mind begins to wonder as to what had happened at this 'Northern Pompeii'. He takes the story beyond scientific enquiry and presents us with evidence of a poignant human tragedy.

The chapter continues with the description of a winter's night in a Hebridean broch and once again, the place becomes alive and animated. With his informed narrative, he again reveals himself to be the arch storyteller, akin to the broch builders of yore, who sat around their hearths telling tales and stories of their ancestors. It is easy to see why academics would cringe at this unconventional approach to history, but in his writing, he reveals a wealth of possibilities and brings to life the long dead race we now know as the Picts.

Tom was a natural and gifted writer and a remarkable example of his aptitude is demonstrated in his composition of *The Painted Men*. After reading through the original manuscript, archivist John Gadd remarked that, 'Tom's typescript submitted to Andrew Melrose was almost identical to the printed copy.' After comparing both documents, Gadd was only able to discover 120 discrepancies between Tom's submission and the printed copy.

The publication of *The Painted Men* was a watershed in Tom's career; it was the last 'conventional' book that he would write. From here, the going became tough and a world of possibilities was about to open for the Honorary Keeper of Anglo-Saxon Antiquities at the University Museum of Archaeology and Ethnology, Cambridge.

Chapter Eleven

Gogmagog: The Buried Gods?

In April 1955, a team of Cambridge archaeologists began the process of sectioning the ditches at the Iron-Age camp of Wandlebury in the Gogmagog Hills, south of Cambridge. Their task was to shed light upon the origins of the Iron Age encampment. The dig was of considerable interest to Tom; during the previous six months, he had been undertaking his own investigations at the Wandlebury site.

His curiosity had been fired by a remark made to him by Sammy Cowles, an attendant at the Cambridge Museum. Tom had known Cowles since 1925 and had once been asked by his friend: 'When are you going to look for that giant?' Cowles was referring to a chalk-cut figure that was known to have once existed in the vicinity of the Wandlebury earthwork. As a boy, Cowles had been acquainted with an old man who had told him of a giant that could be observed from the nearby village of Sawston. Cowles' story was backed up by information given to the archaeologist Guy Maynard, the onetime curator of Saffron Walden Museum. Cambridgeshire antiquarians John Layer (1586-1640) and William Cole (1714-1782) had also claimed to have seen a hill-figure at Wandlebury.[137]

Tales of the giant were prevalent in the Cambridgeshire area and Tom deduced that the figure had fallen into disrepair and vanished from view during the nineteenth century. He believed that the Wandlebury giant would have been similar in form to that of the Cerne Abbas Giant, which he had visited on 5 February 1928.[138]

A local folktale, once narrated by the medieval historian Gervase of Tilbury, had been translated by Arthur Gray, Master of Jesus College Cambridge, and printed in the 1911 volume of the *Proceedings of the Cambridge Antiquarian Society*. The tale told of an ancient moonlit battle that had once occurred in the Wandlebury ring between Osbert, son of Hugh and a fearsome knight. Tom deduced that the knight in the story had become immortalised as the giant on the Cambridgeshire hillside. It was apparent to Tom that the moonlit warrior and the long-lost hill figure were inextricably linked. The mystery of the Wandlebury giant had intrigued him for many years, for he had first published a concise interpretation of the story in a letter to *The Times*, published on 12 June 1936.

Gog Magog Hills

To the Editor of The Times

Sir, - Gogmagog, or Gourmaillon, was undoubtedly responsible for the name of these hills. His figure cut in the downland turf, either inside Wandlebury camp itself or on the hillside close beside it, was still visible in the middle of the eighteenth century, as the following extract from the manuscripts of William Cole, the antiquary, shows:- 'In a quaint book by Bishop Hall, in 8vo., printed by Edward Blount and William Barrett, called the *Discovery of a New World or a Description of the South Indies*, with his running title, *The Description of Tenter-Belly*, and subscribed the *Cambridge Pilgrim*, at p. 44, is this:-

'A Giant called All Paunch, who was of an incredible Height of Body, not like him whose picture the Schollers of Cambridge goe to see a Hogmagog Hills, but rather like him that ought the two Aple Teeth which were digged out of a well in Cambridge, that were little less than a man's head.' When I was a boy, about 1724, I remember my Father or Mother, as it happened I went with one or other of them to Cambridge, the riad from Baberham there lying through the Camp (now blocked up by the house and gardens inclosed in it of my Lord Godolphin), always used to stop and show and my Brother and

Sisters the figure of the giant carved on the turf; concerning whom there were than many traditions, now worn away. What became of the two said teeth I never heard.

It is probable that Gogmagog was to be seen in the camp itself, for a tradition, published some years ago by the Master of Jesus in the Proceedings of the Cambridge Antiquarian Society, tells us that if we go to the entrance of the camp in the moonlight and cry, 'Knight to Knight come forth,' a giant will emerge and fight with us. It is possible that the Elizabethan edict that forbade students to attend festivities at Wandlebury is not unconnected with the survival of fertility rites performed at this figure. It is curious that a similar figure also existed at Oxford. I have been unable to trace the slightest sign of our Gogmagog either on the ground or from the air.

I am, &c.,

T.C. Lethbridge - University Museum of Archaeology and Ethnology, Cambridge.

In the autumn of 1954, Tom took the opportunity to turn his attentions to solving the conundrum of Sammy Cowles' lost giant. Having thoroughly surveyed the Wandlebury site, he sought permission from the Cambridge Preservation Society (CPS) – the owners of the Wandlebury estate – to conduct a search on the banks of the Iron Age camp. His request was granted and his preliminary investigations revealed a section of land on a southern slope leading up to the ring to be the most likely place for the lost hill figure. It appears that his choice of location was influenced by local accounts: the giant could once have been observed from the nearby village of Sawston. These observations were coupled with the fact that the designated area appeared relatively undisturbed. He felt certain that he had located the site of the Wandlebury giant.

On 30 October 1954, Tom wrote to Sir Cyril Fox explaining that he had begun his quest to search for the lost hill figure.

Rather than conduct a labour-intensive dig, Tom decided on rather an unconventional method of detection. He believed that by ramming his metal probe, the one conceived by Sid Ford, into the hillside turf, he would be able to establish if certain areas had been disturbed in antiquity. By measuring the depth upon which the iron rod penetrated the hillside and noting the sound and vibrations it made, he deduced that he would be able to detect any previous interference with the topsoil. As his initial investigations involved only minor disturbance to the site, the CPS granted him permission to proceed with his investigation.

He began the task of accentuating the figure and before very long the hillside was littered with the evidence of his industry. To mark his findings, he used artichoke stems to indicate the locations where he considered the chalk had previously been disturbed. The formation of these protruding sticks formed a surreal scene on the lonely hillside. In a further letter to Fox on 3 November 1954, Tom declared: 'I have found Gogmagog.' He continued: '...but I am rather alarmed and astounded by what I have found.' The letter included a sketch of what appeared to represent a gent wearing a bowler hat wielding a sword and a spear. Over the following weeks, Tom kept his learned friend posted with further notes and pencil sketches that detailed the progress of his investigations. Furthermore, his enquiry appeared to reveal that the figure was mounted upon a stead. A further letter, sent on 5 December 1954, was headed: BRILLIANT NEW SERIAL COMING SHORTLY 'THE SECOND GIANT OF WANDLEBURY' and he excitedly commenced his briefing by reporting: 'I feel pretty certain that there is a second figure of comparable size behind the horse's arse.'

Tom's investigations continued through the Christmas period and on into the following year. The bitter weather and the constant ramming of his probe into the chalky hillside had made his hands raw, but still he persevered with his quest.

In April 1955, Lethbridge was part of a team of archaeologists, led by Brian Hartley, which began the task of sectioning the Wandlebury ditches. With his mind consumed by his 'discovery', Lethbridge found the official dig mundane and gravitated back to his own investigation on the lower slopes. It was not long, however, before Tom's activity drew the curiosity of locals and members of the Cambridge archaeological team involved in the official Wandlebury excavation. We can only speculate what his fellows thought of his undertaking, but their persistent snooping prompted him to retort: 'The ones I complain about are migrants from the other dig who wander down and express opinions.'[139] It is clear from this comment that many of his fellow archaeologists were scornful of his undertaking and many believed that the figures that Tom was revealing were creditable to solufluction in the chalk, or even figments of his over-active imagination. Tom was astounded at the criticism that was being levelled at him and he considered it incredulous that his efforts should have ignited such vitriol. His perseverance, however, resulted in further hostility between him and many of his fellows and he became involved in many a heated altercation with onlookers regarding the legitimacy and credibility of his undertaking.

Tom's survey had now revealed three figures – a moon, a horse and a chariot. He identified the figures as being; a pre-Norman warrior with a round shield, who he identified as the knight in Gervase's tale; a hooded goddess and a sun god. From his investigations, he was able to construct a comprehensive pencil drawing of his findings. The next step was to request permission from the CPS to begin a formal excavation of the site. His request was granted and Tom and his newly appointed helpers – Tebbutt, three farmers and a vet – began the task of exposing the figures. William Frost was still in his employment, but the ageing foreman, with eyesight failing, was not initially called upon to assist in the painstaking undertaking. In a further update to Fox, Tom made reference to his assistants: 'They are all staid, if not always respectable.'[140]

Henry Urmston Willink – Master of Magdalene College and Vice Chancellor of Cambridge University – was kept frequently updated by Tom. Initially, he was quite excited by the discoveries, but urged caution and, 'to restrain to the utmost possible degree all publicity.'[141] An Outsider Report submitted by chalk deposit experts, Mr Sparkes and Mr Lewis, requested by the CPS, had concluded: the depressions discovered by Tom were most likely of a natural occurrence and not man-made. In response, a four-man committee, which comprised of I.W. Cornwall, W.F. Grimes, C.F. Hawkes and S.E. Piggott, was formed on the authority of the Executive Council for British Archaeology (CBA) following a request from the Chairman of the CPS for an independent opinion on the features being exposed by Tom. Sensing that the excavation would undoubtedly meet with opposition from some members of the CBA committee, Willink made clear his own position that he would have to remain impartial at all times.

Tom's enthusiasm and certainty regarding his discovery got the better of him and, ignoring Willink's words of caution, he embarked on a worldwide publicity campaign. Articles, featuring headlines such as 'The Goggle-Eyed Mother of God' caused concern amongst the academics at Cambridge.[142] The story became quite a scoop. Having given an interview to the *London Evening News* in March 1955, an agitated editor wrote to Tom explaining that a strike had held up the publication of the article and he was concerned that the *Daily Express*, who had also got wind of the discovery, might be first with their exclusive. Further ignoring Willink's advice about keeping his findings low-key, Tom embarked on a lecture tour and conducted a number of interviews with the BBC.

Soon after lodging his request with the society, he took the unprecedented step of publishing his findings in *The Times*. His unsubstantiated claim to have discovered a 3,000 year-old hill figure did not sit comfortably with the Cambridge hierarchy. Amidst the fury, Tom continued with his excavations throughout the Christmas period of 1955 and on into the New Year. He was only distracted from his labours by heavy snowfalls the following January and during this period of respite, he took the opportunity to visit and sketch a pertinent etching of a figure holding a sword in nearby Sawston church. He likened the carving to the pre-Norman warrior he had discovered on the Wandlebury hillside. On 16 April 1956, he wrote again to Fox declaring that he was still digging!

Despite Tom's diligence, the controversy escalated and the story caused many factions in the world of archaeology. Terence Grey, the owner of the Wandlebury estate, was enraged at Lethbridge's methodology and discourteous attitude. Many in academia chose to distance themselves from his 'discovery', although it appears that Tom's approach and attitude were responsible for much of the resentment that ensued. He did, however, manage to find a couple of allies in his friend C.F. Tebbutt and Sir Cyril Fox, who initially remarked that the Tom's critics lacked the imagination to perceive his figures.

In July 1955, Willink wrote again to Tom, having got wind of the fact that Cyril Fox was planning to visit the Wandlebury hillside in the spring of 1957. He also realised that the CBA committee's report was almost ready for submission and he urged Tom to get Grimes and Fox to communicate, for he valued any input or observations that Fox may have had regarding the site.

After a visit to the Wandlebury hillside, the CBA committee concluded that Tom had unwittingly excavated a natural feature caused by conditions during the last Ice Age. Their Majority Report was submitted to Willink on 18 September 1957: Grimes, Piggott and Cornwall signed it with renowned geologist F.E. Zeuner's support. Hawkes was unable to attend on the day that the CBA committee attended the Wandlebury hillside. Tom accused the CBA committee of doing a poor job on their visit and sent Hawkes a copy of his recently published book *Gogmagog – The Buried Gods* that had recently been published by Routledge and Kegan Paul. After spending time discussing his excavations with Hawkes, Tom insisted that he should submit his own findings alongside the Majority Report.

Hawkes submitted his own Minority report that appeared to disagree with the CBA committee's conclusions. He claimed that the Majority Report did not disprove Tom's claims of a discovery of a chalk hill figure. In it, he stated: 'My colleagues rejected it on imperfect appreciation of the conditions which were unlike what they were accustomed to.' It was apparent that Tom's undertaking had caused division amongst the academic community.

In January of the following year, V.J. Gastor, Assisting Master of the CPS, tried to calm the situation. He wrote to Tom stating that although the Majority Report appeared to the contrary, the CPS was not saying that they disputed his claims of a hill figure at Wandlebury. The uncertainty and lack of solid scientific evidence was causing divisions in academia. In a letter to the Council of British Archaeology, Tebbutt suggested that two camps had arisen: Grimes and Piggott locked in opposition against Hawkes' more sympathetic appraisal of Tom's findings.[143]

In September 1957, the CPS wrote to Tom informing him that it would be advisable for him to re-turf, at his own expense, the excavated areas in order to protect the exposed goddess figure from frost damage. Although initially quite miffed at the suggestion, Tom took the step of organising some aerial photography of the excavated areas. He commissioned Aero Pictorial Ltd, based at the nearby Redhill Aerodrome, to fly over the site and record his work. On the 17 September, they wrote to him explaining that they were awaiting favourable conditions for the photo-shoot, but by 4 October, Tom had received three 10″ X 8″ black and white prints of the giantess and a quantity of small greetings cards bearing the image of the hill-figure. Aero Pictorial invoiced him the princely sum of £7/9s/9d for their services.

Gogmagog – The Buried Gods was aimed at the layman and provided a powerful argument for the authenticity of the figures. It cast a doubt in the minds of many of his critics, many of who were forced to reconsider their initial, hasty criticisms. Tom utilised his book as a vehicle for evidencing his discoveries and commenced the work with a provocative opening line: 'The story really begins with a fairy tale.' From these introductory words, you can almost hear the groans of disdain from his peers. He had thrown caution to the wind and had ignored the advice of his colleagues, who warned him that publication would not only prolong the saga, but also inevitably damage his reputation. Having no interest in his reputation, he chose to ignore their advice.

Tom began his work with an analytical discourse of the Gervase of Tilbury tale. If taken literally, the story had to be pure fiction, but he realised that if it was not pure fantasy, it possibly concealed a hidden message. Tom's observations of the origins of myth and folklore were very perceptive and unlike fellow twentieth century archaeologists, Heinrich Schlieman and Sir Arthur Evans, who utilised ancient mythology to seek the lost city of Troy and the Knossos labyrinth respectively, Tom did not take the Wandlebury fairy story literally. He was able to decipher the words meaningfully and logically and provide an explanation stripped of the medieval embroidery that masked the original tale. It was an unconventional, but perceptive, approach; by utilising the fairy tale as a research tool, he believed that he had added yet another string to his investigative bow.

Evans' interpretation of the Minotaur myth at Knossos was a fine example of modern man's attempt to rationalise an ancient myth with a literal explanation. Like Schliemann at Troy and so many other twentieth century scholars, Evans failed to understand the muse and the fact that perhaps the words of the poets were intended, as true poetry surely is, a patronage to the Great Goddess herself. However hard Evans tried to fit the myth with his findings through Classical eyes, how could he possibly explain the zoological improbability of the Minotaur, a beast that had the body of a man and the head of a bull that had once lurked in the chambers of the Knossos labyrinth? It is known that the early Greek philosophers were opposed to 'magical sorcery', for it posed a threat to their new religion – logic. This Classical ideology perceived myth as irrational. In *The White Goddess*, the poet Robert Graves had suggested that the Greeks viewed mythical animals, such as the Chimaera, as zoological improbabilities, and Socrates, by turning his back on myth, had in fact highlighted his own rejection of the Great Goddess.

In his own study, Tom continued this line of thought and took the opportunity to investigate the lost gods of Albion. He suggested that 'Gogmagog' was, in fact, a name aligned to the Great Goddess herself. His research championed the research of Margaret Murray, who in her book, *The Witch Cult in Western Europe* (Oxford University Press, 1921), had suggested that modern day witch cults were evidence of the survival of a prehistoric religion. Tom considered the theory plausible; it was not a million miles away from his own conjecture. He had become familiar with Dr. Murray through her work at Cambridge University and having aligned himself with her theories, it is clear that he had already embraced the muse. It was a patronage that would have an inevitable bearing on his future writing and it would also estrange him even further from the logical minds back in academia.

Dr. Margaret Murray was born in Calcutta in 1863 and had become known as a renowned and respected anthropologist, archaeologist and Egyptologist. She arrived at Cambridge during the World War II with others who had been evacuated from University College London. Tom later remarked:

> Of course Dr Murray did not belong to Cambridge, but she settled there for a time and might have remained for the rest of her long life, had she been better treated. Her books on witches struck Professor Minns as being obscene and he did all he could to make the old lady's life difficult. When she offered to give a course of lectures on Ancient Egypt, free, gratis and for nothing, Minns deliberately cut two out so that it should not constitute a full University course. This was insulting as well as absurd for she was a great authority on the subject.'[144]

Tom, however, admired her work and appeared very fond of her. In *The God of the Witches* (Sampson Low, Marston & Co. 1933), she had suggested that a number of historical figures including William Rufus, Gilles des Rais, Thomas å Becket and Joan of Arc were, in fact, 'Divine Victims' whose deaths were intended and planned as scapegoats for the death of the sacred king. It was a philosophy and practice that dated back to the pagan religions of prehistory. It was these latter, unsubstantiated claims that caused most academics to scorn her work. By nailing his colours to the Margaret Murray mast, Tom had disturbed many of his peers at Cambridge. However, it must be stated that his own theories and ideas were always substantiated thorough primary research, a sharp contrast to Murray's later eccentric and uncorroborated claims. It was therefore amiss of the critics to tar him with the same brush, but many, unfortunately, did.

In May 1957, Murray joined the Gogmagog debate. In a letter to *The Times,* she launched a scathing attack on the academic fraternity; her aim was largely directed at Grimes and Piggott for their refusal to acknowledge Tom's discovery:

> Archaeology is not merely a matter of technique, technology, or the details of flint chipping. It covers the whole field of human endeavour, in which each period is of importance, for

> the individual members have left their mark on the civilisations of the present day, in our beliefs, our customs, and our very natures. Archaeology is not itself a religion, but 'scientific archaeology' bids fair to become fetish.[145]

She, like Tom, appeared to be reacting to what they considered to be the straightjacket methodology of 1950s academia.

Grimes was quick to respond:

> For the rest it is disappointing, not to say exasperating that a scholar of Dr. Murray's standing should be so out of touch with all that is being attempted for the archaeology of this country.

J.G.D. Clark and Geoffrey Bushnell were also quick to 'grasp the nettle' but added brevity to the debate:

> Sir – May we suggest that a League of Unscientific Antiquarians be formed to combat the menace of these scientific archaeologists? There may be many who would like to join Dr. Margaret Murray, whose letter you printed yesterday, in her stand, and the initials F.L.V.A. would ensure that due weight was given to their opinions.

Throughout proceedings, Bushnell, like Willink, always attempted to arbitrate and kept an honest and straightforward dialogue between all parties.

After Murray's public attack on Grimes, Cyril Fox wrote to Tom expressing his disdain: 'He is a dear kind man who evidently hates this sort of row.'[146]

By September 1957, the Gogmagog controversy was in full swing and Murray further embroiled herself in the saga by writing to Tom explaining that she had recently spoken with Hawkes whilst on a visit to Dublin. She claimed that he had far-stronger opinions in favour of the Wandlebury figures than those expressed in his Minority Report and that the other committee members were wrong in what they had said regarding the condition of the chalk. She continued:

> But to my mind the refusal of the other two members (Grimes and Piggott) of the committee to send his report with them is unforgivable, unfair and biased.[147]

She hoped that the CBA committee would ensure that fair play prevailed.

Having witnessed the hostility shown towards Murray first-hand, Tom should have been prepared for the criticisms he too would later receive for banging the same drum. However, during her time at Cambridge, she had found in Tom a helpful and accommodating ally who often assisted her with slides and presentations. It was a relationship that would continue long after Tom had left Cambridge, up until her eventual death in 1963.

A review of *Gogmagog – The Buried Gods* in *The Times* by Tom's friend, Sir Thomas Kendrick, Director of the British Museum, also prompted a flurry of responses, including one from M.A. Pinhorn of Hatfield who had personally undertaken research into the Wandlebury figure. In his letter, Pinhorn quoted a passage from John Layer's History of Cambridgeshire, written during the seventeenth century. Referring to the Gogmagog Hills he wrote:

> I could never learn how these hills came to be called Gogmagog, unless it were from a high and mighty portraiture of a giant which the schollars (sic) of Cambridge cut upon the turf or superficies of the earth within the said trench. And not unlikely might call it Gogmagog, which I have seen but is late discontinued.

Pinhorn also mentioned that references to the figure by Dr. Dale and Bishop Hall show that the figure was still in existence during the latter part of the eighteenth century. He continued by quoting Dale's sighting in 1730:

> Wandlebury hath three ramparts and two grafts between and a giant figure of Gogmagog cut on the turf in the middle of the camp.

The quote added further weight to the growing suspicion that the original figure had been cut within the Wandlebury ring and not on the outer bank as Tom was suggesting.

The publication of *Gogmagog – The Buried Gods* proved to be a turning point in Tom's life and marked a commitment to a cause that many of his peers at Cambridge frowned upon. In Tom's eyes, his work was a natural evolution built upon observations he had made in the field over the previous 40 years. Up until this publication, his earlier books had been well received, for they reflected his work in the field of archaeology and British history. Many of his critics, however, didn't perceive them as serious studies, even though they displayed a good-natured, pragmatic knowledge and an understanding of their subjects. Each publication had demonstrated the observational powers of a man who saw beyond the literal. By employing an intuitive approach to his subjects, he believed it enabled him to see right through the conundrums that confronted him in the field. This had enabled him to present rationalised, commonsense solutions without boundaries or affiliations. His book continued this tradition, but its acceptance was undermined by the continuing uproar surrounding the legitimacy of his findings and the inclusion of a controversial study on the lost gods of Albion.

Publications that chose to review *Gogmagog – The Buried Gods* on the whole remained impartial; none, however, were brave enough to throw their whole support behind his 'discovery'. An uncredited review in *The Listener* was typical and even went as far as supporting the argument presented by Murray in *The Times* earlier that year:

> It seems that Mr. Lethbridge (whom no one accuses of burrowing beneath the turf) must still depend rather upon hunch rather than a secret certainty...

Picking up on the debate that had raged earlier that year in *The Times,* they continued:

> It is not always scientific truth which alone produces scientific truth. Scientific error has its stimulus; and it is really high time that more attention was accorded to English hill-figures and to their likely provenance and affiliations. Archaeology as well ought not to be conceited in its scientific flush to accept a prod even from unorthodoxies which may approach the ridiculous. Were it all the wildest rubbish, it would still be revelatory of its author's engaging complexity of mind and being.'[148]

One of the main areas of concern for the CBA committee was that their inspection had revealed plough marks through the site of the figures. They believed that the existence of this activity poured further doubt on the credibility of the hill figures. Tom admitted that these markings were indeed present, but were attributable to the Stone and Iron Age and that the figures he had uncovered were well below any disturbances made by any modern plough. He once again cited his use of the steel bar as being the ideal detection tool to counteract the ploughed surface. He reiterated that the disturbed topsoil of the hillside was a conducive for such investigations and that this information had been plotted and published in the *Archaeological News Letter* long before any excavations had been carried out. He had realised that the evidence of ploughing activity would present an obstacle for his critics and Tom felt exasperated by those who failed to fully comprehend his methodology.

Despite the misgivings of some of its members, Tom appears to have maintained a healthy and friendly dialogue with the CPS administrators. Gastor wrote to Tom enquiring about *Gogmagog – The Buried Gods* and requested that he present a copy to them.[149] Tom obliged and included a number of the aerial photographic postcards with his tome. Gastor was also delighted that Tom was in full agreement regarding the returfing of the site to protect the excavations of the figure.[150]

By the end of the decade, Tom was still defending his corner regarding his Wandlebury discoveries and it is clear from his writing that he was becoming increasingly frustrated by those who chose to disparage his findings. He began his report to the Cambridge Antiquarian Society by stating: 'Although members of the Society may have become somewhat bored by hearing so much talk on this difficult subject…' He continued by justifying his persistence: 'These controversies often lead to a considerable advance in knowledge.'[151] It is clear through his persistence that Tom was passionate and still convinced by his own discoveries.

More recent dig pits and a magnetometer survey conducted by Cambridge University have cast further doubt upon Tom's revelations and it is now generally accepted in the world of archaeology that the anomalies in the chalk discovered on the hillside were of a natural occurrence and not the activities of an ancient's hand. W.A. Clark, former Head Warden of Wandlebury ring, has disproved many of the nineteenth century observations made of the hill figure from the village of Sawston by demonstrating that trees planted in the late eighteenth century would have blocked the view. He also confirms that he has met old estate workers who recall ploughing on the site in their youth.[152] Many are still convinced that a chalk-cut giant did once exist at Wandlebury, believing, however, that the icon was cut, not on the outer-banks of the earthwork where Tom believed it to have been, but inside the ring itself. Tom firmly believed that dogma was the curse of all learning and it is likely that, if he had lived to view conclusive scientific results that exposed his discoveries as misguided, he would have been the first to admit his error of judgement. On the other hand, if still not convinced by their analysis, he would have endeavoured to provide his critics with further proof to evidence his discovery.

Many have suggested that far from being misguided, Tom – always the perpetual joker – had contrived the hill figures as an elaborate hoax. Anyone who has taken the trouble to read his works will be aware of his good-natured humour, but to doubt the sincerity of the Wandlebury figures is an insult to a man who truly believed in his discovery. Tom never doubted for one minute the authenticity of his findings, but inadvertently found himself in opposition to his profession, who believed them to be figments of his over-active imagination. An attribute that had served him so well in the past was now in danger of ruining him. By going out on a limb, he had backed himself into a corner. It was, however, the vitriolic nature and aggressive reaction to this work by his peers that upset him the most. Disillusioned with what he called the 'trade unionism' of his profession, Tom began to reconsider his future at Cambridge.

On the home front, things were not going smoothly either. Although fond of his daughter, Belinda, now a frequent visitor to their home in Sedley Taylor Road, her increasingly erratic behaviour became a problem for both Tom and Mina. It was clear that the balance of her mind was disturbed and her behaviour was becoming a strain. Things reached a head in the late spring of 1955 and Tom decided to take action and made arrangements for his daughter to be admitted to a sanatorium in Switzerland. In a letter to Cyril Fox, he vented his frustration at his daughter's deteriorating mental health: 'Belinda absolutely tires us out.' He continued by likening her condition to: '...a leaky cell in a battery shorting the next one. In fact, I would bet a good deal that this is what it is. She cannot hold the charge put into her by her food.'[153] The remark was clearly a reference to the failure of the medication in the management of her condition.

Tom's patience with Cambridge finally snapped and in the autumn of 1957, he and Mina 'upped sticks' and moved to *Hole House* in the village of Branscombe in Devon. Still plagued by the reaction to his work at Wandlebury, he was able to consolidate his position and commenced a process of seeking allies for his discovery on the Wandlebury hillside. Whilst at *Hole*, Tom developed a growing band of like-minded supporters who wrote to him frequently about aspects of his work. Morris Marples, author of *White Horses and Other Hill Figures* (London Country Life, 1949), also wrote to Tom requesting the use of one of his aerial photographs of the giantess for one of his presentations.[154] During the course of *Gogmagog – The Buried Gods*, he had championed the work of Margaret Murray and he took it upon himself to renew the relationship that he had forged with her during her period of lecturing in Cambridge.

From their correspondence, it is clear that their relationship was initially remarkably formal, suggesting that the pair were not that well acquainted during Murray's lecturing days at Cambridge. However, it may simply have been that she had forgotten about Tom's presence there. In 1954, Murray had her third and perhaps most controversial book in her study on witchcraft published. In *The Divine King in England* (Faber and Faber, 1954) she advanced her theory that many early English sovereigns, dating back from William the Conqueror in the eleventh century through to James I in the early seventeenth century, had died as a result of ritual murder. She claimed that this action was in observance with the ancient sacrificial themes of the 'Slain God' and 'Divine King' practiced in the pagan religions. Both *Gogmagog* and *The Divine King in England* received similar criticism from academics for their unconventional approach and because of this, Tom saw Murray as a natural ally.

As their friendship developed, it is clear that Murray was tentative of Tom's assertion regarding his identification of the Wandlebury figures. It was a point that she claimed was the weakest link in his study. She believed that all deities started from the same root, but it was the advancement of knowledge and variations in social conditions that forced changes in their depiction and identification, but not always in their functions. Contact with higher civilisations often resulted in cultures adopting less gross forms of ritual, which often resulted in the creation of new deities. Murray cites the example of how Durga – the killer of demons – is only a more civilised version of the Hindu Mother Goddess Kali, with Christ simply being another form of Osiris.[155] She suggested to Tom that his attempts to name and rationalise the hill figures had been the greatest bugbear to academia.

Throughout her correspondence, she demonstrated a respect for Tom's achievements and approach, claiming that his work was indeed, 'pioneering.'[156] She was always honest in her criticisms, sometimes brutally so, but it is clear that she eventually warmed to his good-natured approach and her correspondence reflects this gradual thaw in relations. Margaret Murray died in 1963 aged 100, and through her letters Tom had gleaned an enormous amount from her focused and analytical approach. His contact not only provided him with access to an inspiring oracle, but an insight on how to deal with his detractors.

Back in Cambridge, Tom's ally, Tebbutt, continued to fight his corner. In a letter to his dear friend, he mentioned that Miles Burkitt had suggested that it might be advantageous to consult peri-geologists at the Sedgwick Museum.[157] Two reports by the peri-geolgist, C.L. Forbes, were submitted, but neither reached a firm conclusion as to whether the grooves in the chalk identified by Tom were either natural or man-made.[158] In May 1958, Tebbutt even took a Mr. Greenfield from the Ministry of Works over to Wandlebury and petitioned him to involve the Ministry into solving the conundrum of the chalk hillside.

At *Hole House,* Tom continued to pursue his new direction and eventually embarked upon a series of eight remarkable books that would place greater strain on his relations with his peers back in Cambridge. Time eventually tempered his anger and resentment of those who had opposed him during the Gogmagog affair and he chose to demonstrate this thaw in the notes he made for his proposed autobiography *The Ivory Tower*. The project provided him with an opportunity to fondly reminisce about his life and times at Cambridge and demonstrated a fondness and affection for his fellows, even those who were critical of *Gogmagog*. It is, however, his humour and natural spirit, an endearing feature that had been evident throughout his work, that is to be admired throughout this adversity. It is sad to think that so many were afraid of tarnishing their own reputations by continuing their associations with a colleague who many considered to have strayed from the fold. Until the day a comprehensive geophysical survey of the site is undertaken, the jury still remains out on the authenticity of Tom Lethbridge's hill figures at Wandlebury.

To this day, there are many factions who still trust in Tom's findings and, even amongst those in opposition, many still believe that a giant did once exist at Wandlebury, but that its whereabouts has yet to be discovered.

T.C. Lethbridge:
A Life in Pictures

Tom Lethbridge with his mother Violet.

Photo courtesy: The John Gadd Archive, Cambridge University Library.

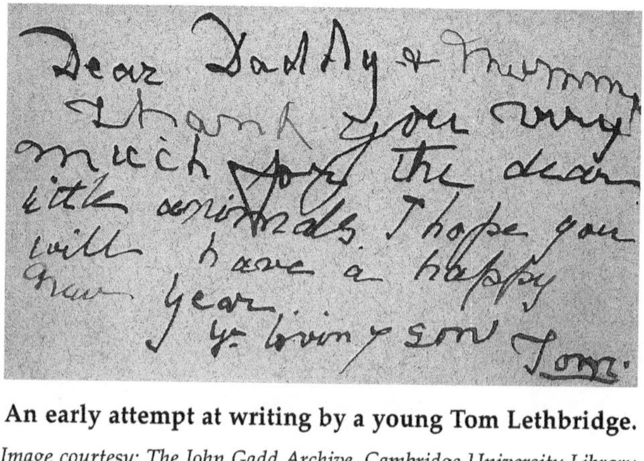

Dear Daddy & Mummy
Thank you very
much for the dear
little animals. I hope you
will have a happy
new year.
Yr loving son Tom.

An early attempt at writing by a young Tom Lethbridge.

Image courtesy: The John Gadd Archive, Cambridge University Library.

Tom Lethbridge - August 1905.

Photo courtesy: The John Gadd Archive, Cambridge University Library.

Tom Lethbridge 1906.

Photo courtesy: Andrew David's personal archive.

Tom Lethbridge (centre) with sister Jacintha and family friend Bridget.

Photo courtesy: The John Gadd Archive, Cambridge University Library.

1904: Tom Lethbridge aged 3 with his baby sister Jacintha.

Photo courtesy: Mary Rose Rogers' personal archive.

Thomas Charles Lethbridge.

Photo courtesy: Mary Rose Rogers' personal archive.

Tom and sister Jacintha pictured with their younger brother Ambrose William Speke.

Photo courtesy: Mary Rose Rogers' personal archive.

Wellington College: Tom (right) with his House Mistress.

Photo courtesy: Mary Rose Rogers' personal archive.

March 1922, Cambridge: Sylvia Frances Robertson and Tom Lethbridge – Engagement Photograph.

Photo courtesy: Mary Rose Rogers' personal archive.

6th February 1924, Salisbury: Tom & Sylvia's Wedding.

Photo courtesy: Mary Rose Rogers' personal archive.

6th May 1925, Salisbury: Christopher Lethbridge's Christening. Left to Right: Geoffrey Walford, Jacintha (Tom's sister), Tom, Violet (Tom's mother), Mrs Townshend Murdoch (Tom's Grandmother), Sylvia, Jane Walford & Humphrey David.

Photo courtesy: Mary Rose Rogers' personal archive.

Belinda's Christening at Mount Blow, June 1930. L to R: Hugh, John Wordie (eldest son of Sir James Wordie), Belinda and Christopher.

Photo courtesy: Mark Walford's personal archive.

Tom with his Godson Mark Walford (son of Geoffrey and Jane Walford) at Woolacombe, July 1932.

Photo courtesy: Mark Walford's personal archive.

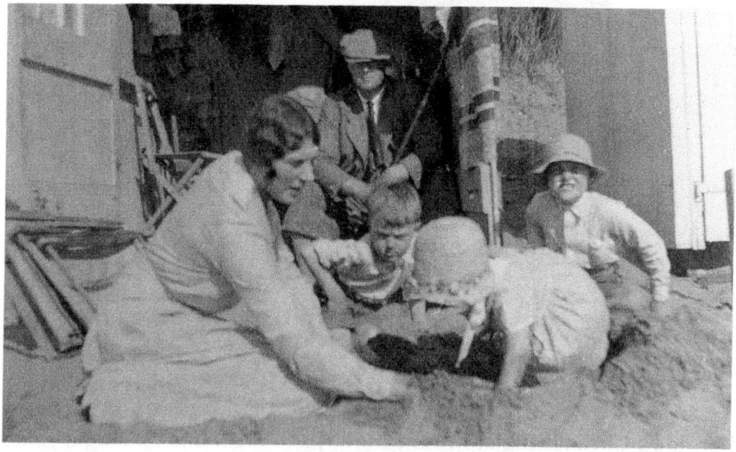

Family friend Wendy, Tom, Hugh, Belinda and Christopher at a beach-hut at Woolacombe, July 1932.

Photo courtesy: Mark Walford's personal archive.

Mount Blow, summer 1929: Tom with divining rods.

Photo courtesy: Nicholas Leadbitter's personal archive.

Tom's sister Jacintha.

Photo courtesy: Mary Rose Rogers' personal archive.

Circa. early 1930s, 'Mount Blow' Tom's friend Charles Leaf with Christopher Lethbridge.

Photo Courtesy: Andrew David's personal archive.

Belinda Lethbridge's christening at Mount Blow. L to R: Hugh, Sylvia, Nanny holding Belinda, Christopher and Tom.

Photo courtesy: Mark Walford's personal archive.

Summer 1926, Waterbeach: Sylvia and Hugh.

Photo courtesy: Nicholas Leadbitter's personal archive.

'Mount Blow' Shelford: Teresa, Sylvia & Christopher.

Photo courtesy: Nicholas Leadbitter's personal archive.

6th July 1933, 'Mount Blow': Tom with Belinda and Hugh.

Photo courtesy: Mary Rose Rogers' personal archive.

Hugh Periam Lethbridge.

Photo courtesy: Mary Rose Rogers' personal archive.

Skipper John Robertson onboard 'Elspeth'.

Photo courtesy: The John Gadd Archive, Cambridge University Library.

Tom Lethbridge's sketch onboard 'Elspeth' 1933. The two men onboard are John Robertson (with cap) and Tom's friend Geoffrey Walford.

Sketch Courtesy: Mark Walford's Personal Archive.

Tom and Sylvia onboard 'Elspeth'.

Photo courtesy: The John Gadd Archive, Cambridge University Library.

Tom Lethbridge undertook two voyages to the Baltic (1934 & 1935) onboard 'Passat'.

Photo courtesy: The John Gadd Archive, Cambridge University Library.

Tom and Sylvia onboard 'Elspeth'.

Photo courtesy: The John Gadd Archive, Cambridge University Library.

July 13th 1937, Greenland: Tom, Robin and Feachman onboard Isbjorn.

Photo courtesy: Peter Wordie's personal archive.

Summer 1937, Greenland: Tom onboard Isbjorn.

Photo courtesy: Peter Wordie's personal archive.

1937: Carmichael & Dymond's scientific equipment to record cosmic radiation in the upper-atmosphere onboard the Isbjorn.

Photo courtesy: Peter Wordie's personal archive.

1938, Cambridge: Mina Elizabeth Leadbitter.

Photo courtesy: Nicholas Leadbitter's personal archive.

Mina Elizabeth Leadbitter.

Photo courtesy: Nicholas Leadbitter's personal archive.

Circa 1937, Moretonhampstead: Mina, her Brother Mathew and Father Revd. Mathew Leadbitter.

Photo Courtesy: Andrew David's personal archive.

Christopher John Lethbridge.

Photo courtesy: Mary Rose Rogers' personal archive.

Circa. Second World War: Tom Lethbridge.

Photo Courtesy: Andrew David's personal archive.

Circa. World War II: Self-portrait of Major Tom Lethbridge in Home Guard attire

Photo Courtesy: Andrew David's personal archive.

15th August 1956, South Uist: Tom shows HM The Queen and the Duke of Edinburgh the Kilpheder wheelhouse.

Photo Courtesy: Andrew David's personal archive.

1954, Wandlebury: Mina and Tom plot out the Wandlebury hill figures.

Photo Courtesy: Andrew David's personal archive.

Excavations reveal the The Wandlebury Giant. Aerial photographs taken by Aero Pictorial based at Redhill Aerodrome.

Photo Courtesy: Andrew David's personal archive.

Easter 1965, Hole House, Branscombe: Belinda and Tom Lethbridge.

Photo Courtesy: Andrew David's personal archive.

1966, Hole House, Branscombe: The BBC film Tom with his pendulum.

Photo Courtesy: Andrew David's personal archive.

Tom at Hole House shortly before his death on 30th September 1971.

Photo courtesy: Andrew David's personal archive.

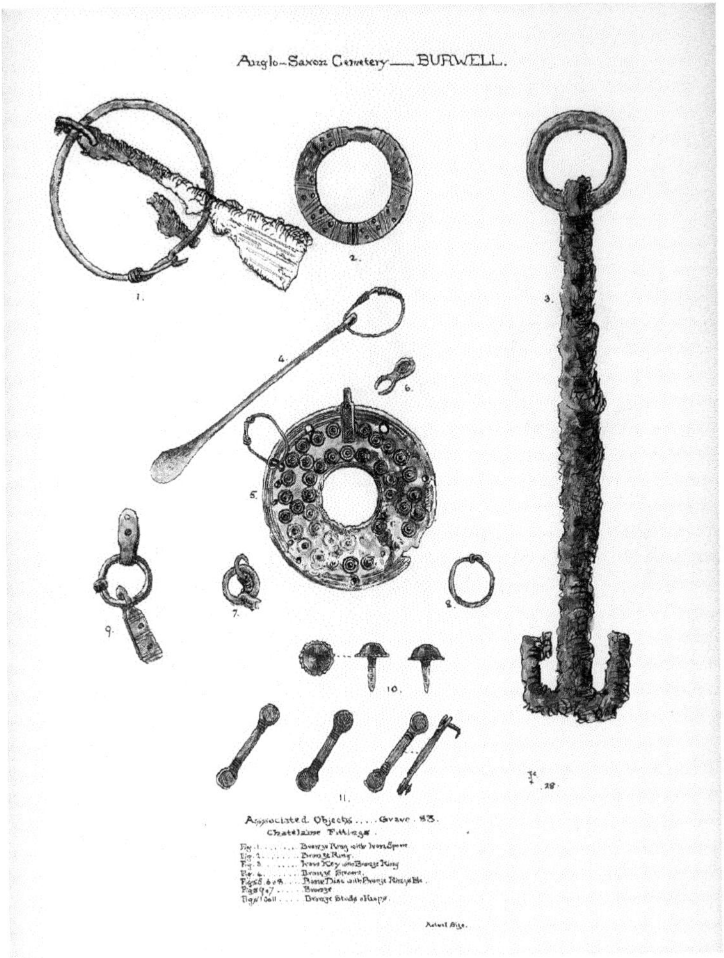

Example of Archaeological Illustrations produced by T. C. Lethbridge: Burwell.

Image courtesy: The John Gadd Archive, Cambridge University Library.

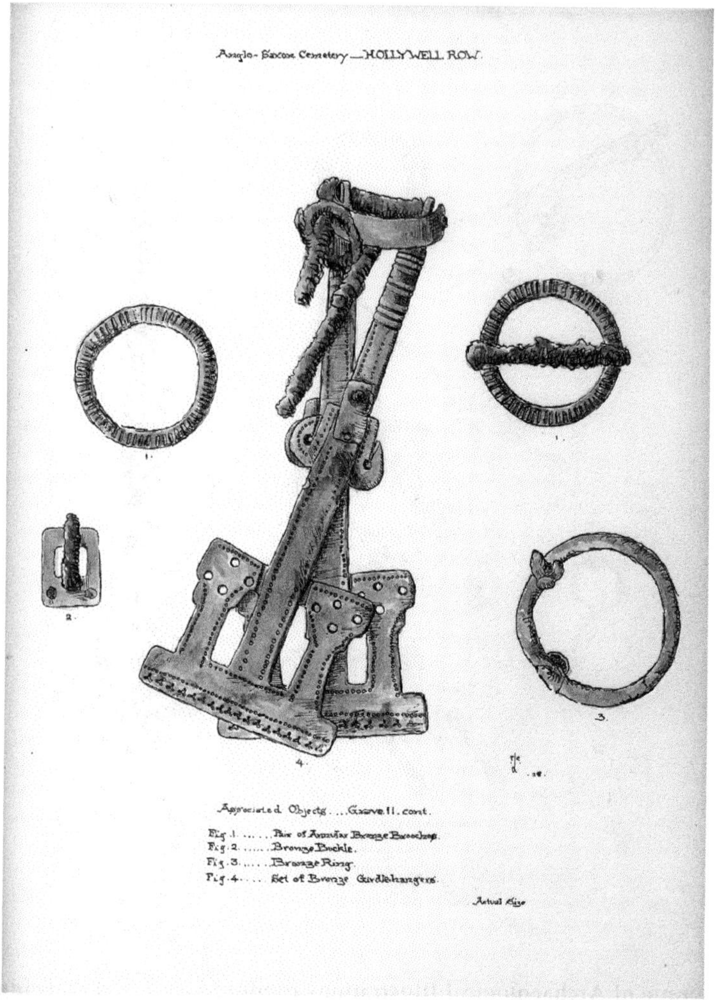

Example of Archaeological Illustrations produced by T. C. Lethbridge: Hollywell Row.

Image courtesy: The John Gadd Archive, Cambridge University Library.

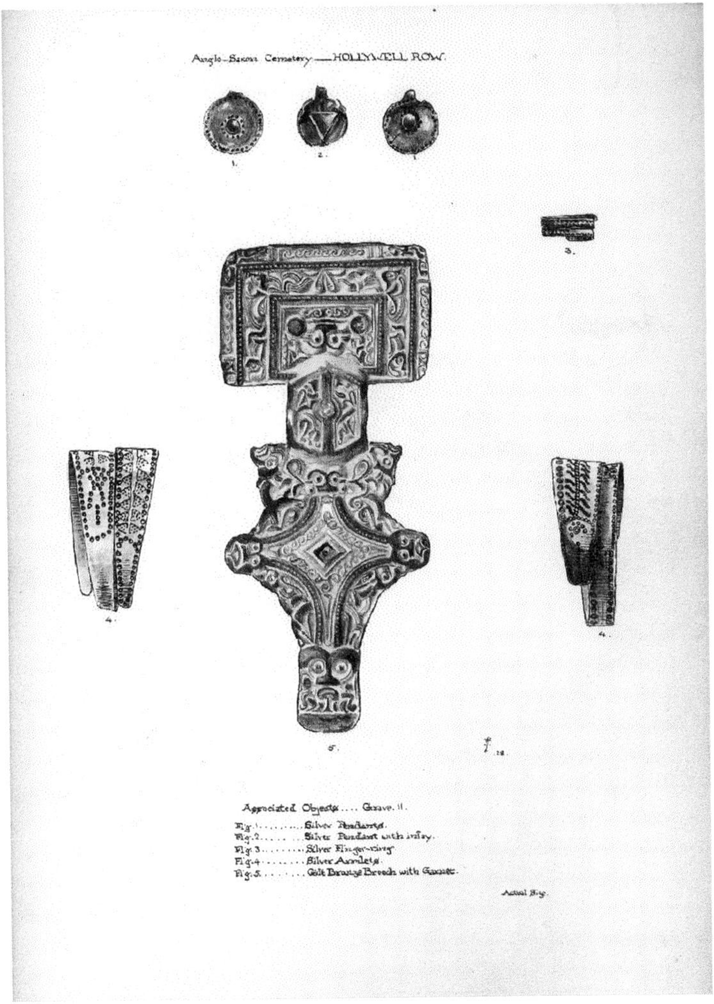

Example of Archaeological Illustrations produced by T. C. Lethbridge: Hollywell Row.

Image courtesy: The John Gadd Archive, Cambridge University Library.

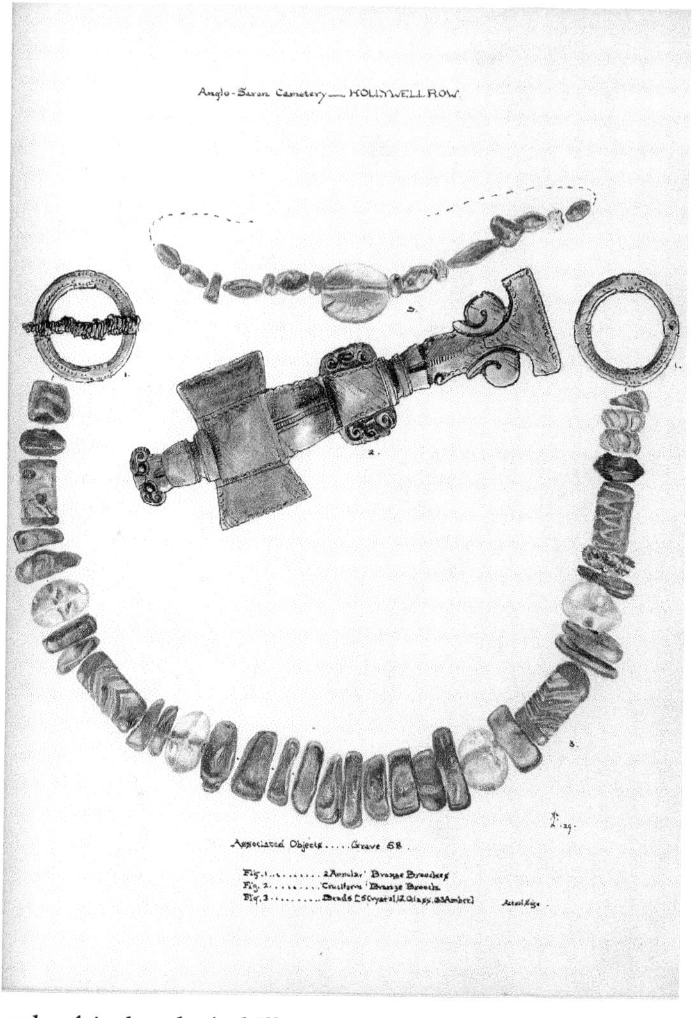

Example of Archaeological Illustrations produced by T. C. Lethbridge: Hollywell Row.

Image courtesy: The John Gadd Archive, Cambridge University Library.

Watercolour produced by T. C. Lethbridge. Greenland 1937: Disko Mountains in distance.

Image courtesy: The John Gadd Archive, Cambridge University Library.

Watercolour produced by T. C. Lethbridge. 'Ocklinge' 10/04/32. Ashore Lowland Point.

Image courtesy: The John Gadd Archive, Cambridge University Library.

PART TWO

Chapter Twelve

Hole – A Haunted House?

Hole is a haunted house. Whether Tom and Mina Lethbridge were aware of this fact when they moved from Cambridge to Branscombe, Devon, in the autumn of 1957, we will never know. Maybe the strange occurrences at *Hole* fuelled Tom's growing interest in ghost and ghoul phenomenon, or perhaps the paranormal events that occurred there were attributable to his investigations into the occult. Many prospective house hunters would run a mile if their survey revealed a haunting; however, for Tom and Mina, this occurrence would have been perceived as a definable asset.

Hole House, along with *Edge Barton,* are two of the oldest houses in Branscombe. Both are fortified, walled properties perched on a ridge on the side of a steep coomb that leads down to the South Devonshire coast. It is understood that Simon de Holcomb – a Saxon bowman who fought at the Battle of Hastings – built *Hole House* in 1075.[159] The Holcomb family inhabited the house for over 500 years. Evidence of this continued occupation can still be found on a stone mantelpiece lintel in one of the front bedrooms where, in 1577, three of the Holcomb children carved their names. It is likely that the Holcomb family derived their family name from the topography of their homestead in Branscombe; for *Hole House* is situated on a coomb, once home to the river Bran that ran down to the South Devon beach. *Hole House* is literally 'the house in the hole'. The property was eventually sold to the Bartlett family in 1605 and then to Judge

John Stuckey in the eighteenth century. It is known that the cottage part of *Hole* was once a smithy. When the estate was eventually broken up in the 1890s, it comprised of seven hill farms and two miles of cliff top.

Hole House was to be the setting for the most eventful phase of Tom's life and has since become intrinsically linked with him; it is here that he embarked upon the most controversial phase of his career.

His study of the old gods of Albion and his associations with Margaret Murray had led him to reflect upon his own brushes with occurrences that he would later describe as 'the odd'. Subsequently, his interest became an obsession that was to lead him to explore areas of paranormal activity that many of his contemporaries considered 'out-of-bounds'. Many of his fellows back at Cambridge believed he had simply 'lost the plot', but Tom didn't see it this way. He remained purely scientific in his approach and believed that paranormal activity was simply an aspect of the mind that had yet to be explained by science. The results of his experimentations with ESP, precognition and dowsing with a pendulum were documented in the series of eight remarkable books that he would write at Hole. It is a legacy for which he is still best remembered today.

On numerous occasions during his residence at *Hole,* Tom claimed to have heard unexplained utterances in the garden.[160] The voices of two, or possibly more, girls chatting and giggling had been heard on three sides of the house. The voices were faint, but were never accompanied by any feelings of creepiness, cold, or other sensations usually associated with this phenomenon. Mina once remarked that on a Sunday, the smell of a cooked breakfast would often fill their home between the hours of six-thirty and seven o'clock in the morning. The cooking smell was usually followed by the distinct smell of shag tobacco and no explanation could be found for this occurrence. Tom had suggested that the ghostly aromas could have been emanating from a block of beer stone above the fireplace in their bedroom. It was as if the stone had somehow 'stored' the aroma of a previous resident's Sunday morning breakfast ritual: someone had first enjoyed a hearty breakfast and then settled down after for a relaxing smoke.[161] This occurrence, accompanied by the children's voices, was not an isolated incident.

Hole House appeared to be steeped in mystery, and their neighbour at the nearby *Hole Mill* further enhanced this belief. Mrs Nancy Norris, the resident at *Hole Mill*, was acknowledged to be a practising witch and had been a disciple of Dion Fortune's Society of the Inner Light in Bayswater during the 1930s. She was also an artist, a writer and a poet of some distinction. Throughout her life she had attracted spirits and had been born in a 'haunted house' in Guildford, Surrey in 1918. At her home, she kept a copy of her 'bible', a book written by H.J. Ryman entitled *Puss in 'Pye' Corner* (Thought Values, 1920) – a bizarre and often incomprehensible volume of occult proclamations.

On the morning of Sunday 22 February 1959, Tom and Mina awoke to discover that the ram, which supplied *Hole House* with water, had stopped working. The pair, accompanied by Mina's cat Sweedle, took a stroll down to the ram house that was situated about 300 yards away down the coomb. It was an exceptionally mild and clear day and after Tom had managed to restart the ram, he and Mina sat admiring the view from the concrete roof of the pump house. At 11:15am, Mina decided to return to *Hole* to prepare Sunday lunch, whilst Tom remained on the roof to ensure that the ram continued to work. From his elevated position, he observed the paper delivery man going about his business in the lane below and being chased off on his bicycle by Mrs Norris' four large dogs.

As he watched, Mrs Norris appeared from behind *Hole Mill* and, seeing Tom on the roof of the ram house, she acknowledged him with a wave. Tom returned the compliment, but as he did so, a second figure, an elderly woman aged 65 to 70 years of age, emerged and stood a yard or so behind his neighbour. The woman appeared to be staring straight at him. The woman wore clothes that appeared quite dated and which Tom likened to garments his grandmother might have worn before the Kaiser's war. Tom climbed down from the ram house roof and made his way back along the lane where he bumped into Mina, returning from *Hole* after putting their Sunday roast in the oven. The pair leant upon a farm gate admiring their tenant's cattle and Tom explained the occurrence of the old lady to his wife and how he had considered the appearance of the visitor at *Hole Mill* most unusual. A barking dog on the lane signalled the arrival of their neighbour and Mina, expressed her surprise when Mrs. Norris appeared in the lane unaccompanied. Further questioning revealed that Mrs. Norris had been alone all day and the only people she had encountered were Tom and the paper delivery man. On hearing of Tom's encounter, she remarked: 'So, you are seeing my ghosts now, are you?'[162]

Having had time to contemplate the apparition, he likened the woman's image to that of the porter he had seen in New Court at Trinity College back in 1922. Although the figure had appeared sharp, it lacked depth, almost like a photograph, and there was an overall greyness and lack of colour about the figure. A year to the day, Tom returned to the scene, but there was to be no repeat performance; however, he and Mina did experience a kind of electrical tingling sensation that seemed to correspond with a drain beside the roadway. They were able to follow this sensation until the rivulet disappeared into the bank. It appears that in the tranquillity of *Hole House*, Tom's sensitivity to odd occurrences had become heightened.

He believed that he was not alone in seeing ghosts, it was just that many people failed to notice them, for he believed they had never been taught to observe. He suggested that this inability to comprehend could be described as a psychic blindness akin to being tone deaf, or colour blind.

The tale of Nancy Norris' ghost was indeed strange, but events at *Hole Mill* the following year took a more sinister turn. Mrs. Norris ran *Hole Mill* as a guesthouse, but in August 1960, she had a row with a number of local people who assisted her with her business. As a consequence of this quarrel, she sacked them from her employment. Following the dismissals, she duly took on two Welsh boys from the Rhonda Valley, one of whom had a cousin living in the village. The boys had arrived in Branscombe looking for work, but had failed to find any due to their bad reputations and wild ways. Tom, Mina and many of the villagers tried to dissuade Mrs. Norris from employing the youths; however, the boys had taken her fancy and she would not be moved on her decision.

Several days later, Tom encountered a furious Mrs. Norris in the lane. It appeared that she had had an altercation with a farmer who lived on the other side of the valley. Tom considered this not to be unusual; both had hot tempers and the pair were constantly at loggerheads. However, he did note that this row appeared to be more vitriolic than usual. Mrs Norris informed Tom that, as a consequence of the farmer's actions, she intended to send a murrain on his cattle. Tom implored her not to do this and warned her that if this was not carefully done, the curse could rebound on her. Tom's words fell on deaf ears and she walked away with a broad grin on her face.

One evening, shortly after his encounter with Mrs. Norris, Tom and Mina saw the two Welsh boys descending the wood path from the direction of *The Fountain* – the local hostelry. Tom noticed that both of the youths seemed particularly excited and were carrying bottles of whisky. The following day, Tom received a phone call from the local constabulary informing him that Mrs. Norris had been found dead at *Hole Mill*. When Tom had seen the boys carrying the bottles of whisky, he had been suspicious; he knew that his neighbour was fond of a drink, but her tipple was gin and all though she was known to be a heavy drinker, he described her as being: 'Tough as old nails.'[163] He pondered over whether the youths had proffered their alcohol on Mrs. Norris and, not being accustomed to the beverage, she had over-indulged and died as a result of her intoxication. He even considered the notion that the boys had deliberately contrived the outcome, for Mrs. Norris was prone to leaving money lying around the house, thus providing the youths with a motive for their actions. The police were suspicious of the youths, but had no hard evidence against them, although they did impose a curfew on the boys while they conducted their enquiries. The cause of death was eventually linked to the quantity of alcohol she had consumed that evening. Curiously, on the morning of her death, her son, Michael, who was living in London, heard his mother calling his name and presumed that she had come to stay. Michael noted the time of the call as being 8.15am on 23 August 1960 – the estimated time of his mother's death.

Tom became convinced that Mrs. Norris had induced a murrain on the farmer's cattle, for several weeks later, foot and mouth disease broke out in farms directly to the east and the west of the village. It appeared quite odd, as no other cases were reported in the locality. Tom described the outbreak as a terrible business; the smell of burning carcasses permeated the coomb for weeks. After Mrs. Norris' death, *Hole Mill* remained empty, although the farmer's wife, who had taken it upon herself to keep an eye on the place, reported that one of the upstairs windows was always open every time she visited. Even though she always closed and fastened it before she vacated. Tom described her as being a most sensible person, but she would never visit the mill alone. Michael Norris visited *Hole Mill* to clear his mother's personal effects and noted:

> After she died, the atmosphere in the house at Hole Mill was awful. I felt as if I was being, not exactly 'denied entry', but more 'hands off – this place is mine.'[164]

Michael returned to Branscombe a month later and noted that the atmosphere at *Hole Mill* was no longer oppressive and that a more peaceful atmosphere now prevailed.

Tom's association with Mrs Norris at *Hole Mill* had always presented him with a problem. When he had first moved to Branscombe in 1957, he had been told of the ghost of the 'red lady' that was said to have been spotted in the lanes around *Hole.* The reported sightings by a Mrs Pike were all dated before, or around, 1926 and there had been no reported sightings since that date. On meeting his neighbour, Tom was astonished to find that Mrs. Norris was often to be seen wearing a cherry-red coat. This got him thinking and led him to remark: 'We have frequently seen the little red lady, but she is alive and well.'[165] He deduced that the ghost, reported in the 1920s, was likely to have been Mrs. Norris. This conjecture, however, presented a problem: how could a person see the ghost of someone who had not yet died, or possibly not yet even existed? In three-dimensional science, cause must always precede the event, but in this case, Tom believed that the ghost was a projection, not one from the past, but from a place or dimension where time did not exist.

Tom claimed never to have seen the ghost that was supposed to come through the wall of the bathroom above the kitchen at *Hole*. However, he believed that the ghost was being projected on a narrow band and therefore, required someone sensitive to that frequency to detect it. During his initial years in Branscombe, Tom began to research the history of the property and conduct investigations on the surrounding land. His enquiries revealed a wealth of history, awash with further mysteries and intrigue.

He corroborates a number of witness statements that claimed to have seen phantom white dogs in the lane leading to *Hole*. The unearthing in his garden of a number of fragments of medieval, ceramic tile that depicted a canine presence further enhanced this mystery.[166] Tom estimated the tiles to be mid-fourteenth century and, as well as depicting white dogs, they also featured what appeared to be white hares surrounded by star, sun and moon symbols. This led him to conclude that the white dog, a symbol associated with Nodens or Nuada[167] – he of the silver hand – was still being venerated in the Branscombe area as late as the fourteenth century. To assist him in his research, he began corresponding with Geoffrey Bushnell. The letters provide a glimpse into the working of Tom's inquisitive mind and on one footnote he suggests that the juxtaposition of the hares and the dog may have an association with the phrase: 'Let the dog see the rabbit.'[168]

Tom was aware that the tiles most likely came from the floor of a building – a private mortuary chapel – that once stood in the garden at *Hole.* Initially, he was unsure of his discovery and through his correspondence with Bushnell, he attempted to pin down a date for the type of pottery he was unearthing. As was his nature, he couldn't let any occurrence pass without supplying an explanation and, undecided upon the origin of the ceramic fragments he was unearthing in his garden, he chose to refer to them as: 'Scratchyarsehole.'[169] Further correspondences with Bushnell revealed that the ceramic fragments he was unearthing were likely to have been produced around 1350. His prognosis was evidenced by the comparison of similar remains discovered at the Princesshay Conduit in nearby Exeter.

Tom had discovered that the Holcomb's private chapel had been destroyed by fire and he suggested that this calamitous event might well have been integral to the phantom white dog that he and several others had seen in the lane. He believed that the sale of the property was a direct consequence of the fire and that this misdemeanour provoked someone to induce the Holcomb's white dog to haunt the property. Tom wasn't too concerned that his explanation of events was correct. However, he believed it to be a well-informed validation of events and the only plausible one available.

Rationalisation and reasoning were both part-and-parcel of Tom's approach; however, sometimes they were not always easy to come by. In a letter to his friend, C.F. Tebbutt, he once remarked how a woman from Maidenhead – who as a child once used to live at *Hole* – had recently visited him and had suggested that there was a deed of gift on the property relating to John of Gaunt that handed over property to Lady Petrie. She claimed that the document had a seal bearing what appeared to be a three-legged animal. For once, Tom was stuck for an explanation:

> I can't do this one. I should doubt the whole story but Branscombe used to be a royal estate. Fox said the kitchen wing was fourteenth century. There were floor tiles from the Chiltern kilns in the midden which must have cost a lot to bring here and finally I have two deeds in my title papers from two different Petries selling off bits of land just over the hill. Nobody knows a thing here. But there is a local mediaevalist woman I might try.[170]

It is clear that having abandoned the 'hands on' archaeology of Cambridge, he felt the need to 'keep his hand in' by turning his attentions to matters now closer to home – his own back yard. This was typical of his approach, and exemplifies a remark he had previously made in *Gogmagog*:

> There is no need to go to the ends of the earth for interesting quests and excitement. It is here, anywhere in prosaic old England, at one's back door.[171]

Tom's excavations in his *Hole House* garden also led him to unearth an usual carving of a stag which had been skilfully carved onto a piece of whitewashed stone that had once been part of the window splay of the mortuary chapel.[172] He also discovered the foot of a recumbent knight and this, along with the deliberately broken tiles, led him to remark: 'I think some sod smashed up a chapel.'[173] He suggested that the animal carvings were not light of nature; their presence had a more significant purpose; they were indeed the goddesses own beasts. In his own unequivocal style, he further stretched the point by suggesting that Devon was the land of the Damnonii – the Scottish branch having been driven north by the Belgic invasion. If indeed the Scottish Damnonii were known as 'the people of the stag', then the Devonshire division was probably the same and thus provided an explanation, albeit a somewhat tenuous one, for the stag carving at *Hole*. It is clear that Tom and Mina's arrival at *Hole House* had presented them with a wealth of material worthy of research.

As 1959 drew to a close, Tom's precedence had changed since moving to *Hole*. His defence of the Gogmagog figures still occupied him and his investigations into the old gods of Albion and 'the odd' were now his main concern. Since moving to Branscombe, his annual cruises around the Western Isles had ceased and his boat – *Zoraida II* – remained neglected on Henderson's slipway at Mallaig. The disused vessel was spotted by Mr. R.C. Dunn – a prospective buyer – who wrote a long, kindly and diplomatically worded letter to Tom, informing him of the poor state of the ketch:

> I don't know if you have seen her lately but the last two or three years have taken their toll as she has no covering. Laying down by the head slightly, rain has run forward in her scuppers with an accumulation of grit, soil paper and general dirt several inches deep. This has moss growing on it round the timber heads, and grass is sprouting... I was quite horrified to see a boat going to pieces in this way and could not resist scraping the soil and dirt out...in all 4 or 5 shovelfuls.

Dunn offered to purchase Zoraida II for £300 (today's money: £3,300: Munby, 1996) and made a promise to return her to her former glory. It was sad to think of her abandoned and deteriorating after all of the adventures Tom, his family and friends had shared with her over the years. It appears that as a new decade dawned, Tom's priorities had changed.

Chapter Thirteen

The Swing of the Pendulum

One of the objectives of James Wordie's aborted Arctic adventure in the summer of 1923 had been to repeat the pendulum gravity experiments carried out by Edward Sabine in the nineteenth century. The original experiments, carried out by Sabine and Captain Clavering, were conducted between 1818 and 1823 on Parry's ship, *The Griper*. To conduct this enquiry, his vessel had sailed along the inter-tropical coasts of Africa and America and also up the eastern coast of Greenland. Sabine's findings were first published in *An Account of Experiments to determine the Figure of the Earth, by Means of the Pendulum vibrating Seconds in different Latitudes; as well as on various other Subjects of philosophical Inquiry* (London, John Murray, 1825). Printed at the Expense of the Board of Longitude, the results of these experiments represented the most accurate assessment of the Earth that had ever been made.

There is no doubt that the theory surrounding Sabine's experiments left a lasting impression on the young Tom Lethbridge. Just after World War I, he had encountered a small pamphlet, written by a French Brigadier, who had utilised a pendulum to locate German mines in the sea. This unexplainable concept had caught his imagination and 40 years later, in the relative isolation of his South Devon home, he chose to further explore the medium and carry out supplementary, far-reaching trials that left him agog at his own findings. Tom had, however, first experimented with dowsing whilst living at *Mount Blow* during the 1930s. He had become aware that most villages had a resident who could dowse and he realised that in country life, the technique of dowsing for water was simply one of the facts of existence. He also understood that most townsfolk and scientists doubted its credibility. Tom, however, believed that the proof of the pudding was in the eating and that dowsing was not 'magic', but simply a power of the mind that had yet to be explained by science. His comprehension of the art revealed to him that it had the potential to unlock the door to a complete knowledge system on a higher level of human mentality. He likened his discoveries to the time when he had fallen into the polar sea whilst stranded on the ice during the 1923 expedition to Greenland. He realised that he had broken through into a world where there were many more dimensions.

Whilst at the Cambridge museum, Tom had once amused his colleagues by using a pendulum to detect the sex of spiders and ancient skulls retrieved from excavations. He had once heard of a Japanese custom for detecting the sex of an unborn child. The process involved the use of a wedding ring, hung from a piece of cord, suspended over the belly of the expectant mother. If the makeshift pendulum swung backwards and forwards, it detected that the unborn child was a boy and if the swing took on a circular motion, the baby was considered to be a girl. Tom's experiments at the museum with the spiders remained inconclusive, for there was no one present to verify his results. Several experts, however, were on hand to verify the pendulum's success regarding the sexing of the skulls.

Tom preferred the pendulum method of divination rather than the use of hazel twigs or dowsing rods. The pendulum simply consisted of a weighty object, or bob (a small ball of wood, for example), suspended on a length of string, which in turn was attached to a windlass. After undertaking comprehensive and painstaking experiments, he revealed that by altering the length of the string upon which the weight was suspended, it caused the pendulum to react to different types of objects. By simply adjusting the length of the filament, the swinging pendulum would adopt a circular motion indicating the object, or material being detected. He found that having a sample of the object being sought close-to-hand, aided the process. He later deduced that simply having a 'picture' of the object or substance in one's mind was often quite sufficient. Through his continued experimentation, he was able to compile a table of string lengths that corresponded to any given substance. Using the pendulum at 22 inches, he was able to detect a small piece of lead, and at 17 inches, it responded to truffles. At 30.5 inches, the pendulum even responded to a small piece of copper tube located beneath the turf in his garden. It appeared that the pendulum was, indeed, an excellent tool of detection.

After painstaking experimentation, it became evident that many tested objects shared the same string length. He was, however, able to isolate individual elements – having once established the string length – by counting the number of oscillations that occurred over a given object. The findings could then be demonstrated in a two-figure representation. For example, the metal silver and the colour grey were both detectable at 22 inches, but the presence of silver resulted in 22 oscillations and grey only seven. Their ratios could therefore be displayed as 22:22 and 22:7 respectively.

As his experimentations progressed, he began to realise that the pendulum was capable of responding not only to physical objects, but also to thoughts, ideas, emotions, countries, depth, age, sex, time and even evolution. Strangely, 'death' was detectable at 40 inches. The table he had constructed revealed that everything he had been able to detect, both physical and ethereal was demonstrable between zero and 40 inches. It seemed plausible that death, at 40 inches, marked a kind of end or finite point. However, further experimentation revealed this not to be the case.

As he increased the length of string beyond 40 inches, the whole sequence commenced once again. For example, lead – detectable at 22 inches – was also distinguishable beyond the 40 inch 'watershed' on a second scale and registered again at 62 inches (40″+22″=62″). However, when extending the string length beyond the 40 inch divide, he found that the pendulum had to be held slightly to one side of the object being tested. He concluded that the pendulum was detecting a realm beyond death: possibly another dimension where everything was slightly displaced and appeared almost distorted, which he likened to how a pencil appears to bend when placed in a glass of water.

He progressed by further lengthening the string length and he discovered that, once again, the cycle repeated at 80 inches. This sequence of multiples of 40 inches appeared to continue infinitum. To progress his experimentations, he had to rely on Mina's assistance and he utilised the stairwell of *Hole House* to gain the height required to dangle his appendage. Strangely, his pendulum refused to respond to the thought of time in our own world – the area detectable between zero and 40 inches. He assumed this must be because we are 'in time', so therefore we cannot actually measure it. The logic being, that you wouldn't be able to measure the speed of the current whilst sitting in a moving boat. Above the 40 inch scale, time appeared to exist, but it appeared to be static. He suggested that anything (objects, thoughts or memories) in the next dimension was located in a kind of museum and was therefore detectable. When he attempted to find time on the next level, beyond 120 inches, he discovered that there was normal 'flowing' time once again, and beyond 120 he discovered yet another 'dimension'. He concluded that this sequence progressed infinitum, and that these dimensions were parallel worlds to our own. He recalled an African tribe who believed that invisible people lived amongst them. He speculated that these 'invisible people' were in another dimensions and existed on a faster 'vibrational rate' than our own world. They could not be seen for the same reason that we cannot read the name of a station as a train flashes through it at high speed.

Having achieved astounding results with his pendulum, Tom decided on the most succinct method of representing his findings. Initially, he laid out his measurements like spokes within a circle. The circle was pivotal to a central bisecting line that represented 40 inches of death, juxtaposed to the rate for life at 20 inches. However, after discovering the recurring nature of this phenomenon, he chose to arrange the measurements in an Archimedean spiral, thus ensuring that an ever-increasing straight line drawn from the fulcrum of the spiral out to the infinite whorls would always relate to the given rate on the corresponding dimension.

Tom corresponded with a number of people regarding his table of rates and many wrote back stating that the measurements that he had tabulated brought them identical results. Initially, he wasn't sure if he had simply taught his prodigies a code, or that the rates he had formulated were built into the actual objects used for detection. In a letter to his good friend, C.F. Tebbutt, he once posed the question: 'Am I dealing with a psychological phenomenon or something cosmic?'[174] He eventually realised that the pendulum was not only responding to the object and their properties, but was acting as an extension of the dowser's own mind. It was clear to him that each object appeared to be numbered like a giant telephone directory and his experimentations had exposed a facet of a vast organisation.

Chapter Fourteen

The Odd

Tom's ongoing experimentations and investigations into 'the odd' were documented in a series of eight remarkable books. The first, *Ghost and Ghoul,* published in 1961, was the follow-up to *Gogmagog – The Buried Gods.* It was the first book written in the relative isolation of *Hole House.* It was, however, not a typical follow-up; Tom considered it to be more of a by-product of his line of research work concerning the old pagan gods of Britain. The understanding, that a belief in gods had been compelled by man's belief in the existence of greater beings than himself, was a prognosis that Tom questioned. The idea that the natural had somehow provoked a supposed supernatural did not sit easy with an enquiring mind.

During the course of his fieldwork, he had become aware that he was prone to experiencing unusual happenings and that an enquiry into these occurrences was worthy of a serious study. He believed that a scientific explanation lay behind what can only be termed 'the odd'. History has proved that the supernatural of one generation often becomes the natural of the next and it was this notion that fired his investigations. He did not perceive his enquiries as contrary to his archaeological study; he simply wished to find things out.

In 1951, Tom had submitted a typescript of seven short stories documenting his paranormal experiences to publisher James Whittaker at Andrew Melrose. The twelve accounts: *The Squint, Unwanted Visitors, M'Bulazi's Bones, The Spirit, The Ghoul, Fear on the Cliffs* and *The Edge of the Crater* were all to later feature in his first publication on paranormal activity.[175] The collection was never published, but later formed the basis for Tom's first study of the paranormal, *The Natural Supernatural,* which eventually became *Ghost and Ghoul* published by Colin Franklin at Routledge and Kegan Paul in 1961.

It was in *Ghost and Ghoul* that Tom first aired his belief that 'mind' and 'brain' were two separate entities. He believed that mind was distinct from brain, which, like our bodies, only existed as a convenience for our time on earth. He believed that earth level existence had a relatively low frequency and that the brain acted as a resistance which was able to filter out information that was required from a much greater volume of happenings. He understood that the brain was housed within a shell that required constant feeding, which one day would wear out and be redundant. He believed that our body was not 'us', it was simply something that was useful to us on an experimental expedition and would eventually become no more valuable to us than a pair of old, worn-out walking boots. To fully appreciate and to comprehend his ideas on the separation between mind and brain, it is important to place his ideas into context.

In his discourse on 'Magic', the Irish poet, W.B. Yeats, had suggested that the borders of our minds were constantly shifting and that our memories were part of one great memory, the memory of Nature itself.[176] Yeats further suggested that many minds could flow into one another and function as if they were a single entity. It is this pooled energy that Jung would later to describe as the 'collective unconscious', a united state where the power of the individual was diminished and became subordinate to a united objective. Colin Wilson even goes further to suggest that this 'collective unconscious' (or universally focused state) could well provide an explanation for the megalithic achievements of our ancestors.

Tom became aware of something he described as a 'collective mind', as opposed to a 'collective unconscious'. During one of his frequent crossings of the Minch, he had learnt of a local custom associated with the fishermen of North Lewis who used to wade into the sea at the beginning of the fishing season to make offerings of beer to a sea god they knew as 'Shoney' – the Holy One. This custom intrigued him and whilst reading Lillian Beckwith's *Green Hand* – a novel based upon fishing life in Mallaig and the Western Isles – he encountered an unusual rhyme that set him pondering on the origin of such divinities. The rhyme went like this:

> Ickle, Ockle, Blue Bockle,
> Fishes in the sea,
> If you are looking for a lover,
> Please choose me.

It was the name 'Blue Bockle' that intrigued Tom; he realised that 'Bocan' was a Gaelic godling and 'bogle' was the same word in Scots. He concluded that the rhyme, a mixture of Scots and Gaelic, when translated would read;

> Little youthful, blue godling,
> (Of the) fishes of the sea,
> If you're looking for devotion,
> Please choose me.

The rhyme was central to the North Lewis beer pouring ceremony and it was clear that further tales that told of the 'Blue Men of the Minch' were direct references to sea gods.

It is generally accepted that Celtic Gods have three phases, or personalities, that relate to their youth, their prime and their old age. He surmised that the Blue Bockle was a direct reference to the young god. The elder aspect, commonly known as 'Bodach Gorm', was often venerated through cattle sacrifices, but it was the prime or virile aspect of the triumvirate that intrigued him. Since moving to the West Country, Tom had become acquainted with May Day rituals that involved a hobby-horse (Obby Oss). It was apparent that these rituals once had a close association with local fishing communities and that these theatrical horses were directly linked to the mythical white horses of the sea. It became clear to him that the sea horse was a representation of the old god of the sea known as *Manannan*, or *Clackmannan* as he was known in Scotland and was simply a Gaelic form of the sea god *Poseidon*.

Many other investigators of myth and legend would have been content to leave their investigation here, but for Tom the most intriguing aspect of the saga was how this mythical god had come into being. This mythical entity didn't physically exist, but he realised that if enough people had envisaged, or evoked its image over the years, the combination of minds were able to create and bring the being to life. He believed that this pooling of memories was able to evoke a presence, in very much the same way that a ghost or ghoul was created. Although the entity didn't exist in earth living minds, he believed its presence to be associated with a second mental level, or higher vibrational state. Tom had already deemed this second level as a timeless zone and therefore the divinity's presence here would be considered immortal.

It was clear to him that this timeless zone was the area that he was able to detect between 40 and 80 inches with his pendulum. His explanation may initially appear preposterous, but his hypothesis was truly remarkable when one considers it in the context of the time. What he was describing was an ethereal zone – a mental super-highway. With hindsight, we can marvel at his explanation, as his reasoning has since been exemplified by modern technology: surely the Internet creates for us a similar collective reality that is capable of not only captivating us, but also influencing our lives. Tom realised that this natural pooled memory was indeed 'real', a vast cloud of past memories, animated by those who created it. It was authentic in the sense that it could be seen and most certainly felt by those sensitive enough to reach it.

Yeats had also reasoned that the induction of The Great Mind could be evoked by symbols, codes that transmigrated generations and transmuted themselves in art, architecture and culture.[177] It is *a given* that family traits are passed down from generation to generation, but the idea of an inherited memory has always been a stumbling block for the men of science. In our modern world, our reliance upon the disciplines of society has resulted in a disassociation from our natural instincts and intuitions. It is only in times of intense consciousness, or *reality*, that these impulses rear their primeval heads. Tom believed that the mind from which you were projected was compounded of the vital sparks of hundreds of ancestors mixed together and that a selection was sent out to you when you were born.

As a teenager, he had been surprised to discover the striking similarity between his own artwork and the paintings undertaken by his father who had died when he was only eight years old. He believed that mind and body were influenced by heredity and that environmental influences inflicted a negative effect upon this occurrence.

Tom's conjecture could be likened to Yeats' views on social memory, although it appears unlikely that he was aware it. Yeats' views, however, were not exclusive; it appears that *The Theory of Social Memory*, written by Aby Warburg in 1927, was also born out of isolation.[178] It is unlikely that Warburg was aware of Yeats' essay, or for that matter the work of Samuel Butler, or the more widely know Lafcadio Hearn who shared similar theories. There are of course parallels between Warburgs's hypotheses and Jung's theory on archetypes and racial memory, but it is his allegiance to the work of Richard Wolfgang Semon (1859-1918) that that can best be related to Tom's theories.

Semon deduced that memory was not a property of the consciousness, but one that distinguishes living from dead matter. He believed that every event left a trace, or *engram* on living material and that this vestige, under suitable conditions, could be reactivated or discharged at will. It is immediately apparent that there are parallels here between Semon's theory and Tom's experimentations with a pendulum. In fact, Tom had conducted an experiment to detect whether slingshots, discovered at an Iron Age hill fort near to his home in Branscombe, had been used in anger, or were simply *passive* like the similar ones discovered on a nearby beach.

Tom used his pendulum as a detecting tool and, like Warburg, he understood that to decipher these *engrams*, an interpreter, or decoding system, would have to be employed. Warburg went on to suggest that *engrams* could be found locked within social and racial memories that, consequently, became physical features embroidered into the art and architecture of a given culture. It is clear that Yeats' own understanding of the symbolic qualities of these memories is crucial to Warburg's own understanding; it is surely the aspiration of the artist's mind to interpret, or discharge these codes.[179]

Yeats had lived in a land embroidered with mystery and he had suggested that there was indeed a secret, unwritten code that existed. He had overheard a saying on the Aran Islands, that told of how your tongue would turn to stone if you spoke too much of the Faery ways. It is obvious that his discourse troubled him, for he queried: 'Who can keep always to the little pathway between speech and silence, where one meets none but discreet revelations?'[180]

It is interesting that many megalithic sites are named after people, or creatures that have been turned to stone. Often, the stories are Christian warnings of those who defy the Sabbath, but their metamorphosis to stone encapsulates a memory of a heathen past where every standing stone, potentially, becomes a portal to a lost or secret knowledge.

Warburg understood that the power that existed within the symbolism that he had encountered was responsible for the pagan frenzy that emerged during the Renaissance, and was compelled and driven by covert forces. He realised that the artist's responsibility was crucial, for their power to overwhelm was truly immense. Artists can, however, draw upon these powers and use them to their own advantage and inverted symbols can display contrary meanings and therefore be used influentially. Our churches and cathedrals are cluttered with such images, exhibiting duality and perpetuating primeval principles. Of course, the *engram* was, in fact, a charge of latent power, which could be discharged as negative or positive energy at the artist's discretion.

E.H. Gombrich suggested:

> To be carried away by the symbols of the past with all their sinister associations is a sign of weakness. The powerful personality can withstand the shock and turn the energy he deviates from more primitive strata to good account in the service of enlightenment and humanisation.[181]

Gombrich's wise words are more relevant today than when they were written more than 35 years ago. Assault against a belief should not be met with defiance and anger, but absorbed, administered and incorporated; eventually this processed vilification will only add to the wealth and depth of the besieged doctrine.

Tom's neighbour, Mrs Norris – the witch at *Hole Mill* – once explained to him that by throwing an imaginary pentagram around himself, he could ward off evil spirits, or deter unwanted visitors.[182] She explained that by visualising a pentagram, or pentacle, constructed clockwise in her mind, she was able to position the symbol to block or obstruct the path of any approaching visitor, therefore deterring their passage.

Tom successfully experimented with this pentagram theory and found it not too dissimilar to his own thoughts on psyche-fields that he was currently investigating. He concluded that the psyche-field consisted of bundles of thoughts held together by electricity. These psyche-fields appeared to other bundles of thought as no different to how our own bodies find tables and chairs and other matter in the material world. Basically, he was suggesting that psyche-fields were intrinsically linked to the material bodies of their owners, and were, in fact, simply facets of life itself. He concluded that magic and miracle were one and the same thing and, in theory, should not be beyond the range of any serious scientific investigation.

Yeats considered the icon to be the greatest of all powers, but initially he had to decide between what he described as inherent or arbitrary symbols. He deduced, however, that it mattered little whether their power had arisen out of themselves or from a random origin. He believed that The Great Memory associated them with certain events, moods and people. He was indeed perceptive, for sometimes it is difficult for us to segregate metaphorical thought from rationality. The images created in art also occupy this middle ground.

The ancient hands that carved the cup and ring markings on the rocks below Goat Fell on the Isle of Arran, upon the terraces of Auchnabrech in Argyl and into earth-fast rock on Weetwood Moor in Northumberland, understood the need to make sense of nature's chaotic presence through their use of symbols. This inherent memory still survives in the symbols they carved, and also within the souls of their descendents; they still contain that undiluted energy that once gave birth to the symbols of civilisation. It is these intense, basic experiences that once powered the ancient's hand, but are now laid covert, anticipating an awakening in a future, receptive generation.

Gombrich suggests that it is the artist and the historian who are the most sensitive to these covert influences from our past. It is therefore no coincidence that Tom was indeed a historian, but essentially he was a visionary of extraordinary breadth. His Jack of all Trades approach provided him with a great store of experiences that he believed put him in a unique position to be able to use himself as a guinea-pig. He was eager to state that his ideas were tentative and he considered it his prerogative to change his theories should evidence prove contrary. In all of his works, he was astutely aware of not wanting to inflict dogma upon his readers and throughout *Ghost and Ghoul,* he continually criticised dogmatic pedants and their inability to investigate and undertake primary research for themselves.

Tom began his book by recounting his own experiences. The first was that of the porter at New Court, Trinity, Cambridge in 1922, and another, of Mrs. Norris' ghost at *Hole Mill.* He believed that these 'visitation' were not people from another world, but projections, like a television picture or photograph. He posed the question: was his own presence responsible for the perception of these ghosts, or was he acting as a receiver to some unknown, possibly unconscious, projector?

Tom used *Ghost and Ghoul* as a vehicle to discuss psychokinesis and the precognition experiments of Professor Rhine, but he astutely realised the limitations of our vocabulary when occurrences become impossible to rationalise. This definition of *experience* as opposed to the methodology and scientific logic of physics is astutely discussed at the beginning of J.W. Dunne's *An Experiment with Time (A & C Black, 1962),* a book much cited by Tom.[183]

Throughout *Ghost and Ghoul,* he makes reference to the George de la Warr's work on resonance, a force akin to electromagnetics. Many of these works were not considered by academics as serious studies and De la Warr's 1956 publication, *New Worlds Beyond the Atom* (Vincent Stuart, 1956), written in conjunction with Langston Day, was condemned as being wholly unscientific in its approach. Although Tom cared little of what others thought of him, he would certainly not have wanted to have been tarred with the same brush as researchers who were not thorough in their methodology, or who were unscientific in their study. As his enquiries into 'the odd' progressed, there become fewer references to other researchers exploring in similar fields. At some point, he made a mental note to rely solely upon his own primary research and observations. This is a point that he emphasises in his summary at the end of *Ghost and Ghoul.*

Tom provided evidence of the folly of relying on second-hand research in a reference to a topographic anomaly on the West Man Islands back in 1939. Here an account of an event, that is said to have occurred in 874 AD and documented in 1908, is proved to be unsound by observations he had personally made in the field. He made a mental note never to rely on second-hand knowledge and that his own undertakings provided him not only accurate information, but new and startling revelations. After the publication of *Ghost and Ghoul,* the ball was set rolling and Tom's journey into the unknown had begun!

Chapter Fifteen

More Earthly Matters

After the brief detour of *Ghost and Ghoul,* Tom returned to his study of the old pagan gods of Britain. His 1962 publication, *Witches – Investigating an Ancient Religion,* was a natural progression from *Gogmagog – The Buried Gods,* and continued to expand upon Margaret Murray's theory that witch cults were the survivors of a prehistoric religion. This wasn't entirely new ground for Tom; he had aired the notion that the witch religion had prehistoric roots in *Merlin's Island* back in 1948.

Tom turned his attention to magic and the powers of the mind, defining magic as simply a facet of the mind that was not yet understood by science. He believed that 'magic' and 'miracles' were one and the same thing; it was just that Christianity perceived magic as dark and threatening. He also suggested that divine and devilish were the same thing, it just depended upon your perspective.

He believed that the witch cult was a religion of the suppressed classes and set out to demystify the goddess and her consort, the Great Mother and the Great Father, in their many guises. The book was really a concoction of ideas that merge his study of the old pagan gods with ideas first aired in *Ghost and Ghoul.* The study of Dianic belief and the transmigration of souls had led him to believe in a universal, controlling mind – a theory that would be explored and expanded upon seven years later in *The Monkey's Tail.* He linked the concept of the evolving mind with the Laws of Karma, the Avatars and other religious teachings of the world and concluded that Druidic belief was not a million miles away from modern psychical research. He also suggested that similarities existed between the Barddas and Pythagorean doctrines.

This sharing of ideas and common ground between Eastern and early Western religions provided him with evidence of the trading of ideas in the ancient world. The ocean, so important to Tom, was perceived as a kind of filter for ideas heading into Britain and that no idea on the continent ever arrived into Britain intact. It was this influence that made the study of British customs so intriguing. It was clear that these habits and traditions continued to fascinate him. The belief that witches were unable to cross running water was one such occurrence that he chose to investigate.

His train of thought was instigated by the notion of objects giving 'male' and 'female' responses when tested with the pendulum. He didn't for one minute think that these designations were actually male or female, but simply positive and negative reactions that were responding to the sex of the experimenter. He considered that this fact was crucial, for men and women should, in theory, receive opposite reactions in their pendulum experimentations. He tested a 200 year-old piece of wood and he and Mina received opposite reactions. He reasoned that this 'reaction' was possibly why witches were unable to cross running water. Tom's experimentations revealed that running water was, to him, female and he surmised that, of course, witches could walk across water, but he believed that the flow created a barrier for their thoughts and transmissions. He also considered that inanimate objects, like a piece of gypsum found on the beach, had no 'sex' rate, but once touched, the item developed the sex rate of the handler. This was not, however, true of wood:

> But if I carve something out of a bit of wood it keeps its original sex rate and does not add mine to it.[184]

In other words, you could, in a sense, create with inanimate objects, but not with those that had sex already. A stone idol therefore would have 'absorbed' the sex of its carver, but a wooden version would only have the sex of the tree from which it was carved.

Witches is therefore typical of Tom's work and, although it is filled with rants, digressions and amusing stories, a picture emerges of a man at the hub of life's great adventure. The inclusion of one particular story, paints for us an endearing picture of him. In 1933, Louis Clarke had sent Tom to Lundy – a small island situated off the north coast of Cornwall – to search for Viking Graves. The geologist, A.J. Dollar, a man described by Tom as 'a polite man', accompanied him on his mission.

Their initial investigations revealed that the burials were not, in fact, Viking, but most probably dated to medieval times. Although the discovery was not what Tom had expected, he considered it inappropriate to leave without pinning an explanation on his find. He therefore suggested that the medieval burials were those of prisoners who had been shipped across the Atlantic as slaves after the battle of Sedgemoor in 1685; it was known that these poor unfortunates had been dumped somewhere on-route. Later, in correspondence to Geoffrey Bushnell, Tom revealed that their objective of unearthing Viking burials was eventually achieved: 'I got them, but they were buried through medieval rubbish.'[185]

The story of this visit to Lundy Island is enhanced by the inclusion of a short anecdote concerning their wait for the boat back to Bideford. Tom and Dollar passed the time by successfully attempting to dowse for the volcanic dykes, which passed through the slate rock in the south of the island, as well as attempting aerial photography with a kite. We don't know if their attempt was successful, but the picture painted of two grown men imaginatively passing their waiting time, is one of sheer delight. The inclusion of such tales was a key feature of Tom's writing. Their addition brought his stories to life and provided the reader with a unique insight into his world. The work was finally completed and with the working title, *Diana and the Witches,* still in place, the typescript was submitted to his publisher, Colin Franklin, on 17 July 1961.[186]

Despite the ethereal happenings at *Hole,* it was more routine and secular matters that provided Tom and Mina with their greatest challenges. On 30 January 1956, Mina's father Mathew had resigned his position as rector of the church of St. Andrew in Moretonhampstead. He continued to live in the Devonshire village with Mina's mother, Eirene, and her youngest brother, Mathew Aidan. Mathew suffered from mental health problems and in September 1962, he was admitted to hospital. His absence from the family home had implications for his elderly parents, now both in the late 70s. It was therefore decided that they should spend time at *Hole* until Mathew was discharged. It is clear from his correspondence to friends that Tom found the whole episode trying, but he was, as usual, philosophical regarding the presence of his in-laws. He remarked:

> However, we are getting used to living in a world where most people here are round the bend and no longer take it quite so seriously.[187]

During her parents' stay at *Hole,* it became apparent to Mina that her father's health was failing and the following year, on 26 September 1963, he died. He was cremated in Torquay the following Saturday. Mina attended the funeral with their new tenant who had recently moved into the *Hole House* cottage.

Much has been written about Tom's researches conducted at his Devonshire home and assisted by Mina; their story is acknowledged as one of the most enchanting ever told, but privy to the remarkable occurrences was their unwitting tenant, Jo Erskine Collins.

Jo moved into the cottage at *Hole* in 1963. It had been her intention to move to New Zealand, but 'red tape' had prohibited her from shipping-out her newly acquired car until it was six months old. She therefore decided that she would postpone her emigration, but having already sold her house, she required urgent, short-term accommodation for the next six months. Audrey Morton – a mutual friend – was aware that Tom and Mina's cottage was vacant and that they were seeking a new occupant. She therefore recommended the *Hole House* cottage to Jo. Tom and Mina hurriedly made the cottage ready for their prospective tenant, whitewashing the walls and laying rugs and carpets. Their makeover was successful and, on seeing the cottage and taking a shine to Tom and Mina, Jo agreed to take up the short-term tenancy. She couldn't help being intrigued by the myriad of curiosities and the intriguing books that littered their home. On her moving in day, she arrived with her belongings, one of which was a carrier bag full of fossils. On seeing the collection, Tom was immediately enthralled and delved into the bag to identify the contents. Jo's interest in such curios appealed to Tom and, holding up an oddly shaped fossil, he remarked:

> My God! Not only does our new tenant come down with her baggage loaded with soirée and shit, she also appears to know an elephant.[188]

It was clear that Jo had made an impression.

Jo's cottage was, in fact, an annexe to *Hole* and was linked by an adjoining corridor to the main building. A shared telephone was located in the passageway and in the event of Jo being absent, Tom would always politely take her calls and leave cheeky scribbled messages for her on her return. Likewise, Jo would often reciprocate the favour, should someone call for either Tom or Mina.

As a result of his enquiries into the old gods of Albion, witches and 'the odd', Tom began to receive letters and telephone calls from a myriad of interested parties. Many of these communiqués were welcomed, but many he considered irksome and he would often take steps to avoid taking calls from people he deemed to be a nuisance. Jo would often vet his calls, making excuses that Tom was away, or unable to get to the phone. On one such an occasion, Jo informed a caller – referred to by Tom as, 'The Bloody Druid' – that Tom wasn't available. After acknowledging Tom's elusiveness, he was known to have retorted: 'There is an evil force keeping us apart.... But I am dealing with it!' The caller was unaware that the 'evil force' was attributable to Tom's own desire not to converse.

It was during his time at *Hole House* that Tom continued with his pendulum experimentations and, as result of his remarkable undertakings, Jo's ambition to move to New Zealand was put on hold. As a result of her tenancy, she became intrinsically linked with Tom's experimentations, often assisting Tom in Mina's absence. She also became a close friend to them both, but especially to Mina, who she referred affectionately to as *Muffy*. Jo astutely realised that what she was experiencing was quite unique and her desire to postpone her move to New Zealand was fuelled by her curiosity of Tom's experimentations and the friendship that had developed at *Hole*.

As a consequence of her husband's death, Mina's mother, Eirene, became a frequent visitor to her daughter's home in Branscombe. Throughout her life, Mina had had a 'volatile' relationship with her mother, but any lasting resentment appeared to have been contained for the sake of the family. The visits were stressful for Mina, for Eirene's intense dislike of Tom was founded upon the past eccentricities of the Lethbridge family and Tom's 'devil may care' attitude.[189] In correspondence to his friend, C.F. Tebbutt, Tom revealed that Mina had, on one occasion, demanded a 'divorce' from her mother because of her perpetual rudeness to him as a consequence of her forbidding him from attending her husband's funeral.[190] However, it appears that Eirene's discourtesy was 'water off a duck's back' and he frequently referred to her as 'the old hay-bag'! The fact that he appeared to derive enjoyment out of her rudeness further fuelled Eirene's loathing of him and further incensed an already agitated Mina.

Against a backdrop of family upheavals and turmoil, Tom's ideas began to expand, not just psychologically, but geographically. In January 1963, an extract from *Ghost and Ghoul* was featured in the American science fiction publication, *Fantastic Stories of Imagination.*[191] It was ironic that Tom's pragmatic theories should be aired in such a fanciful publication. Inspired by the words of Sir Cyril Fox, Tom began his follow-up to *Witches.* His mentor's metaphorical advice regarding the 'striping off of the layers' inspired him and he used this as a philosophy for his 1963 publication, *Ghost and Divining Rod.* By removing superstition, hearsay and traditional views, it had enabled him to return to the root of his paranormal investigation. *Ghost and Divining Rod* is therefore an essential read; it collates all of his previous theories and ideas and presents them as a working prognosis. In it he recounted his tale of the ghoul in the Golden Ball covert that he had experienced with his mother back in 1919 and likens it to a similar, more recent occurrence he had shared with Mina on the beach at nearby Ladram Bay.

On a warm and muggy afternoon on 27 January 1962, Tom and Mina had decided to visit the beach with the objective of collecting seaweed to manure an asparagus bed in their garden. They had heard that there was plenty to be found on the beach at Ladram Bay, a sheltered cove two miles south/west of Sidmouth. On arrival, the couple descended the steep red, sandstone cliffs via a lane that proceeds down to the pebbled beach.

As they stepped onto the beach, Tom recalls walking into a kind of blanket of fog that he described as having an air of depression and fear. He likened this experience to having a high temperature and being full of drugs. Surprised by their experience, the couple were undaunted and continued in the task of collecting seaweed. Mina and Tom became separated, but it wasn't too long before Mina returned saying: 'I can't stand this place any longer, it's horrible... let's go home.' Having collected enough seaweed, the couple left the beach and headed back to *Hole*.

The next day, Mina's brother Nicholas and his wife Judith came for lunch and were unsurprised when their hosts retold their experience at Ladram Bay; they too had once experience a similar phenomenon in a field near to the stone circle at Avebury. Tom asked them what the weather had been like on the day of their visit and the couple recalled that it had been a warm and muggy day, exactly the conditions that Tom and Mina had experienced at Ladram Bay. This train of thought set alarm bells ringing in Tom's head and he decided to pay a return visit to the beach.

The following Saturday, Tom and Mina returned to Ladram Bay. The weather was again warm, but it was drizzling and Tom had a notion that the damp conditions were responsible for the strange feeling of gloom and depression that was still present on the beach. He recalled that field telephones were prone to short circuit in warm, damp weather and that this occurrence might be associated with the events at Ladram Bay. After walking the entire length of the beach, Tom noticed that the gloom appeared most intense near to the place where Mina had been collecting seaweed on their previous visit. The field of gloom appeared to have limits that one could step in and out of in a single stride. The occurrence was also accompanied by an unpleasant tingling sensation, not dissimilar to the one that he had experienced at his neighbour's house above *Hole Mill* in 1959. Mina drew Tom's attention to a place on the cliff, about 75 yards up the lane to the beach, where the sensation of gloom was most intense. Whilst standing by a small stream that cascaded onto the beach, Mina had felt that 'something' had urged her to jump off the cliff.

Tom deduced from his Ladram Bay experience that human emotions were somehow capable of being recorded, not only onto physical objects, but also onto 'fields', as a kind of 'electric haze' associated with dampness and moisture. He believed that this was a possible explanation for this and the other ghouls that he had encountered. He recalled that the ancients had associated supernatural beings with streams and waterfalls, so he therefore chose to name these 'fields' after these nymphs, or 'naiads', as they were often known. Beings associated with woods and trees were known as 'dryads'; 'oreads' were associated with deserts and mountains, and 'nereids' had an affiliation with the sea. Tom's proposal to utilise these names to designate electro-magnetic fields found in corresponding places demonstrates his genius.

At the time of their visit to Ladram Bay in 1962, Tom and Mina knew of five people who had experience similar phenomenon on the beach; by 1967, this figure had increased to 12. However, an unexpected twist of fate several years later provided Tom with an opportunity to reach a satisfactory conclusion regarding the Ladram Bay ghoul. In *A Step in the Dark* (1967), he would later comment upon the suicide of a local man that had taken place on the cliffs back in 1964, two years after he and Mina had experienced the ghoul on the beach. Tom concluded that the man had more than likely visited the cliff-top, where Mina had experienced the urge to jump, many times before he actually chose to end his life. Although his suicide was a couple of years after Tom and Mina's visit, he believed that the man's negative-energy, gloom and unhappiness had somehow become impregnated upon the ambience of that lonely place.

It was the notion that events and emotions were able to pregnate themselves into objects and energy fields that had inspired Tom to utilise divination as a detection tool. It was in *Ghost and Diving Rod* that he had first introduced his readers to the power of the pendulum. He believed that everything had an invisible field around it and that his pendulum experiments enabled him not only to detect, but also to establish contacts with other dimensions.

A constant gripe, common to all of Tom's work, was the dogma that surrounded not only his own vocation, but also the world of science and the church. In *Ghost and Divining Rod,* he once again took a swipe at those who relied upon tradition and second-hand knowledge in their research process. He believed that it was their approach that inhibited the quest for wisdom. He highlighted his desire to avoid reading subject matter of a similar nature, in the fear that it would influence his thinking. This may also be partly due to the criticism that he had evoked from his links with the likes of George De la Warr and Margaret Murray in previous works.

Ghost and Divining Rod is basically a continuation of where *Ghost and Ghoul* left off. In the preface, he displays his astonishment at the areas to which his investigations were leading him and likened them to the realms of science fiction. Even reading his books today, it is quite unbelievable that many of his investigations have still not been researched, or acknowledged by science. He believed that a reliance on the demands of the material world would inevitably condemn this line of enquiry to the fringe areas of our society. Sadly, only a radical change in ethos will enable the genius of Tom's discoveries to be brought to the masses.

Colin Wilson suggests that his sequence of later books should be viewed as a series of notebooks, or working journals and not as a complete, definitive thesis. This style of writing is typified in the final chapter of *Ghost and Divining Rod*. One can almost imagine him reaching the final chapter still bursting with ideas; yet the constraints of his publisher prohibit him going into further detail. Undeterred, he threw in a handful of ideas anyway: force fields as cones, or spirals, the charging of sacred sites with energy; these were all theories that he would pursue in subsequent works.

Whilst undertaking his experimentations with the pendulum, Tom had continued to lecture at local societies and institutions in the Branscombe area. Through these lectures and his report writing, word got around of his unusual experimentations and it wasn't long before the BBC took an interest in his remarkable discoveries. In the spring of 1963, Tom travelled to the BBC's Exeter studios to be interviewed by Robert Forbes about 'Black Magic' for a programme entitled *News Talk London*. The Interview took place on 18 March 1963 and the half-hour programme was broadcast that evening at seven o'clock, to viewers in the south/east region. Tom received no fee for his appearance, but he BBC paid Tom his mileage for the Branscombe to Exeter round-trip.

Suddenly Tom's experimentations had reached a wider audience and the years of research in the relative isolation of *Hole* appeared to be reaping their rewards. It was not, however, Tom's intention to capitalise on his findings for notoriety, or fiscal gain. He simply wanted to break down prejudice and preconceived ideas and to trigger a train of thought that would encourage people to start thinking for themselves.

Chapter Sixteen

Déjà vú

In the course of their many dowsing experiments in their garden at *Hole,* Tom and Mina discovered that one of the most conducive places was in the courtyard, an area enclosed on one side by a fourteenth century composition and two others dating from the mid-sixteenth century. The finds included a number of coins dating from the reign of Edward I, III and IV, seventeenth century pottery and Rhineland stoneware. It became apparent to them that the grounds of *Hole House* contained a midden of discarded objects that charted its 900 year history. A number of alterations have been made to the fabric of the property over the years and the recollections of a BBC cameraman called Graham Tidman in 1964 revealed him to have an uncanny knowledge of the layout of the property prior to reconstruction work that was carried out in 1929.

It is likely, that director John Irvine was inspired by the BBC's 1963 interview with Tom,[192] as in May of the following year, he led a film crew down to Branscombe to record Tom's dowsing experiments with a pendulum and to view the site of the ghostly apparitions at the nearby *Hole Mill.*[193] Prior to filming, Tom had invited Irvine down to Branscombe, where the pair had planned the recording over lunch. As was often the case at *Hole,* events didn't pass without incident and even before filming commenced there was the unusual occurrence concerning Graham Tidman the BBC cameraman.[194]

At eleven o'clock on the morning of 20 May 1964, Tidman arrived at *Hole House,* unaccompanied and ahead of his director Irvine. Tom came out to greet the cameraman, but he found his visitor to be in a rather dazed and confused state. It appeared that on his arrival at *Hole,* Tidman had experienced a feeling that he'd, 'been here before,' and was able to describe buildings and features of the property that on closer inspection were only later revealed on an old map dated 1896. Tidman had also dreamt of reconstruction work at *Hole,* undertaken 32 years previous in 1929. Being a young man, in his early 30s, Tom was convinced that Tidman had experienced a kind of déjà vú. So baffled by what he had experienced, Tidman returned to *Hole House* the following day accompanied by his family. In the pouring rain, he took pictures of the place that he had 'experienced' in his dream. The unusual occurrence intrigued Tom and he later documented Tidman's experience in *A Step in the Dark.*[195]

The programme that Irvine and Tidman were recording was called *Outline,* and during his good-natured correspondence, Irvine informed Tom that the filming had turned out well.[196] He stressed that the film would be greatly enhanced if Tom could make a personal appearance in the BBC's Bristol studio. He begged Tom to visit and promised him that the role would be, 'almost entirely sedentary,' and that the recording would be over by 5.30pm the same day. Wanting to make their visit as conducive as possible, he offered Tom and Mina overnight hotel accommodation in Bristol. He closed his correspondence by confirming that the Programme Executive would be issuing a contract, 'in the course of the next few days.' Tom was initially concerned about the studio demonstration, but after further reassurances by Irvine, he agreed to the undertaking.[197] However, the offer of the hotel was declined and instead, Tom and Mina chose instead to hire a car and, accompanied by their tenant Jo, they drove to Bristol during a thunderstorm and returned to Branscome that very same evening after the studio session was completed. It is likely that the need to hire a car was necessary due to the unreliable nature of Mina's own vehicle.

Details on the BBC's Television Casting Form confirm that Studio A at the Bristol Television Centre was booked for 6 June

1964, from 11.30am until 5.30pm, that evening. A recording slot, running from 4.30pm until 5.30pm, had been pencilled in with a view for Tom, 'To appear in studio and carry out an experiment in extra-sensory perception. To be interviewed by Kenneth Hudson and talk over film.' Tom was described as being, 'a retired archaeologist and author,' and also rather uncharitably as 'an arthritic'. The Television Casting Form also contains additional financial information, plus Tom's fee of being, '....not less than fifteen guineas.' The programme log recorded the broadcast as *Ghost hunting with T.C. Lethbridge* and *The Radio Times* – the BBC's regional listing magazine of 6 June 1964 – detailed the 10.45pm slot *Outline* broadcast, thus:

> The rest of the programme will be devoted to an experiment in a new force which an archaeologist claims to have discovered and explored with the help of a small hand-held pendulum weighted with a ball of Hazelwood. He is T.C. Lethbridge, F.S.A., author of books on archaeology and on what is now known as E.S.P. (Extra-Sensory Perception).
>
> Mr. Lethbridge, who lives in South Devon, believes he is investigating a whole new range of psychical phenomena that at present are not recognised within normal sciences. In the studio he will be interviewed on his investigations, and the workings of his instrument will be put to objectively controlled tests.

It is understandable why Tom had trepidations regarding the studio demonstrations, as the need to convince others was not a remit in which he chose to indulge. He also realised that the art of divining was a skill that required the dowser to be in a conducive frame of mind. It was not a practice best suited to a busy TV studio. It was clear that Tom's desire to return home to Branscombe that same day reflected his dislike of cities and their associations, for they were a stark contrast to the peace and tranquillity of his life at *Hole*. The BBC no longer retain the recording of Tom's TV appearence, so no record remains as to whether his on-screen experimentations were successful.

Tom's two surviving children, Christopher and Belinda, were occasional visitors to *Hole* and, although their stop-overs were not regular, their appearances never passed without incident. Belinda was still living in Switzerland and, responding well to her treatment, was deemed well enough to occasionally return home to visit her father in England. On the Easter weekend of 1965, she arrived at *Hole* with an American, male suitor.[198] Tom took a shine to the man who he described as, 'quite a nice Yank,' but was unconvinced by his daughter's attempts to woo her man and accused her of almost stalking the poor fellow. Belinda bought with her a vast quantity of alcohol and Tom realised that the American had no idea that he was to be 'the goat on the altar.' After an enjoyable weekend of fishing and drinking, Tom and Mina eventually saw the couple off back to London from the station at nearby Axminster.

The following week, Tom received a phone call from his ex-wife Sylvia, informing him that 'Binny' had been found in hysterics on the platform of an underground station. One can only presume that her American friend had not been impressed by her antics over the weekend at *Hole* and had ended their relationship. Belinda was admitted to hospital with a temperature of 102°F and was eventually collected by her brother Christopher and admitted to a mental hospital in Devizes. Sylvia's fussing over her daughter resulted in Belinda retorting that she never wanted to see her mother again. However, this outburst was soon retracted; in a following letter to her father, she informed him that her mother had been wonderful during her illness and that she had made a full recovery and was returning to Switzerland to collect her belongings.

Christopher Lethbridge had, on the request of his mother, collected Belinda from the hospital and, in reporting events to Tom, demonstrated that he had inherited his father's sardonic sense of humour. After his departure from the hospital, he informed Tom that he had left his sister with two artificial flowers, which he thought would wash well and a packet of strong peppermints! Christopher, now a medical graduate, considered himself to be somewhat of a 'ladies' man' and once informed his father that he intended to bring a different girl down to *Hole* each weekend. Tom managed to talk him out of this plan, but was certain that his son's advances would not have impressed his son's intended 'victims'.

The visits to Branscombe by Tom and Mina's friends and relatives, although often eventful, were few and far between and in the relative peace and quiet of the coomb, Tom still managed to find time to persevere with his studies. In the most evocative of his prefaces, he began *ESP – Beyond Time and Distance* (1965) with the alarming account of how he had fallen through the ice-flow into the polar sea whilst on an expedition to East Greenland in the summer of 1923. Not one to miss the opportunity of a classic metaphor, Tom assimilated this experience to his recent discoveries.

Tom always demonstrated incredulity at his own findings and his enthusiasm for his endeavours always remained childlike and at fever pitch throughout his works. At times, he would apologise to his reader for leading them into this multi-dimensional world. But after all, it was accessible to everyone willing to shed their inhibitions, or the shackles of traditional thought. He believed that his findings and discoveries were so important that the implications would eventually destroy the whole argument for materialism. Never one to be carried away with his own discoveries, he had a naturally inquiring mind and even made a light-hearted reference to his biblical namesake to reiterate the point:

> Remember that my baptismal name is Thomas and it was most correctly given. I doubt even my own evidence.

He 'set out his stall' early in *ESP*, by stating that the book was an attempt to link science with magic, and magic with religion. Once again, he used the pendulum as a divining tool. His primary objective was to exhibit rays of energy which appear to omit from every living and inanimate object. This train of thought was triggered by the apparent existence of a green ray of light sent by the sun across The Minch at the moment of its setting. Tom claimed that he never did witness, or ever meet anyone who had seen, this unique phenomenon. However, as a postscript, he remarked that since embarking upon his quest, he had become involved in a maze of invisible rays, numbered by the million.

Tom was astutely aware of the pickle that modern religious thinking had got itself into. By trying to fit a four-dimensional subject into a three-dimensional frame, it had been forced to retreat from its intended line of evolution. In its attempts to be more modern and up to date, the less credible it had become. Unlike the church, he was always prepared to change his theories in the light of new available evidence. He had previously concluded that nothing could be impressed onto the field of an inanimate object. However, further experiments with the pendulum revealed that portions of the psyche-field of artists were retained within their paintings. He remained unabashed by his change of heart, for he truly believed that dogma was the curse of all learning.

Throughout his writing, Tom became notorious for his rants and diversions, which litter his works. One minute he is discussing the probability of extra-spatial rays in the animal world and next he is discussing the vermin-infested and 'slum-like' dwellings of the swallows at *Hole House*. These distractions add a curiously beautiful detail to his writings and present him as a truly great observer of the detail of nature. It is this facet that Tom believed was constantly missing from the lives of the general public and was an inhibitor to discovery. He likened his and Mina's relative isolation at *Hole House* to that of eastern sages who retreat to caves to think and to contemplate in peace. He believed that people who congregated in large numbers in towns and cities were subject to a mental wearing down by the constant din and demands of town and city life. This 'Hurry! Hurry! Hurry!' lifestyle caused nervous and mental inefficiency and created a materialistic herd mentality amongst the populous. He believed the solution to the mass 'brain-drain' was to somehow isolate each person at-will from all of the others. This would result in the individual's mind being given a chance to send correct ideas to its attendant body. He describes this 'unknown territory' as being as dark and dense as wildest Africa during the days of his grandfather, and that the rolling back of this darkness was the prime objective of his scientific studies and experiments.

In the spring of 1966, Tom contracted an infection and became bedridden. The illness caused him immense pain. It was to be the beginning of a long battle with heart disease, but his condition eventually improved enough for him to participate in further recording with the BBC. Two years had passed since his first foray into the media world and during the period 22-26 August 1966, the BBC's Travel and Exploration Unit paid a visit to *Hole*. Their mandate was to film and record the latest experimentations that Tom had been undertaking involving ESP and dowsing. Brian Branston and Bob Saunders were to direct the programme that was to be called *Three Steps in the Dark*.

The filming that occurred at *Hole House* in the summer of 1966[199] was intended for a BBC feature entitled *More Things...* Brian Branston outlined the objectives for this programme in a letter to Tom, dated 18 August 1966, in which it was agreed that he would be paid 250 guineas for his involvement. There appears to be no evidence that this programme was ever broadcast.[200] As a result of the recording, following on immediately after his spell of ill health, Tom was left exhausted.

Tom briefly mentioned the filming activities in *A Step in the Dark*, but in a letter to his friend, C.F. Tebbutt, written on the final day of filming, Tom appears quite excited at what had just occurred. In a gushing and humorous letter, he outlines the filming procedures in his own unequivocal style:

> We are just recovering from a really frightful experience. We have had eight and sometimes 9 BBC men for a week. Like a fornicating film-star, a hero of the Soviet Union and perhaps the Pope as well. I've had my balls photographed by a man lying on the lawn while swinging a pendulum over the lens.
>
> From ten till six I wandered about with microphones stuck in my pockets and wires threaded through my braces and fly buttons. It's all very well being a film star if you have your script and learn it by heart. I had to make it up as I went along. After about two minutes they said 'Cut!' and I had to go back and say it again. As I didn't know what I had said it was bloody easy.
>
> I had four huge lamps focussed on me all the time and that makes you giddy and they are bloody hot. The language is incomprehensible and most of them appear to be bugger boys.
>
> Anyway I put on a superb demonstration and found a Georgean (sic) tinned fly- button right where I said it was under the lawn and plumb under the camera. In fact they were very pleased with me and said I was a 'natural', which I thought meant a village idiot, but means something else in BBC language. They expected everything to have to be said five times they said and most producers allow for twenty times. I once had to do it three times and a few twice, but usually I got away with one.
>
> I shocked them rather by my simple talk. They did not know what a 'bunch of buggers' was and they didn't like me

> saying 'balls' or 'Christ' and got red and embarrassed. Knowing that they tried to diddle you I put my London lawyers on to them for a start and got a contract at 4 times their usual rate. I think I could have got double, but 250 guineas seemed quite a lot before the thing began. Now it seems like chicken feed.
>
> Mina had to throw some stones at a wall and get walked at with a divining rod but she is tired out by all the excitement. They are all bloody well crazy. The only sane one was the photographer and he was a Highlander.
>
> Now the press have heard of it and are beginning to be a bother. The old Icelanders wouldn't have stood for a thing like this. Neither would I if I had had the slightest idea what they wanted. I thought it was one of those 10 minute shows, but it's a whole half hour film. They say it takes a month for anyone not used to it to recover, but I think I am still 'unscathed and vulgarly abusive' like Daniel in the den of lions.
>
> Fortunately we can't get BBC2 on our machine so will be spared the horror of seeing ourselves like performing seals.
>
> p.s. The BBC only broke two cars in the week.[201]

It is clear, despite his gripes, that Tom enjoyed the whole experience.

A Step in the Dark was Tom's fifth book written at *Hole* and takes its name from the 1966, eponymous BBC TV series directed by Brian Branston and Bob Saunders. The experiments encourage the reader to step out of the three-dimensional world into one where time and distance play no part. The work is really the third part in Tom's study of the pendulum. Much of what has been described before in previous works is repeated here. But he makes no apology for covering old ground; he admitted that he disliked having to do it, but he understood that for the readers' benefit each of his books must be self-contained and self-explanatory. He did, however, use the opportunity to elaborate on many of his previously discussed themes.

During the many digressions that are familiar to his work, Tom often took the opportunity to vent his spleen against the outside world. Many a humorous and amusing example can be found in *A Step in the Dark*. At one point, having paused to assess the remarkable nature of his findings, he ponders the fact that maybe the study would be better off in the hands of churchmen or philosophers. He immediately had second thoughts and embarked upon a barrage of abuse aimed in their general direction. What initially commenced as a whinge was quickly turned around and given a typical poetic and philosophical, finale.

From these digressions, it is clear that Tom liked a good grumble. If he were alive today, he would be a prime candidate for *Grumpy Old Men*, a television series that focuses on the dissatisfied worldview of a generation of embittered males. It is easy to relate to his disenchantment and it is this aspect of his writing that provides us with an insight into his world, where almost every day appeared to have bought an injustice or incongruity.

During the *Hole House* years of the 1960s, Tom would have experienced a world very different to his life back at Cambridge during the middle period of the twentieth century, but it is inevitable that each generation will look back with 'rose-coloured spectacles' on a time when personal values or standards where superior to what is being experienced today. By the time Tom had moved to Branscombe, Western culture was experiencing a technological revolution led by the post-war generation. With a growing population and the introduction of innovations that had not been truly road-tested, the brave new world began to backfire. Pollution, neurosis and disenchantment were just some of the manifestations that were resulting in a major 'fall'. Tom lived during the cusp of this era and would have been first to witness a decline in society's standards. His reaction to the incredulity of modern life was therefore vented in his writing.

At *Hole House,* Tom was relatively socially isolated and it is therefore likely that Mina often bore the brunt of his grievances. A prolific letter writer, Lethbridge often vented his spleen in his correspondence to his good friend, C.F. Tebbutt. His rants were usually targeted at Mina's mother, or towards visitors, especially those who outstayed their welcome. For Tom, the grumbling process was a necessary evil, a safety valve that allowed him to let off steam. However, for those who choose to keep their anger and disenchantment to themselves, the rantings of the less restrained can indeed appear to be, to say the least, infuriating. Reading through his work, it becomes clear that his writing often became a vehicle for his discontent.

In one instance, Tom dexterously jumps from discussing fields of force and the Dryad Field to a lengthy rant about his plight as a writer. It is certainly worth quoting the passage *A Step in the Dark* in its entirety to give you an appreciation of his frustration.

> This whole thing (the study of the Dryad Field) is becoming so remarkable that I often feel I ought to abandon it, or hand it over to churchmen or philosophers. But when I meet specimens of both disciplines I usually think: 'Well, I don't believe they know any more than I do, and most of them have far less general knowledge.' They may earn a reasonable income at their trades and mine does not cover the price of stamps for answering the flood of letters from people who do not even buy my books, but write with pride to say that they have managed to borrow them from libraries. Well, you know this is a bit tough on the author who is expected to pay the postage on the answers. Why I answer them I don't know. I give them the benefit of thoughtlessness and on rare occasions rise a good trout who becomes a pen-friend for years. A very few extremely intelligent and thoughtful people put a stamp in with their letter and they often become pen-friends too. But I know only too well how many people have later written to

say that I was the only archaeologist who would answer their letters.

I have wandered off again, but I was brought up to the expression, when a gale was screaming round the house and the rain pouring down the chimneys: 'Pity the poor sailors on a night like this.' Pity the poor author too. He may work for many years on a serious book and practically the whole of what he earns does not cover the lowest paid operative of the Printers' Trade Unions in wages for half a year. Why does anyone write books at all? The answer is that they are compelled to do so by the natural urge to create. They cannot make a living by it. It wastes enormous energy. But they have, like the lemmings of Norway to obey the call which drives them to the sea.

The rant may appear rather negative and irrelevant, but it is these moments of passion that enable the reader to not only bond, but also sympathise with him. It is this endearing, honest approach to his work that makes him so remarkable. In his foreword to *The Power of the Pendulum,* Colin Wilson was later to affirm that Tom was a born writer and he champions the clarity and originality of his work. From this passage alone, he enables us to create a picture in our mind's eye: sitting ranting and raving at his desk at *Hole House*. One can image Mina too, going about her own business unmoved by her husband's outbursts, for I am sure that she had heard it all before.

Should we perceive this outburst of frustration as negativity, or can we learn something deeper from it? Tom provides the answer to his own question of why anyone should want to write books at all. Every writer has a natural urge to create and is therefore compelled to persevere against all odds. He reveals here the crux of the predicament and the dilemma of the artist, for their vocation is at odds with the everyday world in which they exist. It is therefore apparent that there will always be conflict. For a true artist, time spent on the mundane is time wasted.[202]

In his foreword to *The White Goddess*, the poet Robert Graves made it clear that to be a true artist/mystic and to intuitively understand and perceive, one needed to spiritually rid oneself of the trappings of society. Some may perceive this as arrogance, but Graves is simply stating that poets, artists and mystics exist in a different sphere to those around them. It is a full-time occupation, not something that can be categorised and switched on and off in our 'nine-to-five' world. Graves offers us a tantalising challenge and tests the artists' commitment to their cause. By moving to *Hole* and ridding himself of the grievances and niggles he had experienced back in Cambridge, he too had made a commitment to discovery.

In the past, those who have chosen to 'opt out' of society have experienced the psychological trauma of literally being 'outsiders'. A compromise is therefore required and it is this conciliation that, on occasion, leads to moments of frustration when the real world rubs too close to the ethereal. We can therefore make excuses for Tom's frustration, because the incongruity that he experienced was metaphorical of the disorder that he was trying to counteract and harness through his writing.

Mina once remarked that she could never understand why people were always looking for security. She believed that the whole point of life was to learn how to deal with insecurity. Her intuition reveals not only the artist's problem, but also the key to their motivation. Once there is an acceptance that 'Nirvana' can never be reached, the frustrations associated with their quest will be eradicated.

Of course not everyone can possibly be 'on the top of their game' one hundred percent of the time. Sometimes, even the visionary is entitled to an inane grumble every now and again. The intellectual excuse of 'frustrated artist' sometimes cuts no weight and the term 'miserable old git' is a more apt description.

It is therefore appropriate to leave the last word on this matter to Tom who once vented his spleen on 'modern' artists:

> One wonders whether a week or two at sea in a curragh on the Northern Ocean, coupled with a couple of months on an Icelandic hill-top feeding on scurvy grass and puffins, would have any beneficial effects on the perpetrators of those monstrous daubings and stones with holes in them, which now pass for modern art.

The rant is clearly a swipe at the likes of Barbara Hepworth et al.

From these words, we can deduce that Tom was indeed a *Victor Meldrew* prototype. However, his discontent was always delivered with a generous slice of humour. It is an infectious quality that appears in abundance in *A Step in the Dark,* an endearing quality that enables him to discuss cannibalism alongside the absence of a fixed universal scale in another dimension.

Tom's ability to vent his frustrations through his writing was indeed a godsend, but the stresses and strains of a life of overindulgence was finally beginning to take its toll. In March 1967, he suffered another bout of ill health and doctors diagnosed a serious heart condition. After this, Mina had observed that he was no longer strong and was reluctant to leave him on his own for any length of time. Tom was a good patient and always remained cheerful and uncomplaining and utilised his time confined to bed as a chance to contemplate and enter into deep thought without the disturbance of everyday life. For Mina, however, it was a time of deep concern.

Chapter Seventeen

A Medieval Mystery

When Tom moved to Branscombe in the autumn of 1957, he continued corresponding with numerous pen pals, not just in Britain, but all over the world. One particular overseas correspondent was Frank Glynn, a graduate of Wesleyan University. As well as being President of the Connecticut Archaeological Society, Glynn was also the postmaster of Clinton, Connecticut. One of his particular enquiries, at *Pilots Point* in Westbrook in 1953, had established that an advanced agricultural society had existed long before the mound builders of Ohio had established their art. Through his investigations into 'heap stones', he had become an authority on Native American culture.

From his home in Connecticut, Glynn had developed an interest in the origin of the North Salem, New Hampshire megalithic complex, and began his correspondence with Tom regarding this and other related sites in the New England locality. This intriguing correspondence commenced in 1950 whilst Tom was still at Cambridge and had continued up until 1966 – two years before Glynn's death in 1968.

Glynn had been inspired by *Merlin's Island* and had written to Tom expressing his interest in his conjecture regarding northern seafarers. Glynn had enclosed a photograph of an underground house in Jenett City within his opening correspondence in the hope that Tom might be able to shed light upon its origin. Tom had responded by suggesting that the dwelling bore a striking similarity to the entrances to the Icelandic hellis, the caves he had visited with Tebbutt in 1939. The pair continued to write and a firm friendship was soon established. It was clear that Tom saw his pen friend as a like-minded soul, fuelled by the desire to simply find things out. Within their first year of corresponding with each other, the pair became quite convivial and had adopted pseudonyms for each other: Tom being addressed by Glynn as *Brendan* and Tom reciprocating with *Finbar*. The pair also entered into sending each other parcels and gifts and, on one occasion, Tom was cautiously called upon to thank his pen pal for an unusual offering:

> Your Homeopathic Poison Oak Pellets arrived this morning. I don't know if the same things are in it as when it left you. They look like ships of some volcanic rock but they are not the same stuff as the things we call flint.[203]

In *Herdsmen and Hermits,* Tom had made reference to a fascinating North American relic that had intrigued Glynn. The discovery of *The Kensington Stone* had provided Tom with a medieval mystery that appeared to support his conjecture that northern seafarers had 'discovered' America, in pre-Columbian times. The mystery began with an intriguing legend.

> Eight Goths and twenty-two Norwegians on exploration journey from Vinland through the west. We camped by two skerries one day from this stone. We were fishing one day. When we came home we found ten men red with blood and dead. A.V.M. Save from evil. Have ten of our party by the sea to guard our ship fourteen days from this island. Year 1362.[204]

Tom had described how the above legend was found carved on a dressed stone slab in Minnesota, by a Swedish settler. The main body of the inscription was carved in runes, but with the A.V.M. (Ave Maria) appearing in a Roman letterform. Since its discovery in 1898, it had long been the subject of controversy and was therefore of great interest to Tom.[205]

The slab was discovered beneath the roots of a very old tree and, for the enquiring mind, it begged the question: 'who put it there?'[206] Tom acknowledged that it was quite easy for unscrupulous people to make fakes, but because of the knowledge implied in the inscription, he realised that if it were a hoax, it would have had to be carried out by a scholar, or learned fellow. In view of this fact, he believed that such a person would have little motivation for creating such a contrivance.

He astutely observed that the runes used in the carving were not those one would expect to find in an ordinary textbook. They appeared to be the correct late runes and related to the period to which they were supposed to have belonged. He also realised that whoever had undertaken the carvings, would have required access to a manuscript that had only been discovered in 1928 in the Royal Library in Copenhagen. The document, an order dated 1354, commanded Paul Knutson to take a Royal Knott with a picked crew of adventurers to visit Greenland to ensure that the colonists were observing the Christian religion. The order had been signed by Orm Ostenson on behalf of King Magnus Erikson.

Those who believe *The Kensington Stone* to be genuine, understood Knutson to be a missionary who, on his American journey, had passed the Hudson Bay and pursued the Red River to its source. Many believed that he was, in fact, searching for the missing settlers from the Godthaab district of Greenland. Tom believed that it would have been very unlikely for anyone to have access to this information, let alone have the inclination to create a hoax. He therefore considered *The Kensington Stone* to be genuine.

To support his belief, Tom entered into a commonsense deconstruction of the scenario. His reasoning was thus: any scholar who wished to prove the existence of Norsemen in North America would have had the slab carved in eleventh century runes. They would also have chosen a more prominent place to deposit the stone, possibly near to a shore on the east coast of

America that they believed to be Wineland.[207] He also suggests that the number of people with knowledge of King Magnus' fourteenth century order, before it was published, was limited. He therefore considered the chances of *The Kensington Stone* being a fake as hundreds-to-one against.

The actual stone was considered to be a native of where it was found and the tree that it was discovered beneath had been growing for at least 25 years before the stone was unearthed. During this growth time, the surrounding land was still relatively unpeopled and was home only to Native Americans and hunters. Tom concluded that if the stone did, in fact, turn out to be a fake, then it must have been the work of a demented scholar of great learning! This was a real whodunit, and Tom had challenged the sceptics to find the 'criminal' responsible before commonsense accepted their case. He continued his discourse by suggesting that if the stone was genuine, then Wineland may not have been the east coast of America, but reached by way of the Hudson Bay. He concluded by washing his hands of the controversy and suggested that the problem was one for the Americans to solve. This was typical of his approach; he was always willing to set the cat amongst the pigeons and leave it up to less imaginative minds to prove him wrong. Tom realised that his time was valuable and he had far 'bigger fish to fry' closer to home.

Throughout his life, Tom remained fascinated by the notion of ancient passages to America. The consequent correspondence with Frank Glynn further fuelled this belief and in *A Step in the Dark,* he once again allowed himself to become sidetracked. During his discourse on the creed of materialism and the speed and vibration of objects, he chose to turn his attention once again to the ancient seafarers in the northern oceans. In an unusual story concerning mediaeval seafarers of the North Atlantic, an ancient carving, and the Knights Templars, he related an intriguing tale that still inspires debate and controversy to this very day.

Tom chose to relate an ongoing debate between himself and Frank Glynn. The pair shared an interest in early voyages of discovery to America and, prior to their most recent discussions, Glynn had sent Tom a book entitled *The Ruins of Great Ireland in New England* by W.B. Goodwin.[208] The book was dispatched, with a view to him identifying any old Irish buildings or objects within its pages. On the whole, Tom found the book uninteresting, except, that is, for a line drawing and two photos of a slab of rock depicting a sword. Tom identified the weapon as 'a hand and a half'. The carving begged the question: How had a mediaeval broadsword come to be hammered on to a slab of rock in America? Intrigued, Tom requested Glynn to obtain a good photograph of the carving and send it to him.

It took Glynn over a year to locate the rock with the carving, for Goodwin had been rather vague in his description of the site. In 1954, after months of fruitless searching in New England, Glynn came to hear of a carved stone at Westford, Massachusetts.

Goodwin states that the stone was situated near an old Mohawk Trail, some six miles south/west of the town of Lowell. However, he associated the carving with the trail because he appeared to confuse the place names of Westford and Weston. Researcher Dave Goudsward states:

> If the carving was in Weston, it would have been on the trail, which would correspond with his theory that the Culdee Monks used the Indian Trails as routes for their massive conversion effort. Goodwin's original interpretation of the carving was that it was an Irish Face Cross, similar to one of Skellig Michael, and the Norse carving in the book was erroneously included in the book.[209]

It appeared that the carved image had been created in the rock by a number of punch holes, created with a hammer. It was identified locally as 'Old Indian' until Glynn's arrival, when it became known as *The Westford Knight*. It was situated near a bend in the Merrimack River at Tyngsboro, Massachusetts. It was alleged that a boulder once existed nearby which featured a carved map of the river path.

Since the 1880's, children had played stepping games on the stone and someone had jovially attempted, with little success, to carve a pipe on what was considered to be the *Old Indian's* mouth. Tom, however, had interpreted the body of the Indian as the pommel of a sword. It was Glynn's daughter who eventually persuaded her father to visit the site, insisting that it would be what he was looking for. Glynn was eventually persuaded and, acting on his daughter's hunch, he successfully captured a photograph of the carving, which he promptly sent to his friend in England.

Tom responded immediately and congratulated Glynn on his discovery: 'Well done Finbar! Well done Finbar's daughter!'[210] He was convinced that his analysis of the carving was correct, as he had become familiar with mediaeval weapons after previously dredging specimens from the river Cam near Cambridge. However, his fellows, like the New England children, interpreted the carving not as a sword, but as a human figure, and did not share his enthusiasm for the 'discovery'. He suggested to Glynn that he return to the site and clear away surrounding turf; he was convinced that what had been discovered was an impression not dissimilar to mediaeval, brass carvings that can be found in English churches and West Highland graveyards. Their 'finding' was of course controversial; it indicated to the Americans evidence of pre-Columbian voyagers to their homeland. Tom was suggesting that his friend had discovered an effigy of a British, pre-Columbian knight in New England a century older than the voyages of Columbus.

Acting upon his pen pal's instructions, Glynn removed the turf and revealed the full knight. Tom believed it to be of British origin and not Scandinavian, as initially thought by Goodwin. It therefore had no relation to the Swedish expedition of Paul Knutson, which, in turn, was related to the discovery of the equally controversial Kensington Stone. Tom believed that the effigy was in some way connected to the expedition of Sir Henry Sinclair, Earl of Orkney, who, according to the Venetian Zeni, had sailed to Greenland and America after his conquest of the Faeroe Islands, around 1385. The Sinclair story was discovered in the *Zeno Narrative and Maps* that were translated by R. H. Major in 1873.[211] Many, including F.W. Lucas, deemed it as roguery and a fake. However, geographical evidence in these accounts suggests that these sea voyages actually took place.

In his book, *Geschichte der Entdeckungen und Schiffahrten im Norden* (History of Discoveries and Navigations in the North, first published in 1784 with an English edition published two years later), the German naturalist and writer, Johann Reinhold, was the first person to associate Sinclair with the explorer-prince Zichmni. Forster discusses the voyage of the Zeni and as a casual aside in a lengthy footnote he makes the suggestion that Prince Zichmni was, in fact, Henry Sinclair. Major translated the Zeno narrative and brought it back into the public eye and was steadfast in his belief that Zichmni was, in fact, Sinclair.

Although he had never personally visited the stone, Tom believed that *The Westford Knight* was a memorial to one of Sinclair's Knights who had died whilst on the expedition. The idea of it being a fake seemed implausible to him. Since Colonial times, the only visible part of the stone had been the knight's sword and, because of this, Tom believed that the *Old Indian* interpretation was incorrect. By revealing the complete carving, Glynn had exposed the evidence for him to conceive the *mediaeval knight* interpretation.

Tom then turned his attention to the shield supported by the knight; it appeared to feature a buckle or perhaps a shoulder brooch and there was also a galley with a furled sail. Initially, he had believed the coat of arms to be that of the Sinclair family, but on inspection by Sir Iain Moncreiff, of the Unicorn Herald, it was accredited, not to Sinclair, but to James Gunn from Caithness, Scotland. Tom never actually committed himself to the claim that *The Westford Knight* was attributed to Sinclair; like with many of his theories, he believed that it was sufficient to inspire and initiate a train of thought and then leave it up to others, more appropriately qualified, to ascertain the facts.

The sequel to this story typifies Tom's forever enquiring mind; in August 1963, he received a further letter from Glynn; enclosed was a photograph and an explanation of how a second carved stone had been found about a mile from *The Westford Knight*:

> A year ago an old farmer in the southwestern part of the same town (Westford, Mass.) got wind of the fact that a carving up on the hill was creating interest. He also had a carved stone on his farm. He offered it to the local Historical Society. They decided to accept it, and made arrangements to have it stored in the entrance lobby of the library.

He continued with a description:

> All lines are made by punches; the depth and diameter of the punches appear to be identical with the punches that make the sword handle outline at the original site.[212]

It appeared that the latest discovery, known locally as *The Boat Stone,* had been carved in the same manner as *The Westford Knight,* but bore an image of a ship, an arrow and a number. Tom observed that the ship was of mediaeval origin and not contemporary with the eighteenth century, as it featured only a single mast, a square sail and featured no headsail. It also had a series of dots, which he had interpreted as ports for oars. The figures were in Arabic numerals, which had been familiar in Europe since The Crusades. This new stone had been found in ancient woodland and Tom believed that a race of people, who utilised stone as a natural medium, had placed it there. He was dismissive of the idea that traders had placed it; he believed that they would have used wooden or temporary signage.

This time, the coat of arms was immediately recognisable as that of Sinclair; this was a heraldic ship. Tom assumed that the arrow was obviously a directional indicator and therefore the number '184' indicated a number of paces. He then communicated with Glynn, requesting that he followed the direction of the arrow for 184 paces and suggested:

> …184 paces from the track on which the stone was placed you will find a snug little corner where Sinclair's bothy, hut, tent or whatever, was set up.

Glynn replied, explaining that on 11 May 1963 he had followed his friend's instructions. The directions had taken him down a slope into a thicket where, just inside, he encountered a stone enclosure that measured 32″ by 40″. It contained two or three courses of large boulders and in the south/eastern corner there was evidence of a dried-up spring with stonework surrounding it. Glynn wrote a further letter to Tom, congratulating him on the way he had called this shot. It commenced: 'This is intended as nothing but homage to your clairvoyance.'[213]

Tom concluded by stating that there was no evidence found to associate the site with Sinclair, but humbly conceded that his detection work was the result of reading countless detective stories! He also encouraged Glynn, or at least his perceptive daughter, to undertake some pendulum experiments at the site, but regrettably the outcome of this request was never recorded. It is believed that Glynn had made plans to revisit and excavate the enclosure in 1967, but unfortunately, in the preceding year, when excavations were scheduled to take place, housing developers destroyed the site. *The Boat Stone* had been moved from its original location in 1932 to save it from road-widening work. To date, the stone remains on display in Westford's J.V. Fletcher Library.

Since the discovery of *The Westford Knight*, many have pursued the Sinclair connection, attributing the site to the Knights Templar; it was Earl William St. Clair (Sinclair), the first 'Jarl' of Orkney, who was, supposedly, the Grand Prior of the Scottish Templars. William's son Henry's involvement in The Crusades brought him into contact with Nicoló Zeno, to whom he offered protection after Nicoló had been shipwrecked on Fair Isle between Orkney and Shetland.

In 1398, Henry Sinclair financed and mounted an expedition in the North Atlantic and he chose Zeno's brother, Antonio, as the fleet's guide. Their first landfall was in Nova Scotia, where they wintered, and this landing is substantiated by the discovery of a canon from one of their ships; a find which is now housed in the Naval Museum in Venice. In the spring, they journeyed on to what is now Massachusetts and then on to Newport, Rhode Island. It was during this leg of the journey that their connection to *The Westford Knight* was made. Like Tom, many believe that the carving represented a memorial to a crewmember that had died on this expedition. For those who seek further evidence of a Templar connection, then look no further than decorative carvings found in the Rosslyn Chapel in Roslin, Scotland, a building conceived in 1446 by the last 'Jarl' of Orkney, Earl William St. Clair. In the chapel, carvings exist of maize or 'Indian Corn' not native to these shores and a carving of an Aloe Cactus, which again is not indigenous to northern Britain. These observations again add weight to Tom's theories of the medieval Atlantic crossings.

A quick perusal on any search engine on the Internet reveals countless stories of Masonic and Templar mysticism associated with *The Westford Knight* and the Sinclairs; although there are many others who dismiss the carvings as simply 'faces in the fire'. David K. Schafer, the Curatorial Assistant for Archaeology at Harvard's Peabody Museum of Archaeology and Ethnology, agrees that an image has been carved onto the stone using a metal punch, but refutes the claim that it depicts a mediaeval knight. He also claims that a local historian has evidence that boys undertook the 'T' shaped carving on the rock face in the late nineteenth century. Schafer also believes that the rock on which the 'knight' is depicted would have been buried under one to three feet of soil during the fourteenth century. The landscape at the time would have been heavily forested and the erosion that eventually revealed the rock would have occurred due to the deforestation of the area during the early Colonial period. Schafer suggests that glacial scratches have created the 'sword' and remarks that similar marks can be seen elsewhere on the rock. He suggests that the only mediaeval knight on offer here is the one crudely daubed on the rock with white paint.

It appears that Tom's observations opened a can of worms and the debate on the authenticity of *The Westford Knight* continues to this day. But as he was later to suggest, in his introduction to *The Legend of the Sons of God* (1972), that it was his obligation to cast the stone in the pool to see what moves there, but he left it for others, more qualified, to identify the beast that emerged!

Tom believed that all of his studies, however diverse they may have appeared, were all inextricably linked. His lines of enquiry saw no boundaries and he was contemptuous of those who chose to criticise him for overstepping the boundaries of his vocation. He would later remark:

> If you find out anything, I feel it is your duty to pass it on to your fellows. So although I know many will snort contemptuously at what I have written, I also know that it was my duty to write it. It is their loss not mine.[214]

Chapter Eighteen

The Final Years

The unique locality of *Hole* enhances its sense of mystery. Situated along the steep coomb, high above Branscombe, the defended property basks in its sense of isolation and solitude. The vocation of its inhabitants during the 1960s would have fuelled the curiosity of the villagers below and added to the intrigue of the folk who lived in the house on the hill. In winter, *Hole* was, at times, impossible to access: the steep approaches proving treacherous and impassable during periods of ice and snow. Although relatively isolated, Tom and Mina still received regular visitors, many of whom drove up the steep coomb along the narrow track from the village. Tom's study was situated in the room above the front door and from here he could observe visitors approaching the house.

After the death of Mrs. Norris, Tom and Mina's new neighbour, Mr Fanshaw, was not as amenable as the previous resident of *Hole Mill*. Fanshaw was a keen marksman, but Tom had an aversion to anyone carrying guns on his land and this caused several disputes between Tom and his neighbour. Tom had an aversion to the needless killing of animals for sport; even the killing of polar bears to supplement his diet during his Arctic adventures had deeply troubled him. Prior to his arrival at *Hole,* the local hunt took for granted the right to cross the *Hole House* estate in pursuit of their prey; however, on Tom's arrival, he put an end to this tradition, forbidding them from crossing his land. Tom's decision was not viewed favourably by many of the locals.

Branscombe resident, Joy Kiddle, began working for Tom and Mina in 1968 and it was her job to keep *Hole House* clean and tidy. Mina had an arrangement with Mrs Kiddle regarding the cleaning: 'I'll do the middles – you do the corners' she would often remark.[215] The arrangement applied to the entire house, except that is for Tom's study, a room that he was quite happy to see left in disarray. His desk was stacked with books and papers and many of the piles were weighted down with relics and antiquities he had collected on his travels. The room was also covered in a layer of snuff, for it was a habit that both Tom and Mina indulged. From his study window, Tom was able to observe the comings and goings in the coomb and it is here, amongst his collection of fossils, bones and antiquities, that he wrote his series of eight remarkable books.

Tom enjoyed the task of writing, but hated the mundane tasks associated with the art. In May 1969, he wrote to his friend, C.F. Tebbutt, informing him of the horrendous indexing task that had taken him four days to complete. He remarked on how anyone could possibly adopt this undertaking as a profession. The fruits of his labour were, however, realised when he received an advance copy of his most recent work, *The Monkey's Tail* (1969). He informed his friend that he was generally happy with the result, although he found the reproduction of his landscape illustrations far too small.[216]

The Monkey's Tail was Tom's sixth book written at *Hole* and was based on the prognosis that Darwin's theories on evolution were manipulated and narrowed by Herbert Spencer and Thomas Huxley for their own 'political' ends. Tom believed that what was initially intended as a working hypothesis was later transformed into dogma and common belief. In Victorian times, a large gulf existed between the church and the men of science and because of this, an alternative vision, or a 'middle-way' was overlooked. Tom therefore attempted to uncover this 'middle ground', based on observations he had made whilst undertaking his archaeological fieldwork. His study was fuelled by comments made to Darwin by the Cambridge professor, Adam Sedgwick. Sedgwick had warned Darwin that if he persisted in publishing his theory it would wreck the world and utterly debase mankind.

The Monkey's Tail is exactly the type of book that played into the hands of his critics, not that this concerned Tom. Intentionally repetitive, he chose to retread old ground, further reinforcing his theories discussed in more recent works. To those unfamiliar with his earlier studies, they were provided here with a mind-spinning, crash-course into the world of T.C. Lethbridge. It is difficult to imagine what the initiate made of this 'in at the deep-end' approach. To those more familiar with his work, the regurgitated theories and stories are a familiar trait. In his foreword to *The Power of the Pendulum* (1976), Colin Wilson would later describe Tom's books as a kind of working journal into which he poured fresh discoveries and insights year by year. Wilson suggested that they, in fact, share this *fault* with the notebooks of Leonardo da Vinci and many other important discoverers. There is no complete 'system' in any of his books, but collectively they portray an intuitive, developing mind.

The Monkey's Tail is split into two parts. The first is outstanding and is, in essence, his real prognosis. Here he 'goes-to-town', exploring genetic memory and devolution in opposition to the accepted theories of Darwin and Wallace. Once again, he relied upon personal experiences for his source material and the study beautifully portrays the workings of his enquiring mind. We are, in fact, witnessing the evolution of a theory before our very eyes. His research with the pendulum had led him to conclude that there was indeed a blueprint for existence. He believed that some controlling force was responsible for our destiny. He had dispelled the notion that occurrences in nature happened purely by chance; it was a notion that he considered absurd.

The second part of *The Monkey's Tail* is a disappointment. After whetting our appetites with the opening chapters, Part Two comes somewhat of an anti-climax; it primarily covers old ground. The reader is left without a conclusion and, to the frustration of his critics, this was deemed typical of his approach.

It is important, however, to remember Wilson's insightful words and to view Tom's works collectively. The reader was not to be disappointed for too long, as Tom had already commenced work on his next publication, *The Legend of the Sons of God – A Fantasy?* (1969). The work would provide answers to many of the questions posed in the first part of *The Monkey's Tail*. It was also a logical conclusion to his previous train of thought. With hindsight, the two volumes combined would have made an interesting prognosis, but one can only speculate that his publishers put pressure on him for a release. However, one has to commend Colin Franklin at Routledge and Kegan Paul for his foresight and perseverance for facilitating this evolving and enquiring mind.

The tranquillity of *Hole House* appeared destined to be forever punctuated by family crises and upheavals. It is amazing how Tom ever found tome to develop his theories on the occult and the paranormal. One August morning in 1969, the relative peace and quiet of *Hole* was once again shattered by tragic news from Moretonhampstead. It transpired that Mina's younger brother, Mathew, had been found dead at the family home. He appeared to have taken an overdose of tablets. As a consequence of his death, Mina's widowed mother, Eirene, came to stay at *Hole*, pending the inquest. The process was painfully slow and Tom eventually wrote to the local constabulary expressing his desire to see the course of action accelerated. In a letter to his friend, 'Fred' Tebbutt, he related what he had written to the Chief Constable, explaining:

> ...it was getting most expensive filling my ma in law with whisky every day and also an outrage to keep an old woman of over eighty in suspense. I did not say that if he didn't stir things up she would probably come over to Exeter and either scratch his eyes out or kick him in the balls. Result immediate and obsequious.'[217]

His sardonic letter achieved its objective and an inquest was arranged forthwith. He also received a humble apology, with blame being laid firmly and squarely at the door of the pathologists in Bristol.

Tom offered to attend the inquest in the place of his mother-in-law. Eirene, however, was adamant that she wanted to attend the proceedings herself and therefore Mina considered it appropriate that she should accompany her mother to the enquiry. If the three-week delay hadn't been considered awkward enough, what was in store at the inquest left Mina and her mother astounded. Tom picks up the story:

> Then the path man started reading a long list of notes. Ma in law went into a semi coma, but Mina listened. Suddenly she heard that the victim had had an appendectomy (or whatever silly term they have for this operation). She remarked loudly, 'But my brother never had his appendix out'. Ma in law woke up and said 'Wrong body' in ringing tones. Path man said 'Well, the body I investigated had no appendix' he was cross and flustered. The police told Mina and Ma in law not to interrupt and no more notice was taken of this obvious point of interest. The doctor, who would have known, had gone sailing. The path man had clearly got the wrong notes and so they brought in an open verdict. When Ma in law got home she told everybody that if anyone mentioned suicide she would sue them for libel. But we will never know who the man was who had eaten 20 Russian rockets, nor what killed Mathew.
>
> The remains, whose remains nobody knows, had to be cremated and the ashes sent reverently to Northumberland in a pot. I hope it's worth digging up some day! Nice if at the last trump it turns out to be a Spanish waiter or even a yank.[218]

Tom's remarks clearly demonstrate his irreverent attitude to life, a trait that clearly infuriated his mother-in-law. Mina, however, realised that Tom's flippant responses were a coping mechanism and a direct response to Eirene's uncompromising attitude to her husband. She continually played the diplomat, concealing her own frustration with her mother. It is clear, however, that her sympathies lay entirely with her husband.

On first moving to *Hole,* Mina had been initially sceptical of her husband's new direction and cautiously reserved judgement on his discoveries. In fact, Tom found his own findings so remarkable, that even he regarded them as unbelievable and that they really had no part in the 'real' world. It was this incredulity that led him to once remark:

> Although much of what has been written so far is not strictly orthodox, the present chapter is far worse and deals with matters, which are fit really only for the television plays called Dr. Who.'[219]

Tom understood that he was 'going out on a limb' with his revelations and in the preface to *Ghost and Ghoul,* he had acknowledged his research as being directly attributable to Mina; by recommending books for his consumption, she had inadvertently fuelled his appetite for knowledge. However, her initial reticence led Tom to further remark that the conclusions reached from his 'outrageous' research and experimentation were attributable to him and him alone. It is clear that Mina, having weathered the storm of condemnation regarding the Gogmagog affair, had chosen to exercise discrete caution regarding her husband's latest revelations. As she became more involved in his research, her stance began to soften and in Tom's preface to *Witches – Investigating an Ancient Religion,* he had chosen to acknowledge his wife's commitment to his work. He had remarked that Mina had found this to be the most interesting of his recent works. This comment, once again, provides us with evidence that she had initially exercised caution regarding her husband's new direction. From the opening quote featured at the beginning of this essay, it is clear that Tom received jibes from his wife, who jokingly referred to him as being 'slightly simple' for even considering such outrageous thoughts.

One of Mina's more 'challenging' tasks was the deciphering and typing of Tom's somewhat erratic note taking. In the acknowledgements to *Herdsmen and Hermits,* he had painted a delightful picture of her sitting in the idyll of their Cambridgeshire garden, intrepidly typing up the manuscript. Mina continued this undertaking at *Hole* and it is likely that she perceived her task as being a crucial opportunity to rationalise their discoveries.

After receiving criticism for his associations with the likes of Margaret Murray, it became clear to Tom that, to avoid guilt by association, he would have to place a reliance on his own primary research. Further criticism soon followed and it became apparent that his associations would have to be curtailed and reliance placed upon references closer to home. In the preface to *A Step in the Dark,* Tom had revealed that no one had influenced his conclusions; that is, no one, except his wife. This comment reveals to us that Mina's initial and understandable caution had now been abandoned and that Tom had finally learnt the lesson of guilt by association.

Throughout his work, Tom acknowledged Mina's contribution to his researches and it is clear that the pair worked as a team, bouncing ideas off one another and exploring possibilities. It has been suggested that Tom's frequent acknowledgements to his wife appear somewhat condescending and patronising, and that he portrays her as a mere assistant or dogsbody, but this is certainly not the case. Reading through his numerous acknowledgements, it is understandable how these impressions could have arisen; however, we must view his remarks in the context of the period in which they were written. We must constantly remind ourselves that we are now living in far more enlightened times than those post-war years. Any prejudices or political incorrectness that occurs is born out of a lack of general awareness rather than a deliberate attempt to disparage. It is clear that Tom regarded Mina's efforts as worth more than their weight in gold.

It would be simple to suggest that Mina was Tom's muse, but this accreditation fails to provide us with a true portrait of this remarkable woman. The Oxford English Dictionary defines a muse as 'the poet's inspiring goddess', but this definition conjures up images of a fickle, dormant figure, in the Helen of Troy mould, whose role as a docile manipulator is as divisive, as it is incongruous. It is therefore more conducive to view Mina, not as merely Tom's muse, but a fully paid up member of the Lethbridge expedition party.

Much has been spoken of Tom's ability to disentangle the conundrums that confronted him and he would have perceived his union with Mina as a meeting of like-minds. He credits her with the gift of incisive thought and an ability to see right through to the root of a problem.[220] This was a faculty that uncannily enabled her to bypass the normal, more methodical thought process. He believed that this 'gift' was indeed attributable to the 'sixth sense'.

As Tom developed his theories into 'the odd', his sensitivity appears to have been enhanced. Mina, now convinced of her husband's new direction, began to share in her husband's experiences. Tom put this 'sensitivity' down to the relative isolation they were able to experience at *Hole*. He was convinced that the hubbub of daily life prohibited thought and he likened his and Mina's existence at *Hole* to that of holy men and hermits.

All this rooting around in his own backyard suggests to us that Tom and Mina had become somewhat reclusive, but this was certainly not the case. They were frequently visited not only by family, but also their friends, including his old school friend Humphrey David and his young family. Mina also owned a car, and later a van, and these vehicles enabled the couple to take frequent visits to Cornwall and nearby prehistoric sites where Tom could conduct experiments with his pendulum. Although Tom owned a black Wolseley, Mina now took the responsibility of driving due to her husband's poor health. On one occasion, returning from a journey to Hembury Castle near Honiton, the engine of Mina's Austin A40 began to make an unusual noise, similar to that of a stick being pushed into the spokes of a revolving bicycle wheel. On stopping to inspect the engine, they chanced upon a local, Welsh doctor who stopped to greet the couple and comment upon their misfire. Tom, in his usual mischievous manner, commented that it was not their engine that was malfunctioning, but the doctor's own vehicle. As Tom and Mina drove away with grins on their faces, they left the poor doctor with a concerned look on his face, his head beneath the bonnet, inspecting the engine of his own vehicle. Mina's car eventually gave up the ghost and she replaced it with a later model, one that Tom claimed made her look like a 'gangster's moll'.[221]

In between his excursions and his entertaining of visitors, Tom continued to write and soon he had completed the typescript for *The Legend of the Sons of God – A Fantasy?* The work was typical of Tom's style, but the devil of the detail lies in the question mark at the end of the subtitle. Still unwilling to foist dogma upon his readers, he presented his most outrageous set ideas as informed possibilities.

After reading *The Legend of the Sons of God – A Fantasy,* it becomes clear why so many of Tom's peers had distanced themselves from him and his work. By now he cared little of what the world at large thought of him, and in this extraordinary work, he really let his imagination have its head. At the time of publication, many of the ideas discussed here were new and unexplored and it is therefore important to read the book without hindsight prejudicing judgement. As he stated in his brief introduction: '...it is worth throwing a stone into a pool to see what moves in it.' Tom was indeed testing the depth of the water.

Before remarking on this book, it is important to recap on where Tom was coming from. His previous book, *The Monkey's Tail,* had explored the origins of how life had developed on earth, but the work had abandoned the reader midstream, without a satisfactory conclusion. His notion was that all life had developed as part of a master plan, rather than by sheer chance. This concept of an external influencing force was still in its infancy and remained unexplored. *The Legend of the Sons of God – A Fantasy* pushed the boat out further, suggesting that this influencing 'external force' was, in fact, alien intervention.

During his research, he had made a request to his friend, Newall, to send him tiny pieces of bluestone obtained from the inner ring at Stonehenge. Tom had used the stones in a pendulum experiment in an attempt to locate the source of the stone using a pendulum swung over a map. He had identified their source, not as the Prescelly Mountains in Pembrokeshire, a site identified by archaeologists as their most likely home, but Tipperary, Ireland. It was a place once suggested as the source by Geoffrey of Monmouth. After his experimentation with the bluestone chippings was complete, Mina acquired one of the pieces and after having it cut and polished by Colonel Hawley, she had it mounted on a silver disc brooch that she frequently wore.

The Legend of the Sons of God – A Fantasy was Tom's most 'challenging' work to date. It has often been equated with Erich von Däniken's *Chariots of the Gods* (1968), but this comparison is unmerited. Tom had acknowledged this similarity in his introduction and expressed his own initial doubts about the publication of his work, in view of the release of von Däniken's book. Although both publications often touch on the same subject matter, their similarity ends there. Whereas von Däniken had presented his discoveries as facts, Tom had presented his scenarios simply as possibilities. Since its publication, many of von Däniken's theories have since proved to be unfounded and have subsequently left him with egg on his face. However, Tom was canny enough to acknowledge the outrageous nature of his claims and, by presenting his ideas as possibilities, he had provided himself with a metaphorical safety net. He always perceived his own role as that of instigator and he believed it was up to other, less imaginative minds to prove him wrong. If he had lived to witness this process, he would have been the first to admit the shortcomings of his theories in the light of new evidence. It is also likely that he would have provided alternative solutions and conundrums to further stimulate our minds.

From the outset, the reader is encouraged to enter into 'the journey' with an open mind. He even suggested to his audience that they might well be reading a fairy story, or watching an episode from TV's *Dr. Who*. He then tantalised them further by suggesting that curiously, some of what is being discussed might even be true. This unique approach is encapsulated in the book's subtitle. He was at times outrageous with his hypothesis and appeared to deliberately take things 'too far' in order to provoke a response.

After completing the comprehensive first chapter, the reader soon realised that they had hit the ground running. He commenced the book by asking the question: 'Who were the sons of God?' The first chapter is overflowing with concepts so outrageous that even those familiar with his previous works will have been left with their heads spinning. Tom acknowledged this on page 15, by suggesting to the reader that if it has all become too much to take in already, then there was little point in continuing. Clearly, there was no room for passengers.

Tom was an avid reader of the Greek-Armenian philosopher, George Gurdjieff. In *The Legend of the Sons of God – A Fantasy*, he suggested that circles of standing stones were receptacles for stored energy that had been generated by frenetic ring-dancing. When fully-charged, the stone circles could then act as 'beacons' for alien spaceships. Gurdjieff too was also intimately acquainted with earth forces. He describes being with a party in a mountain village, when he got to hear that there were dolmens in the area and he asked to be taken to one. The dolmen in question proved to be a sort of giant stone coffer with a lid. Asked about the nature of such stones, Gurdjieff replied that they were 'road signs' showing the way to places of initiation. It was a view that revealed that he possessed some esoteric knowledge about the stones and their purpose. This is confirmed by what happened next. Gurdjieff asked his guides if there were any other dolmens in the area; they said no. He then made certain measurements and calculations, and led them through thick woods, which had to be cleared with hand axes. He led the party to two more dolmens, both heavily overgrown and unknown to local people. Their guides were astonished. In his own account of the journey, Gurdjieff makes a cryptic remark suggesting that various experts among his pupils – in engineering, astronomy and archaeology – assisted him in resolving 'the problem of the dolmens'. Unfortunately, no record of this 'solution' was ever documented.

Gurdjieff's assertion that we are all in a state akin to sleep and can only be awoken through tremendous effort, or 'intentional suffering' would have appealed to Tom. His own view that the populous was suffering from a 'brain drain' as a result of materialism is likely to have been inspired by Gurdjieff's conjecture.

During the writing of *The Legend of the Sons of God – A Fantasy?* it is apparent that Tom felt pressured by his publishers, and recent ill-health had not added to his wellbeing. Not entirely happy with his typescript, he felt that to appease his publishers, he had 'scraped the bottom of the barrel' somewhat, regarding his current prognosis regarding alien intervention into human evolution. However farfetched his ideas may now appear, it is important to place them into the context of the time and into perspective regarding his ongoing theories on human evolution. In the late 1960s, theories regarding alien intervention were relatively unexplored and his ideas were just one possible solution to a complex line of enquiry. His reticence did not, however, stop him developing new ideas and he had already conceived a speculatively idea for a book on dreams. As Tom commenced his new project, his publishers began assembling *The Legend of the Sons of God – A Fantasy,* and *The Monkey's Tail* began appearing on bookshop shelves up and down the country. It was, however, the last of his books that Tom would see published.

Chapter Nineteen

Beyond the Ivory Tower

Over the years, Tom had become estranged from his mother Violet who, in 1950, had returned to live at the former family home in Finchampstead. The move followed seven years after the death of her second husband, Brigadier Gordon, on 15 January 1943. The Manor House at Finchampstead had since been divided into flats by her younger sister, and Violet now occupied a residence that was the former stables. Tom endeavoured to keep in contact with her through regular letters, but never received replies.[222] During her final years, Violet was attended to by Mrs. McDonald, one of her many housekeepers, who took excellent care of her. Her granddaughter, Mary Rose, also often used to visit her during her holidays and as Violet became frailer, she was granted compassionate leave from her generous employer – a Herald at the College of Arms. It was Tom's son, Christopher, who eventually informed his father of Violet's deteriorating health and eventual death aged 96 in 1970. Due to his own ill-health, his doctor forbade him from attending his mother's funeral.[223]

Photographs taken in the 1950s, at the scene of the Wandlebury dig, reveal Tom Lethbridge to have put on a vast amount of weight. He was hardly recognisable as the slim, fit-looking man who accompanied Sir James Wordie to the Arctic in 1921. During the final decade of his life, this enormous weight gain had an obvious effect upon his health. In the midst of writing *The Dream Book*, Tom's health began to deteriorate rapidly. Although his physical condition was a cause for concern, other family matters had improved and it would have no doubt gladdened him to hear that Belinda's health had improved, in as much that she was now holding down an enjoyable job looking after disadvantaged children. It appears that she still maintained a relationship with her mother, albeit a volatile one, for she often wrote to her father informing him of their squabbles.[224]

The postal strike of 1971 did not impact on Tom Lethbridge, the prolific letter writer; during this period he suffered an immobilising illness than prevented him from putting pen to paper. Triggered by pills given to him by his doctor to control his rheumatics, he became consumed with cardiac asthma, which caused him to 'balloon'. Tom had always relied on homeopathic cures and he believed that nettles aided his rheumatics. By mid-April, he had made a partial recovery and was able to continue with his work.[225] Tom's heart health problems had been ongoing since his first attack in the spring of 1966. After the death of his mother, Tom had taken to going to bed early and did not rise again until after breakfast. During this period, it had become clear to him that his condition was not going to improve and he began to teach Mina tasks around the house that he had previously undertaken. It was apparent to her that he was preparing her for the inevitable.

At the end of August, both Tom and Mina caught a virus, but Tom was unable to shrug off his infection and remained bedridden. During this time, Mina received what she described as a number of 'sendings'; these included a dream where a friend came to see her and told her that Tom was dying, and another where a bell in the house started unexplainably ringing. She put these happenings down to coincidence, but in her heart, she knew that Tom's was dying.

Jo Erskine-Collins had departed the *Hole* cottage in 1968 to embark on her long awaited trip to New Zealand. Her emigration was short lived and after a brief tenure 'down under' she returned to her new home in nearby Colyton. It was a cottage that Tom had helped her choose, although his opinion on the suitability of a residence for his ex-tenant was influenced primarily by the dwelling's potential for archaeological discovery rather than Jo's personal requirements. Jo was a qualified nurse and during Tom's illness, she drove the short distance from her home, down into Branscombe village and up the narrow lane that led to *Hole* to care for him. As Tom's conditioned worsened, she often stayed over to assist Mina with his care.

Due to his illness, Tom became immobile and a hoist was fitted above his bed to enable him to be lifted. Eventually, his conditioned deteriorated to such an extent that Jo and Mina were no longer able to provide the 24 hour care that he required. Unwillingly, Tom was admitted to the Nuffield Hospital in Exeter. During his illness, Mina recalled that the nurses took a shine to her husband and were enthralled by his tales of the pendulum and thoughts on ESP. He remained upbeat throughout his illness and was always willing to entertain everyone his with stories and jokes. He was always able to present new ideas for them all to mull over. Eventually, he became semi-delirious and began reciting tales of small people he had met in dreams who were preparing things for the 'showbiz' world. Mina considered this expression out of character; throughout his life he had shown no interest in the theatre.

On 30 September 1971, Tom died peacefully in his sleep. He was cremated the following Saturday in Exeter. As was the family tradition, only male friends and family were allowed to attend his funeral. One attendee, his cousin, Sir Hector Lethbridge, came dressed in top hat and tails and was accidentally mistaken for an undertaker. It was an incident that would undoubtedly have brought a smile to Tom's face. After the ceremony, his remains were finally interred in a family plot in Heytesbury, Wiltshire.

Mina was only 52 when Tom died; however, it must have been heartening for her to see *The Legend of the Sons of God – A Fantasy* finally appear in print the following year. It must have also seemed strange to see her husband's work acknowledged by a new audience riding on the wave of the von Däniken explosion. I am sure that had Tom lived to see it, he would undoubtedly have prepared an appropriate response to the critics of the movement to which he had been inadvertently linked. It is to Tom's credit that even respected publications like *Antiquity* chose to review this penultimate, posthumous and most contentious of works:

> The book is the quintessence of Lethbridge, the ambivalence of scholar and anti-scholar, critical and uncritical, wise and unwise, sound and lunatic, shrewd and silly, perceptive and preposterous, stimulating and stupid, that made him such an exciting, lovable, and contrary person.[226]

Tom and Mina had lived at *Hole House* since 1957, but Tom had never purchased the house outright; it remained in the part-ownership of the Lethbridge family Trust. Throughout their tenure, Mina had always encouraged him to purchase the property, but without any income, sufficient funding had never been at his disposal. At one point, Tom had even sanctioned the felling of beech trees overlooking *Hole* and sold the timber for cash. It was an act that angered many of the locals. Tom claimed his motive was purely to let more light into his property, although it is likely that his motive was fiscal rather than aesthetic gain. In his will, Tom made provision for Mina to continue living at *Hole*, but it appears the trustees had the final say and she was eventually forced to leave the property in the spring of 1973. She departed leaving behind much of the furniture, most of which belonged to the Lethbridge family trust. To make ends meet, Mina sold Tom's library, personal diaries and numerous notebooks and assorted papers to the Bournemouth-based antiquarian bookseller, John Ruston *(See Appendix 2)*.

Shortly after Tom's death, Mina received a copy of Colin Wilson's book, *The Occult* (Hodder and Stoughton, 1971), marked for Tom's attention. Wilson had inadvertently stumbled upon her husband's work and immediately realised the omission of Tom's study from his latest tome was a major oversight. Mina replied to Wilson's letter, by informing him of her husband's recent death and offered to return the volume. Wilson insisted that she retain the book and the pair embarked upon correspondence that finally resulted in Mina, accompanied by her friend Jo, visiting Wilson at his home in Gorran Haven.

After leaving *Hole,* Mina moved from Branscombe to *Gilcott* in the nearby village of West Hill. She was able to buy the property with funds paid to her by her late husband's family trust. During her search for a new home, she felt that Tom had somehow 'helped' her find *Gilcott,* for she considered it a place of which he would have approved. It was here, with the assistance of her cousin, Peter Acland, that she began to assemble the notes of Tom's last work, the one he had described as *The Dream Book.* During this period, she continued to correspond with Wilson, who offered to write a foreword to Tom's posthumous assemblage. By January 1975, Mina and her cousin Peter had successfully assembled Tom's manuscript into a readable prognosis; they now had to find a title suitable for the proposed publication. *The Swing of the Pendulum* was eventually presented to the publishers in 1975. On receipt of the manuscript, Routledge and Kegan Paul promptly re-titled the work *The Power of the Pendulum.*

It is likely that if Tom had lived to oversee the production of *The Power of the Pendulum,* he would have chosen a more suitable title. During his research, he made reference to his work as *The Dream Book;* it was a discourse that should have inspired a more pertinent heading. It is clear that his publishers saw a marketing opportunity and put pressure on Mina to encapsulate Tom's legacy under a more generic title.

Tom had always seen Mina and himself as a team and therefore this assemblage stands as a testament to their spirit. Published in 1976, *The Power of the Pendulum* commenced with Colin Wilson's foreword. The regret of having not met Tom Lethbridge was eventually to fuel Wilson's next major undertaking, *Mysteries*. Published in 1978, he dedicated Part One of his book to Tom and his ideas. It was this publication that introduced many people, like myself, to Lethbridge's work. For the initiate, however, Wilson's foreword to *The Power of the Pendulum* was an excellent starting point; he believed Tom to be a classic exponent not just of parapsychology, but also English Literature.

The book commences with one of Tom's greatest dilemmas: was our existence on earth planned, or just pure chance? It was, in fact, a reiteration of a question once posed in *The Monkey's Tail* back in 1969. Was there a middle way, an explanation of existence that bridged religious thinking with that of science? On commencing the study, he reiterated a humble claim that he had previously made in *Boats and Boatmen*; that he was not suitably qualified to commence such an undertaking. He astutely realised, however, that if he didn't undertake the enquiry, no one else would and he was quite prepared to continue even if it earned him contempt.

Throughout his career, Tom had been greatly influenced by J.W. Dunne's *An Experiment with Time* (A. & C. Black Ltd, 1927). He had come to accept that on the next level, time and sequence were irrelevances and pertinent only for our earth level existence. Like Tom, Dunne had identified a superconscious mind that lay beyond sleep and death. Tom understood that mind was distinct from brain, which was simply an organ that acted as a censor for earth-level thinking. He described this realm as a 'country' where nothing could be quantified, or proved to the satisfaction of the earth-bound scientist. He astutely realised that the experimenter had to develop his own faith to satisfy himself. Experiments with the pendulum had led him to discover this and other dimensions, but he understood that it was our dreams that provided a glimpse into this 'other' world.

An Experiment with Time was published in 1927, and it is difficult to imagine how it was perceived by a world that was still drawn to the Victorian notion of scientific reasoning. Even in the opening lines, Dunne is quick to assert that this is not a book about 'occultism', or 'psycho-analysis': subjects that were already being frowned upon by academics and those in the scientific community. However, as Dunne states, it is a, 'cautious reconnaissance in a rather novel direction.'

Tom had realised that mankind's 'voyage of discovery' was limited to the sea-worthiness of the vessel in which it chose to travel. He understood that we could only work with the tools that were available to us. Our comprehension of the Universe was based upon how we can scientifically evidence our observations. Without this scientific substantiation, our views and theories would be merely philosophical. Because of human nature, our perception of 'truth' is always going to be subjective. Two people in a cinema watching the same film will each leave with their own recollections; because of their unique personalities, the focus of their attention may differ entirely. One, may focus on the leading lady's actions, the other may focus upon a classic car that pulls into shot in the background. Our ability to comprehend the whole scene, for one hundred per cent of the time, is limited, but, as a result of this, the observers will leave the cinema with their own perception of events.

The greatest part of any scientific enquiry is the role played by the experimenter and this is the role that Tom was astutely aware of in his theory on ghosts and ghouls. The medieval alchemists believed that the elusive ingredient was 'the self', the unique part played by the chemist. The two people in our cinema scenario may well have been observed by a third person who has spent the entire movie not watching the film, but monitoring the two members of the audience. This observer will have acquired their own memories of events in the auditorium, and their understanding of the proceedings in the cinema may have a wider, more universal perspective compared to that of the viewer who spent the entirety of the film ogling the leading lady. Whether we like it or not, as experimenter or observer, we too become part of the trial; our own presence has a bearing on the eventual outcome of events. Of course, this chain of events could, in theory, continue infinitum, each observer progressing up the 'chain', with each participant influencing and memorising events.

Although inspired by Dunne's masterwork, Tom saw one major flaw in Dunne's reasoning. By suggesting a scenario of an endless stream of observers, Dunne was suggesting that time progressed evenly and therefore could be illustrated as a straight line. Tom, however, had already suggested that the second level of consciousness that he had discovered was a timeless zone – a vast library of timeless memories and therefore the concept of the chain of observers was subject to the conditions on this higher level. The observers and their perception of sequences of events were dictated to by the constraints of this zone.

Tom was intrigued by the conscious mind of the observer and, in *The Monkey's Tail,* he had contemplated on who or what would observe a future time? He believed that the chain of observers in our scenario must surely lead to a single, omnipresent observer – God?

He was determined to search for a middle way, one that observed the laws of science, yet he was sympathetic to universal and theological viewpoints. He believed that consciousness was a faculty that we had developed in our own evolution and that any evolution, in plant or animal, must have taken place in the 'seed'. Without the presence of a conscious mind to observe events both terrestrially and universally, how could we possibly define reality?

In *An Experiment with Time,* Dunne discusses 'Animism', a term used to describe the intervention of the observer. It was this intervention, or 'soul' aspect, that intrigued Tom. It was this ability to observe and interpret our dreams that enabled the savage to become the conscious being that we have become today. It is our ability to focus and maintain attention that enables us to enquire and it is from this 'focus' that our memories are created. But this comprehension is a 'double-edged sword'; with this attention comes the failing or inability to understand the world outside this main hub of events. This 'tunnel vision' prevents us, like our two members of the cinema audience, being able to comprehend events in the auditorium as well as on the screen. The memories taken away by three people in the cinema that day, as we have previously stated, may well have varied greatly.

Dunne believed that dreams were the key to understanding time. He believed that they contained memories not just of the past, but also of the future. He was astutely aware that in being able and willing to undertake the dream experiments, mankind had made a leap forward in understand 'time'. Dunne believed that there was a need to record dreams, in order to gain a success rate of dream analysis. This actual recording process was crucial to human evolution; by undertaking this proactive stance, it challenged mankind's relationship with time. Perhaps there isn't a definitive answer to the 'big question'; any answer will inevitably be a contrivance of mankind's intervention. It is therefore a prognosis that reveals an open book of possibilities.

It was his publisher, Colin Franklin, who had put Tom on to studying dreams. However, Tom believed that Freud's use of phallic symbolism was 'complete cock.'[227] It was, however, the displacement of the second whorl of his spiral that intrigued him. He surmised that this timeless zone, or higher mental level, was a depository of an individual's memories that could be visited after death, or whilst in sleep. He had accumulated stories of people who had experienced out-of-body occurrences during near-death encounters, sleep, or fever and all had acknowledged that their viewpoint of 'themselves' had been displaced, usually from above and to the left. He realised that this dislocation was similar to the displacement that he had detected with his pendulum in the higher mental zones, the ones detectable beyond 40 inches.

He realised that each individual was independent and not the equal of any other person; therefore, the second whorl of the spiral contained the personal memories of their existence on the earth level plane. Through his pendulum experiments, he had already established that this vast library on the second whorl was a timeless place; therefore, by accessing this zone, the entrant would have access to future memories – ones that hadn't yet occurred on the earth level plane. He believed that dreams that foretold of future events were proof of this.

He realised, however, that dreams of future events might not necessarily come true, or even be detailed and entirely accurate. The dreamer's consequent actions will eventually determine his or her own fate. The momentary waking glimpses of the future, known as déjà vú, enable us to take stock, but these 'glimpses' are far too rapid for analysis. This glimpse of 'the future' enables us to make conscious actions to determine future events, but their significance is lost instantaneously. But unlike déjà vú, dreams are a mixing of future memories, a displacement in time which often requires triggers, arousals and recalls before they emerge and flood into the conscious waking mind. Tom had been aware of this process being triggered when Graham Tidman, the BBC cameramen, had visited *Hole House*.

Nature provides us with a barrier to stop this 'future time' interfering with our conscious, material world, but dreams provide us with this portal. Dunne discussed ideas such as 'The Memory Train' and 'The Train of Ideas', methodologies designed to open the 'gateway'. Dunne's task was to find the barrier that divided past and future knowledge, but deep down he knew that the barrier didn't exist. He believed that all one had to do was arrest all obvious thinking of the past, and the future would become apparent in disconnected flashes. The observer could then alter their course of action and, as a result of these pre-observations, prevent events from happening. The free will of the individual was a major factor regarding the outcome of future events.

Tom realised that our ability to capture moments in time by using film and photography and to record its progression, somehow gave us a foothold over something that is totally abstract to our material world. The use of technology has therefore created for us a 'timeless' reality, or 'actuality in a bubble'. He realised, however, that the crucial element was 'sequence'. Although time appeared to be absent on the second whorl of his spiral, sequence, however, was still crucial. This concept had hit home to him on 28 July 1923, whilst trapped in the ice onboard the *Heimen.* Whilst asleep in his bunk, he was woken by the crashing and creaking of the ships timbers. Believing that the boat was about to be crushed, Tom and the rest of the crew abandoned ship and carried their essential belongings out onto the ice field. Although the crisis turned out to be a false alarm, it was the speed of events that intrigued him. They had spent weeks trapped in the ice, as time ticked slowly by. Then all of a sudden, they were standing on the ice sheet, surrounded by their belongings. Although 'clock time' had remained constant, his mental clock had been accelerated by the urgency of immediate events. He realised that time as we know it, in daily life, was merely a convenience for the observation of sequences of events.[228]

If mankind has advanced to a point where it is able to create this 'prefabricated' reality, surely nature too must ultimately be able to surpass our 'amateurish' attempts to control 'time'. Like Dunne, Tom understood that nature would always be one step ahead of any man-made discovery, for he knew that our scientific knowledge was in its infancy. By presenting his ideas and theories as possibilities, he challenged the men of science to prove him wrong. Ultimately, he knew that we would have to shed the baggage of our material existence to comprehend the greatest gift – a comprehension of time.

The Power of the Pendulum expanded upon and summarised many of the ideas discussed in his most recent publications, including pendulum-rates, ESP and vibrations. His chapters on breeding and heredity complimented the incomplete theories discussed in Part One of *The Monkey's Tail*. Many have suggested that the ideas presented by Tom were eccentric, but this criticism is without doubt unjustified, for his research reveals evidence of a thorough, scientific methodology. Was he eccentric? Mina believed not: 'He was unorthodox definitely, but too well balanced to be classed as an eccentric.'[229]

Postscript

After his death, many of his peers – eminences in their own right – were quick to acknowledge Tom's contribution to British archaeology. In a response to his Obituary in *The Times*, Professor Christopher Hawkes wrote:

> To your notice of Tom Lethbridge; I would like to add two essentials: the strength and honesty of his character as a man, and the singleness of purpose that united all his work, as experimental testing of what he found by observation. He liked to respect the work of others; yet he preferred to test that too. His well observed drawings had their part in all he wrote: and his exploring of ancient dwellings such as the 'wheel house' at Kilpheder, and around Cambridge of Anglo-Saxon and earlier graves and cemeteries, not only assembled facts in an array foe which research will long be grateful, but made them reveal the lives that the people had lived. His archaeology stretched back into the past directly from the present, from the people and the places he knew familiarly: it could start 'from your empty cartridge left smoking on the ground'.[230]

The Editorial of Antiquity proclaimed that Lethbridge had been,

> a man who had been a colourful, stimulating, provocative and often controversial figure in British archaeology; a man who could very properly be described, in Cyrus Gordon's phrase, as one who throughout his life kept an open mind and avoided confusing majority opinion with truth. Lethbridge, like Cyril Fox, took us out from our studies and museum cases, to see how life was lived in Fenland farms, in Scottish crofts, and by fishermen and sailors everywhere. They have

gone, but the breath of fresh country and sea air they blew through academic archaeology, remains.[231]

Reo Fortune, a social anthropologist, had been a lecturer at Cambridge between 1947 and 1970. His interests included sorcery, magic, witchcraft and mythology. Both Tom and Mina were friendly with Fortune and his second wife, Aileen Pope. Whilst holidaying in Devon, the Fortunes had often chosen to lodge in the nearby village of Beer and during their stopovers they often paid visits to *Hole House.* Tom was always the perfect host, but privately, he found Reo hard work. In a letter to his friend, C.F. Tebbutt, he revealed that he found the couple's visits, 'tiresome and trying.'[232] After the death of his wife in 1978, Fortune sought to forge a closer relationship with Mina, but the feeling appears not to have been reciprocated, although the pair remained the best of friends. Fortune died – as a consequence of a fall – in Addenbrooke's Hospital, Cambridge on 25 November 1979. It is told that during his final years, he wrote almost daily to Mina and although these letters are no longer in existence, his brother once referred to them as being quite 'magnificent'.

Although she partook in local events and activities, Mina found life without Tom in *West Hill* dull and lacking in stimulation. Unable to occupy her mind, she decided to return to Cambridge. In 1980, she moved into *Fortune Cottage* at Duck End, Girton, a property once owned by her friend, Reo Fortune. It is known that her love of cats, a devotion apparently tolerated but not shared by her late husband, was continued during her time in Cambridge. During her final years at *Hole House* she had owned a Siamese cat called *Hecate.* The pet had been purchased whilst Tom and Mina had been on a short break in Cornwall during the autumn of 1967. It was transported back to Branscombe in Mina's car, perched upon Tom's knee; it was a task that required him to draw on his skills of ferret handling.[233] *Hecate* was the subject of

Tom's study of backward dreams that features in *The Power of the Pendulum*. Publicly, he viewed the cat with contempt, but it is obvious that he had a deep affection for Mina's pet; her antics were fondly remarked upon in his letters to his friends.

During her time in Cambridge, Mina ran an antiques shop with her friend, Susanna West, who lived at nearby Cottenham. Mina eventually moved from Girton to Bar Hill, her last residence before she died suddenly on 2 November 2000. Mina had a desire to be buried at sea and she personally informed her nephew, Nicholas Leadbitter, that she wanted her ashes to be scattered in warm waters, stating: 'She wanted to always feel the sun on her back.' Nicholas granted his aunt her final request and one beautiful evening whilst on a sailing holiday in the British Virgin Islands, he ceremoniously scattered her ashes onto the sea off the west coast at Tortola.

The big unanswered question is; where would Tom's remarkable lines of enquiry have led if he had survived another decade? Unfortunately, the trail runs cold, so we shall never know. It is over 35 years since his last published work and we now find science delving into areas once considered to be out of bounds. The occult was perceived as dark and evil, something to be avoided, but this 'head in the sand' approach had led to the dogma that Tom knew to be the curse of all learning. The cynics, who sneered at him throughout the last decade of his life, could soon be made to eat humble pie.

Tom Lethbridge was a man of many opinions, but sometimes, even the visionary is inhibited by the limitations of the vocabulary at his disposal. Gratitude is a gift that lies beyond the written word and in the opening chapter of *The Monkey's Tail*, Tom delivered a poetic acknowledgement to his wife's contribution: 'My thanks cannot be stated in words.'[234]

But it is the *Hole House* idyll painted by Tom in his later work that creates for us a quintessential picture of him dowsing for truffles, investigating moths and beetles and unearthing junk from the midden in his English garden. Some cynics might suggest that this relative isolation and abundance of free time was responsible for an over-active imagination. However, contrary to this argument, I might suggest that Tom's detachment and tranquillity may well have been responsible for him becoming more sensitive to the workings of the universe.

Tom's last years are constantly in my thoughts as I create in my 'mind's eye' a mental picture of a summer's day at *Hole* in the 1960s. The windows are open wide and curtains billowing in the Devonshire air. Tom is seated at his desk by the window overlooking the coomb, whilst Mina sits below, diligently typing-up his notes in the garden. She is frustrated, not by her husband's scrawl, but by the myriads of loathsome stinging creatures that surround her. With this idyllic scene in mind, I will depart this idyll and leave the final words to Tom:

> As I sit at my desk here in Branscombe and look over my left shoulder, I can see the sea through a gap in the wooded ridges. Sometimes fog shrouds it and at other times it is blotted out by the driving squalls of wind and rain. But all the time I know that it is there and with that knowledge I am content.[235]

Appendix I

T.C. Lethbridge – Voyages

1921 Expedition to Jan Mayen

Departure: Bratvaag – 1 Aug 1921 (09:00hrs)

Return: Anchored in Aalesund Bay 9 September 1921 (21:00hrs.)

Vessel: *Isflugen*: Length: 70'; Weight: 45 tons. Contained X12 men including the Cambridge contingent.

Vessel: 'Polarfront': Length: 45'; Weight: 25 ton wooden sealer. Contained 9 men.

Skipper: Hagbord Ekerold – sailed on *Polarfront*.

Cambridge men: *T.C. Lethbridge, J.M. Wordie, J. Chaworth-Musters, W.S. Bristowe and R. Brown. Party also included P.L. Mercanton (Swiss).*

Objective: To ascertain whether Mount Beerenberg was still active. Customary geological, botanical and archaeological investigations.

Points of interest: Tom's records include a logbook, photographs and sketchbook (Gadd Archive).

1922 Summer Cruise – Northern Isles

Dates: 12 July – 3 October 1922 with party from Cambridge. 1 August – 3 October digging in Hebrides.

Vessel: X3 hired sailing vessels: *Elspeth* – 16-ton yawl, *Petrel* and *Trident*.

Skipper: John Robertson

Companions: *A. Harker, W.S. Bristowe, J.M. Wordie.*

Points of interest: *Tom recorded the cruise in a 117-page logbook (Gadd Archive).*

1923 Expedition to East Coast of Greenland (aborted)

Departure: *Tromsö – 16 July.*

Return: *Aberdeen – 29 August.*

Vessel: Heimen*: 72 ton motor-driven sealer.*

Skipper: *Lars Jakobsen*

Cambridge Men: *T.C. Lethbridge, J. Wordie, Lord Cawdor, C.C. Duchesne, R.H. McClaren, L.S. Mayne. Also onboard Tom's friend H. David.*

Objective: To explore the east coast of Greenland, explore the Franz Josef Fjord, conduct geological and archaeological work and repeat the pendulum gravity experiments made on the Clavering-Sabine expedition a hundred years earlier.

Points of interest: *Departed Newcastle at 5.00pm on 7 July onboard* Leda *– arrived in Bergen at 8.30am on the following day.*

Departed Bergen for Tromsö at 6.30pm onboard Haakon IV. *Ports of call included: Florö, Aalesund, Mölde, Kristiansund, Trondheim, Rorvik, Sammersjen, Nesna, Kvaro, Agga, Bobo, Svolvar, Lödingen, Harstad.*

Sailed from Tromsö onboard Heimen *at 8.00pm on 16 July. Landed on Jan Mayen at 6.00pm on 20 July and visited the radio station – departed the following day. On 27 July,* Heimen *ran into difficulties 30 miles off the Greenland coast. The ice closed in and they battled with the floes for nearly three weeks. During their time spent on the ice, Tom fell into the Arctic sea whilst on a hunting expedition.'* On 24 August, his friend H.E. David recorded in his diary: *'I fell down a covered crack in the floe but stopped myself with my arms and luckily saved the rifle but it was devilish cold and not very pleasant. Thomas also did likewise and was in for some time till I came back and helped him.'*

After a 'counsel of war' with the skipper on 14 August the mission was aborted.

Arrived at Alden – Iceland – on 19 August. Set-sail again at 7.00am on 22 August and arrived at Thorshaven at midnight the following day. Departed Thorshaven at 5.00am on 25 August – dropping anchor at Kvalvig at 6.45am. Called at Thorsvig on 27

August for water. Berthed alongside a trawler at Aberdeen at 10.30am on 29 August.

Photographs exist of this expedition (Gadd Collection).

1924 Summer Cruise – Western Isles

Dates: 1 June – 7 July 1924

Vessel: 'Elspeth'

Skipper: John Robertson

Companions: *Sylvia Lethbridge*

Points of interest: *Tom recorded the cruise in a 42-page logbook with accompanying photographs (Gadd Collection).*

1925 Summer Cruise – Western Isles

Dates: 6 Aug – 3 Sept 1925

Vessel: 'Elspeth'

Skipper: John Robertson

Companions: *Manny Forbes, James Wordie, Cyril Fox and Holmes*

Points of interest: *Tom recorded the cruise in a 47-page logbook with accompanying watercolours (Gadd Collection).*

1926 Summer Cruise – Western Isles

Dates: 5 Aug – 7 Sept 1926

Vessel: 'Elspeth'

Skipper: John Robertson

Companions: *Sylvia Lethbridge + Blackmans and Duffs for a short period.*

Points of interest: *Tom recorded the cruise in a 117-page logbook with accompanying sketchbook and watercolours (Gadd Collection).*

1927 Winter Cruise – Western Isles

Dates: 7 Aug – 29 Jan 1927

Vessel: 'Elspeth'

Skipper: John Robertson

Companions: *H.E. David*

Points of interest: *Tom recorded the cruise in a 29-page logbook with accompanying watercolours (Gadd Collection).*

1929 Summer Cruise – Ireland/Skelligs

Dates:

Vessel:

Skipper:

Companions: *W.S. Bristowe*

1929 Summer Cruise – Western Isles

Dates: 1 Aug – 4 Sept 1929

Vessel: 'Elspeth'

Skipper: John Robertson

Companions: *Sylvia Lethbridge, Scroope Egerton*

Points of interest: *Tom recorded the cruise in a 29-page logbook (Gadd Collection).*

1931 South Coast off Chichester

Dates: 15 September – 19 September 1931

Vessel: 'Polly'

Skipper: T.C. Lethbridge

Companions:

Points of interest: *Tom recorded the voyage in an 8-page logbook (Gadd Collection).*

1933 Summer Cruise – Western Isles

Dates: 15 July – 31 July 1933

Vessel: 'Elspeth'

Skipper: John Robertson

Companions: *Geoffrey Walford*

Points of interest: *Tom recorded the cruise in a 17-page logbook with accompanying sketchbook and watercolours (Gadd Collection).*

1934 Dublin to Elsinore

Departure: Dublin – 27 June 1934 (Afternoon)

Arrival: Elsinore 23 July 1934

Vessel: 'Passat' – steel, four-masted barque. Weight: 3,183 tons register. Length: 345'. Main Mast: 175' high from truck to main deck. 'Passat' means 'Trade Wind'. Built in Hamburg by Blohm and Voss. She had been built for the famous Hamburg 'Laeisz' Line of Nitrate clippers and used to make the passage regularly around Cape Horn to the west coast ports of South America and back again.

Skipper: Sjogren (surname).

Companions: *C.F. Tebbutt and first cousin David Greenhill Gardyne aka 'Bonny Danny'.*

Points of interest: Tom documented the journey in a 92-page logbook, plus a detailed pencil sketchbook containing drawings of many of the happenings onboard ship. 40 excellent b/w photos were also taken on the voyage.

The logbook also features prophecies made by the medium Elisabeth Gimson, who was to journey with Tom and his family on Scottish cruise in the preceding weeks. Tom kept a record of her success rate in his notes.

On leaving the *`Passat`* at journey's end, Tom saw her slide smoothly away to Mariehamn, Finland, her next port-of-call: *'We leant over the sea wall and watched the Passat setting sail. Wing after wing spread on the yards and stays. Then like a huge grand bird she slid away down the Sound with the sun gleaming on her black paint and sails. It was grand to see the great ship mounting up with the wind like a small yacht, the stays`ls tumbling, the courses clewed up and the halliard wires screaming… The ship herself is grander than the finest Cathedral. I could hardly speak.'*

After paying a visit to Copenhagen Tom and Tebbutt returned to England onboard the MV 'Parkeston' *to Harwich.*

An abridged account of this voyage can be found in Tom's privately printed book: 'From Dublin to Elsinore in a Sailing Ship' (Christmas, 1934). *Copperplates of the illustrations also appear in this publication.*

Tom recorded the cruise in a 92-page logbook with accompanying sketchbook and copperplates (Gadd Collection).

1934 Summer Cruise – Western Isles

Dates: 4 August – 28 August 1934

Vessel: 'Elspeth'

Skipper: John Robertson

Companions: *Sylvia Lethbridge and children: Christopher, Hugh (and Belinda?). The 'sensitive' Elizabeth Gimson. First cousin David Greenhill Gardyne aka 'Bonny Danny'.*

Points of interest: *Tom recorded the cruise in a 41-page logbook with accompanying photographs. The records also include 45 pages of Gimson's predictions and drawings (Gadd Collection).*

1935 Clyde to the Åland Islands

Departure: Greenock Pier – 3 July 1935 (15:00 hours).

Arrival: Mariehamn 19 July 1935 (dawn).

Vessel: *'Passat'* - steel, four-masted barque of 3,183 tons register. (See details 'Dublin to Elsinore' 1934 entry).

Skipper: Sjogren (surname).

Companion: *C.F. Tebbutt*

Points of interest: *Tom documented the journey in a 54-page logbook, plus a detailed pencil sketchbook containing drawings especially of the masts, sails and rigging from up among them. Approx 35 b/w photos, some very unusual and dramatic taken from both on high and of the vessel out at sea from one of its lifeboats.*

The Passat *was held up outside Greenock due to storms. In contrast to the 1934 voyage, they sailed a northern route past the Orkneys, not stopping at Copenhagen. To Tom's admiration, the captain skilfully negotiated the narrows into the Baltic.*

On arrival at the Åland Islands, Tom photographs and draws a whole fleet of famous tall ships in the harbour: Pommern, Prompt, Pemay, Pestalozzi *and* L'Avenir.

On arrival onshore on 19 July, Tom receives a cable from his wife Sylvia informing him that his son Hugh is ill. Unable to say farewell to the captain, he catches a steamer to Stockholm, a train to Malmo, a plane to Amsterdam and on to Croydon, where he is informed that Hugh is well again.

An account of this voyage can be found in Lethbridge's privately published book: 'North About – Notes on a Passage from the Clyde to the Åland Islands' (Christmas, 1935).

Tom recorded the cruise in a 54-page logbook with accompanying sketchbook, photographs and copperplates (Gadd Collection).

1937 Expedition to Melville Bay, Ellesmere Island and Baffin Island

Departure: *Leith – 27 June 1937*

Return: *Back in Leith 1 October 1937*

Vessel: *'Isbjorn': Weight 172 ton motor sealer.*

Skipper: *Albert Bergerson*

Cambridge Men: *T.C. Lethbridge, J.M. Wordie, H. Carmichael, H. Drever, R. Feachem, I. Hunter, D. Leaf, T.T. Paterson, A. Robin + E.G. Dymond (Edinburgh)*

Objective: *To conduct a major study of the cosmic rays in the earth's upper atmosphere by using high altitude balloons in an area along the east of Smith Sound, which was then close to the Geomagnetic North Pole. Customary geological, botanical and archaeological investigations.*

To explore, record details and update charts the coastline of N/E Baffin Land.

Points of interest: *Tom recorded the cruise in an extensive logbook with accompanying photographs (X2 volumes), sketchbook and watercolours (Gadd Collection).*

1939 Expedition to Iceland and Vestmannaeyjar, or the Islands of the Westmen

Departure: *From UK port (not recorded) 18 July 1939 (07:30hrs.) onboard 'Vega' – Arrived Stavanger 19 July 1939 (13:00hrs.). From Stavanger 20 July 1939 to Bergen onboard 'Lyra' – Arrived Reyjavik 21 July*

Skipper: *'King Arthur' – he sat with invited passengers around a round table.*

Return: *Bergen 15 August 1939*

Companion: *C.F. Tebbutt*

Objective: *Seconded by the Admiralty to search for and observe German Submarine activity and bases. Spent time visiting places mentioned in the Sagas, studied old types of fishing boat and ornithological studies.*

Points of interest: *Tom recorded the cruise in a 41-page logbook with accompanying photographs (Gadd Collection).*

Points of interest: *Tom recorded the cruise in a logbook with accompanying sketchbook and photographs.*

1949 Summer Cruise – Western Isles

No Records

Points of interest: *Watercolours (X12) exist dated from 15 September – 25 September 1949 (Leadbitter Archive).*

1950 Summer Cruise – Western Isles

Dates: *20 July – 16 September 1950.*

Vessel: *Zoraida II*

Skipper: *John Robertson.*

Companion: *Mina Lethbridge*

Points of interest: *Tom recorded the cruise in a 72-page logbook with accompanying sketchbook (Gadd Archive). Watercolours (X11) exist of this cruise dated from 27 July – 17 September 1950 (Leadbitter Archive).*

1951 Summer Cruise – Western Isles

Dates: *9 June – 4 September 1951.*

Vessel: *Zoraida II*

Skipper: *John Robertson.*

Companions: *Mina Lethbridge, John Charrington (to start with) then W.S. Bristowe at the end. Tom's Mother Violet was with them for the first few days before they departed for the Outer Isles.*

Points of interest: *Tom recorded the cruise in a 100-page logbook with accompanying sketchbook, watercolours and plans (Gadd Archive). Mina Lethbridge also kept a diary of this trip (Gadd Archive). Watercolours (X13) exist of this cruise dated from 10 June – 11 August 1951 (Leadbitter Archive).*

1952 Summer Cruise – Western Isles

Dates: *16 June – 11 September 1951.*

Vessel: *Zoraida II*

Skipper: *John Robertson.*

Companions: *Mina Lethbridge, W.S. Bristowe - present 4-18 August.*

Points of interest: *Tom recorded the cruise in a 94-page logbook with accompanying sketchbook. Mina Lethbridge also kept a diary of this trip (Gadd Archive). Watercolours (X7) exist of this cruise dated from 11 July – 15 September 1952 (Leadbitter Archive).*

1953 Summer Cruise – Western Isles

Dates: *6 July – 6 August 1951.*

Vessel: *Zoraida II*

Skipper: *T.C. Lethbridge (No mention of John Robertson in log).*

Companions: *Mina Lethbridge, Reo & Eileen Fortune - until 20 July, W.S. Bristowe and Belinda 'Binnie' Lethbridge - joined 3 August.*

Points of interest: *Tom recorded the cruise in a log with accompanying photographs. Mina Lethbridge also kept a diary of this trip (Gadd Archive). Watercolours (X8) exist of this cruise dated from 20 July – 13 September 1953 (Leadbitter Archive).*

1955 Summer Cruise – Western Isles

Dates: *24 June – 27 July 1951.*

Vessel: *Zoraida II*

Skipper: *T.C. Lethbridge (No mention of John Robertson in log).*

Companions: *Mina Lethbridge.*

Points of interest: *Tom recorded the cruise in a log – 14 loose pages – with accompanying photographs (Gadd Archive). Mina Lethbridge also kept a diary of this trip (Gadd Archive). Watercolours (X23) exist of this cruise dated from 30 June – 15 September 1955 (Leadbitter Archive).*

1956 Summer Cruise – Western Isles

No Records

Points of interest: *Watercolours (X22) exist of this cruise dated from 17 June – 16 September 1955 (Leadbitter Archive).*

Appendix 2

Visit to Mina Lethbridge, Hole House, Branscombe, 1973

In 1973, Mina sold Tom's library, diaries, notebooks and archaeological drawings to John Ruston, a well-known antiquarian bookseller. Assisting Ruston that day to carry the books from Hole House to his awaiting van was John Gadd who for years had nursed a fascination with Lethbridge's work. Gadd recalls:

John Ruston asked me to accompany him to act as a sherpa in carrying Tom Lethbridge's library into his van on the promise of a decent dinner on the way back. He was an epicure and knew his food, so I happily agreed. Anyway these jaunts to people's houses are great fun.

After an initial introduction to Mina, I made myself scarce for them to do business and for John to 'do the books'.

Meanwhile, I asked Mrs Lethbridge if I could walk round the garden and look at the old house. Nosey as ever (what collector isn't?), I looked into an outbuilding in which there was a whole lot of stuff, including some tea chests covered in West of England hessian sacks. I lifted one corner, then another and peeped inside.

Papers, notebooks files and even original drawings were all mixed up, sort of thrown in together as if a whole filing cabinet drawer or cupboard contents had been dumped in. Some of the notebooks lay open as they fell and there was at least one tolerable watercolour with its corner badly bent. After rummaging a bit further, I exited rather guiltily and went back to sit in the van.

John came out and said it was all done and we carried cardboard boxes into the library while Mina went off to make some tea and sandwiches.

I told John about the tea chests and said it looked as if there was some really good stuff in there in disarray and that he ought to look at it. While I was carrying boxes out, he asked her if there was anything else such as any non-printed book material, as this could be of interest and he might be able to write her a further cheque if he could look at it. She demurred quite strongly, he told me later, saying that there was a lot of personal papers there and 'a lot of Tom's old papers' in among them. Anyway, she and John went out to look at them and he half-persuaded her to part with them, saying that he was too busy running the shop to go through them and sort out the personal things, but that he would ask me to do so and be so good as to take the confidential stuff back to her, which I did a few weeks later. On having this explained to me, I turned on the charm and assured her that I wouldn't read any of the personal stuff as I wasn't the least bit interested, and this I hope turned the door. John said at dinner, 'I owe you one', so I said I'd have the miniature book he was charging too much for, for nowt thank you very much, but he said, 'No you won't, but you can have first refusal on the tea chest contents at what I'll offer her – it won't be too bad as she seems strapped for cash.' Ever the dealer!

My memory fails me here as I can't remember if we took the three chests back with us – I don't think we did. In fact, on reflection, I'm sure we didn't as with nearly 1000 books already in the van (there were runs of archaeological journals as well as the individual books), the springs were already low, but we did take a file or two of watercolours on John's assumption that they were promised to him, and were amazed that such quality was being so inconsiderately treated.

He told me that she had said that she didn't think anyone would pay for a lot of old letters and her typescripts of his books, etc. Also, she said that the chests 'were awaiting the attention of 'x'', whom we assumed was the gardener, as there was a can of paraffin in the shed. 'She was going to burn them, you know,' John said with a shudder as I leafed through the drawings. 'I think she'd forgotten about the paintings, and I wasn't going to remind her!'

This is the only time I've known John be the least bit obtuse in business, but after all, 'caveat vendor' as well as 'emptor', I suppose.

On the strength of this, I think John went down soon afterwards in his Mercedes (or sent someone down) to bring them home, as the next thing I definitely remember was seeing them in entirety at his flat in Morland Road, Bournemouth and being asked to cart them off home to do the necessary sorting out. By this time he'd sorted through the contents quickly to get some idea of value, and I remember him getting all excited about the two thick folders of Mildenhall Treasure material. (See the extract below from my diary of the time.)

In the end, I paid quite a lot of money for it all, which seemed a lot at the time but now the years have passed it has been worthwhile. All the material has been kept together except the (several hundred?) watercolours of inshore craft, which I couldn't possibly afford, which were put on the open market after John had kindly selected half a dozen for me to keep and which I've added to Tom's privately printed annual monographs.

We were both proud of what we had achieved, feeling that we had almost certainly rescued some precious material from being lost forever.

John Gadd. 30th March 2007.

Extract from my diary of the time…

> …Good as his word, the chests full of paper and folders were there waiting at the shop. For a moment I thought John's memory had failed him and that he was going to repeat the news about the Lethbridge library – but no, this time he was really excited, swishing his trousers from side to side around his ample waist, an involuntary movement which he performs when he has found something important, to the concern of those of his customers who aren't aware of the phenomenon

and who think that something vital is about to be discarded at any moment.

So I knew he had a big fish on the line on this occasion. 'You've found something hot this time,' I smiled. He said, 'At home – at home because I don't want them hanging around the shop – are an extraordinary collection of letters and documents all about the circumstances leading to the discovery of the Mildenhall Treasure – remember? Lethbridge, you see, was a Crown Witness at the Inquest and he thinks perjury was done throughout the proceedings and that the story the British Museum had printed is not accurate at all.

You really ought to take them on and decide for yourself – you are good at this sort of thing – but I think that this should be kept absolutely quiet. It could be dynamite and I don't know if the people involved are still alive, if so there will be all sorts of writs flying around if some of these letters get out...

After acquiring the collection in 1973, Gadd has taken curator care of the materials, diligently binding and archiving them in custom-made solander cases, thus preserving the material for posterity. Since the acquisition, Gadd has made the Lethbridge archive freely accessible to interested parties and the archaeological establishment.

John Gadd's archive is now housed in the Cambridge University Library.

Appendix 3

Notes on T.C. Lethbridge – The Artist by John Gadd

While his contemporaries at Cambridge recognised Lethbridge as a draughtsman – he illustrated all of his own books with competent line drawings – few of them realised what a talented watercolourist he was. Sadly, the position seems similar today.

Only one book, *Coastwise Craft* (Methuen, 1952), carries examples of his vignette watercolours, in this case of inshore trading vessels working between the North Devon and Cornish harbours, the South Wales ports and that of Bristol.[236]

His artistic range was much more extensive than this and can be divided into four groups.

Meticulously-detailed Ecological Drawings

His father Ambrose Lethbridge (1875-1909) drew birds, insects and fish in miniature, very detailed studies; in some cases a magnifying glass is needed fully to appreciate the fine detail.[237] The young Tom Lethbridge seems to have inherited this skill and must have been influenced by it, as some of his early paintings of fauna and fish, seen when the writer visited Mina Lethbridge in 1997, were very similar in style, size and detail to his father's fine work.

Archaeological Drawings

Many of these can be considered among the very best examples of watercolour drawings of grave goods ever recorded. Lethbridge, with his skill as a miniaturist, not only rendered colours accurately, but also the shape and form of the finds. For example, drawings of Saxon necklace beads, drawn to actual size and arranged on the page as excavated, are so skilfully painted that the beads seem to stand out in 3-D. This is because the artist was able to shade away the sides of each bead and highlight reflected light striking the curve of the upper convex surface, so capturing their lustre fresh from the grave.

In one watercolour, that of a necklace from grave 48 in his 1929 excavation of the Hollywell Row cemetery, there are no less than 129 beads – each one carefully painted in this way. This drawing alone – and there are a dozen like it, featuring beads and similar ornament – must have taken him hours of work.

When this drawing was compared with the original artefact in the Downing Street Museum, Cambridge in the late 1970s, it was noticeable how the colours of the beads must have faded over the preceding 50 years.

Lethbridge could also paint silver objects in watercolour made to look like silver – a notoriously difficult accomplishment which the artist seems to have mastered.

Thus Lethbridge has preserved the original colouring of recently unearthed grave goods in a corpus of around 100 drawings. He thought highly enough of them to have them preserved in several calf-bound volumes, now in the Lethbridge archive, where they have been protected from fading.

Watercolour Drawings of Ships

From an early age, Lethbridge took his paint-box with him on all his excursions, both on land and water, much as we would take a camera. Realising in the mid-30s that the possibility of a war with Germany might occur and that the inshore trading sailing vessels were nearing the end of their useful lives anyway, he stationed himself on one or another of the headlands on the North Devon coast – either Hartland Point or Bull Point – for three weeks or more during June from 1934 to1938, and painted the vessels as they passed by, recording the colours of sails and hull on postcard-size sheets. The names of the ships, their direction and time were carefully written down in a series of notebooks,[238] which in itself is a useful record of this vanished trade which is now transferred to, and helps clog up, the M5! Well over 100 of these paintings are thought to exist and were sold (to a so-far untraced buyer) around 1976 by the antiquarian booksellers Horace Commin of Bournemouth, but not before several were retained as examples; these are now in the Lethbridge archive.

Lethbridge also tried his hand – very successfully – at delicate copperplate engravings,[239] some of which are featured in his privately printed monographs,[240] such as *Short Splices* (the hardback version) and *Some Notes on Ships and Boats*. One of the unpublished engravings is a delightful and clever study of a mouse sitting on its haunches, compiled with great economy of line, using only a dozen gracefully curved lines – a skill worthy of the greatest artists. He also ventured into linocuts, usually of storms at sea, a subject which lends itself to this heavy-contrast genre.

General Watercolours and Line Drawings

His own books and some archaeological reports are liberally illustrated with his black and white sketches, again demonstrating a confident sureness of line. He also painted many small watercolours for his own amusement, which are now contained in two bound volumes,[241] most of them annotated. Some of these are somewhat 'muddy' and were probably done en-plein-air in varying weather conditions, but these are counterbalanced by some lovely larger paintings of the frozen north done onboard ship during his participation in the Baffin Bay Expedition of 1937, where he captures the cold light and the limpid colours far above the Arctic Circle in summer.[242] His paintings of Iceland, contained in the same volume, during his trip up there in 1939, are also excellent.

For all these 'serious' paintings he kept companion notebooks, some sewn, others ring-bound, where he made preliminary pencil sketches and dabbed-in splashes of colour for reference purposes when tackling the watercolour proper as soon as the boats he was on were at anchor and free from movement.

He took great care to get shapes and colours right – no artistic licence here, as befits an archaeological recorder. This is borne out by two pages in one of these preliminary notebooks where not only a beautiful iceberg is sketched, but a photo of it is tipped in too. The iceberg's shape is accurately painted in the finished watercolour and dated during the expedition, but the photograph of it must have been developed *after* they returned, as it has the processor's stamp on the reverse. The complex line of the berg is exactly the same in the finished watercolour as it is in the photo; he got it spot on.

He could also draw figures tolerably well, as is evident from his close-up drawings of the crew of the clipper ship, *Passat,* at work furling sails high in the rigging when at sea. He had to be up there with them, and to achieve such drawings when the vessel was sailing at speed must have taken a steady nerve. These pencil drawings, followed later by copperplate engravings, must be unusual if not unique.

Down below he drew his fellow passengers – not always flatteringly!

As an archaeologist, he made many plans of his sponsored 'official' digs, which were subsequently published in his succession of technical papers. He also drew plans and sections with measurements of his 'private' digs of caves, middens and brochs (mostly discovered by word-of-mouth from the locals befriended by his indigenous Scottish skipper) during his many holiday excursions sailing around the Western Isles of Scotland in the 1920s and 30s and again in the 1950s. These pencil drawings intersperse his written 'logs' or diaries and must still be of interest to Scottish archaeologists, as he was usually the first to open these ancient occupation sites and draw what he found.

Photography

Lethbridge did carry a camera but seemingly didn't use it much, preferring to draw. However, the whole of the Baffin Bay expedition was photographed in detail and very well done too. There are good photos of Inuit families of north-western Greenland and Ponds Inlet north of Baffin Bay, including their costume, and the houses and boats of those seal hunters based in Greenland. Some 300 b/w photos are contained, with captions, in two bound volumes.[243]

However, the photos of his many Scottish cruises in the archive are mostly disappointing, just rather poor snapshots.

Lethbridge took, or had taken, only a few archaeological photos to illustrate his written papers, preferring to favour his own drawings.

While Lethbridge can be classed as a modest amateur artist, he was sufficiently competent and enough of his oeuvre exists to merit inclusion in any twentieth Century 'Dictionary of Watercolour Artists'. Like Churchill, he painted for his own enjoyment and relaxation and, as far as is known, never exhibited or sold a painting.

What he has fortuitously preserved for posterity, however, are the colours of some beautiful Saxon jewellery and artefacts as well as the hull and sail colours of those now long-gone sailing vessels.

Both achievements fully justify our recognition and thanks.

John Gadd – Fontmell Magna – 2010

Notes

1. Lethbridge, A. 'Personal Diaries – Book 5', p.77.
2. Source: Interview with Mary Rose Rogers, 18/02/06.
3. Lethbridge, A. 'Personal Diaries – Book 4', p.64.
4. Bistowe, W.S. 'A Book of Islands' (1969) G. Bell & Sons, p.14.
5. Lethbridge, T.C. 'The Ivory Tower' ch.1.
6. Lethbridge, T.C. (1963) 'Ghost and Divining Rod' Routledge and Kegan Paul, p.1.
7. Source: Cambridge University Archives: UA Graduati 12/142.
8. Note: The MA Degree, which in many universities is awarded by examination, is in Cambridge conferred only on holders of the BA Degree of the University and on certain other senior members of the University. It is not available as a postgraduate qualification in the sense in which that term is generally used.
9. Lethbridge, T.C. 'The Ivory Tower' (unpublished) ch.1.
10. Bristowe, W.S. 'A Book of Islands' (1969) G. Bell & Sons.
11. Ibid. p.15.
12. Wordie, J.M. (1922) 'Jan Mayen Island' The Geological Journal for March 1922 p.186.
13. Bristowe, W.S. 'A Book of Islands' (1969) G. Bell & Sons p.15.
14. Mercanton, P.L. (1924) 'La Premiere Ascension de Beerenberg de Jan Mayen' Extrait de l'Echo des Alpes No. 8 pp.280-281.
15. Bristowe, W.S. (1969) 'A Book of Islands' p.25.
16. Lethbridge T.C. 'Jan Mayen Diary', entry of 11 August, 1921 (Gadd Collection).
17. Ibid. Entry of 12 August, 1921 (Gadd Collection).
18. Note: In 'A Step in the Dark', Lethbridge claims the date to be 1st August 1921, but this is almost certainly an error. In the caption to Fig 5 in 'ESP' Lethbridge writes; 'View from the southern end of Jan Mayen. Drawn 21st August 1921, ten days after three of us (Wordie, Mercanton & Lethbridge) had

climbed the distant Berenberg (sic) for the first time.'

19. Note: References to the 'Brocken spectre' can be found in; 'Gogmagog' – pp. 20-21, 'Ghost & Ghoul' – p. 16 and 'ESP' – p. 23. Brocken: a mountain in northern-central Germany in the Harz Mountain range. It is noted for the optical phenomenon known as the 'Brocken Spectre' in which an enlarged image appears projected on clouds and for witches' revels that took place there on Walpurgis Night.
20. Note: Lethbridge provides us with a fine illustration of the spot where the event occurred on page twenty-four of 'ESP – Beyond time and Distance'.
21. Bristowe, W.S. 'A Book of Islands' (1969), G. Bell & Sons, p.31.
22. Lethbridge T.C. 'The Ivory Tower' (unpublished) ch.3.
23. David, H.E. 'Tromso /Greenland Diary – 1923' Entry 7 July 1923.
24. Ibid. Entry 12 July 1923.
25. Note: Lethbridge eventually negotiated the sale of 'Elspeth' on behalf of John Robertson. Lethbridge sailed the vessel from Dover to Falmouth where it was eventually sold.
26. Note: 'Shiant' pronounced 'shant', as in sea-shanty.
27. Bristowe, W.S. 'A Book of Islands' (1969) G. Bell & Sons p.35.
28. Ibid. p. 36
29. Lethbridge, T.C. (1967) 'A Step in the Dark' Routledge & Kegan Paul, Ch.1.
30. Lethbridge, T.C. 'The Ivory Tower' (unpublished) ch.1.
31. Smith, P. J. (2004) *'A Splendid Idiosyncrasy: Prehistory at Cambridge 1915-1950'*, p.59.
32. Letter from T.C. Lethbridge to Sir Cyril Fox dated, 21/04/32.
33. Note: When Tom left Cambridge to briefly live on the Scottish island of Kerrera and Burkitt was a visitor to his Ardantrive Farm. This suggests that there was no lasting animosity between them. 'How are you getting on? Miles was up here for about 10 days with Peggy and Judy and so I heard that you were retiring.' Letter from T.C. Lethbridge to Sir Cyril Fox

dated 10/09/45.

34. Lethbridge T.C. 'The Ivory Tower' (unpublished) ch.1.
35. Ibid. ch.6.
36. Ibid. ch.6.
37: Source: Interview with Peter Wordie, Dunblane 14/02/06.
38. Letter from T.C. Lethbridge to Sir Cyril Fox, undated.
39. Letter from T.C. Lethbridge to Sir Cyril Fox dated 04/12/48.
40. Lethbridge T.C. 'The Ivory Tower' (unpublished) ch.2.
41. Ibid. ch.2.
42. Ibid. 'The Ivory Tower' ch.2.
43. Ibid. 'The Ivory Tower' ch.2.
44. Ibid. ch.2.
45. Smith, M. (2004) 'Sir James Wordie – Polar Crusader' Berlinn Limited p.206. Note: Whilst searching for Eskimo camps on Ellesmere Island, Lethbridge verified the location of Dr Frederick Cook's camp. On finding the camp, Lethbridge mockingly stated, 'We can therefore claim to have trodden in the footsteps of the master.' In 1808, the American Cook had made a phoney claim to have reached the North Pole, a year before Robert Peary.
46. Note: In 'The Ivory Tower', Lethbridge remarks how his friend Sir William Ridgeway proved beyond all reasonable doubt that the people of Mycenae were Greeks and spoke Greek. It took thirty years before this became universally recognised and Ridgeway was given no credit.
47. Phillips, C.W. (1987) 'My Life in Archaeology' Alan Sutton, p.33.
48. Letter from T.C. Lethbridge to Sir Cyril Fox dated 11/02/26.
49. Lethbridge, T.C. (1961) 'Ghost and Ghoul' Routledge and Kegan Paul, p.51.
50. Lethbridge, T.C. (1928) 'An Anglo-Saxon Hut on the Car Dyke at Waterbeach'.
51. Fox, C. (1923) 'Archaeology of the Cambridge Region', Cambridge University Press, p.179.

52. Letter from T.C. Lethbridge to Sir Cyril Fox dated 22/03/25.
53. Letter from T.C. Lethbridge to Sir Cyril Fox dated 01/07/27.
54. Note: Lethbridge's letter to Sir Cyril Fox dated 20/11/38 states that Hugh was suffering from an abscess in his ear and was in the 'Eveline' Care home and that Christopher was suffering with swollen glands.
55. Bristowe, W.S. (1969) 'A Book of Islands', G. Bell & Sons, p.40.
56. Ibid. p.41.
57. Ibid. p.43.
58. Lethbridge, T.C. 'Logbook' Entry dated 15-19 Sept. 1931 (Gadd Collection).
59. Ibid. Entry 15-31 July 1933 (Gadd Collection).
60. Note: The Logbook of the 1934 trip is with the Gadd Collection now housed at the Cambridge University Library (CUL), West Road, Cambridge CB3 9LN. The logbook reference is: MS Add. 9258/2 'Voyage from Dublin in four-masted barque Passat. June 1934'. John Gadd's T.C. Lethbridge archive was purchased by CUL in the spring/summer of 2007.
61. Lethbridge, T.C. (1934) 'Dublin to Elsinore in a Sailing Ship'. Private publication.
62. Letter from T.C. Lethbridge to Sir Cyril Fox dated 31/07/34.
63. Note: Some of Gimson's predictions and 'visualisations' were later recorded in 'Ghost and Ghoul', pp 66-70.
64. Lethbridge T.C. 'Logbook' Loch Creran. Entry dated 4 July 1934 (Gadd Collection).
65. Ibid. Entry dated, 8 August 1934 (Gadd Collection).
66. Note: David Greenhill-Gardyne, Tom Lethbridge's much younger first cousin – son of his Aunt Rachel – was born in 1918 (he was only 16 during the 1934 Western Isle cruise). Rachel Lethbridge married Lt-Col Alan David Greenhill-Gardyne, laird of Glenforsa on Mull and of Finavon Castle, Angus. They had three children: Susan, David, and Maryel. The Gardynes' sold up their estate after World War II. David Greenhill-Gardyne – Captain in the Gordon Highlanders,

graduate of Charterhouse and Sandhurst – was killed at El Alamein in 1942.

67. Lethbridge, T.C. 'Logbook' Kyle of Lochalsh. Entry dated 25 August 1934, p.25 (Gadd Collection).
68. Letter from T.C. Lethbridge to Sir Cyril Fox dated 20/0338.
69. Lethbridge, T.C. (1935) 'North About – Notes on a passage from the Clyde to the *Åland* Islands' Privately Published, p.9.
70. Note: Bull Point Lighthouse gives a guide to vessels navigating off the North Devon Coast with a red sector light marking the Rockham Shoal and the Morte Stone off Morte Point.
71. Note: In 'The Legend of the Sons of God' (p.64), Tom mentions visiting his sons at a school in Fareham in 1931. I believe this date to be incorrect. Christopher would have been only 6 and Hugh only 4 – both too young to be in a boarding school. Tom also mentions visiting his mother who was now living in Bracknell on his return journey to Cambridge. I think the year would be more likely 1937 and NOT 1931 as stated.
72. The Times: Obituary: 'Mr. T.C. Lethbridge – Explorer and Archaeologist', 2 October 1971.
73. Lethbridge, T.C. (1933) 'A Cemetery at Shudy Camps, Cambridgeshire' Cambridge Antiquarian Society, Preface.
74. Lethbridge, T.C. (1933) 'A Cemetery at Shudy Camps, Cambridgeshire' Cambridge Antiquarian Society, Preface.
75. Smith, M. (2004) 'Sir James Wordie – Polar Crusader' Birlinn Ltd. p.206.
76. Letter from T.C. Lethbridge to Sir Cyril Fox, dated 22/10/37.
77. Lethbridge, T.C. (1938) 'The Fishermen of Durness' Privately Published, p.13.
78. Letter from T.C. Lethbridge to Sir Cyril Fox dated 18/07/39.
79. Letter from T.C. Lethbridge to Cyril Fox dated 18/07/39.
80. Lethbridge, T.C. 'Iceland Diary 1939': entry for 21 July 1939.
81. Letter from C.F. Tebbutt to J. Gadd dated 18/03/81.
82. Lethbridge, T.C. (1939) 'News From Tili' Privately Published,

p.7.
83. Lethbridge, T.C. 'Iceland Diary 1939': entry for 15 August 1939.
84. Note: Lethbridge was responsible for painting 'evacuation instructions' on the circular staircase used by staff at the museum. According to Curator, Peter Gathercole, the writing was still visible in 1970.
85. Letter from T.C. Lethbridge to Sir Cyril Fox dated 01/11/39.
86. Lethbridge T.C. (1950) 'Excavation of the Snailwell Group of Bronze Age Barrows' Off print from the Proceedings of the Cambridge Antiquarian Society Vol XLIII, Bowes and Bowes.
87. Note: As a child, Mina's mother, Eirene, lived at the home of the famous Cambridge theologian Rev. Dr. Henry Barclay Swete. Her separated parents lived abroad. Source: 'The Descendants of Capt. John Swete' (A History of the Swete Family from 1635), privately published by the Swete family.
88. Note: According to the census of 1901, Mathew Leadbitter was 12 years of age (born 1889, therefore 30 years of age when Mina was born) at the time and was living at 11 Fifth Street, Wallsend, Tyneside, Northumberland with his parents Joseph – aged 35, a ship yard labourer – and Elizabeth – aged 32. It appears that Mathew had two younger brothers – aged 10 and 8 – and two younger sisters – aged 6 and 8 months. Also living at the address at the time of the census was a boarder named Joseph Corbert, aged 63.
89. Certified Copy of An Entry of Birth: Registration District: (1919) Headington Sub District of St. Clement in the Counties of Oxford C.B.& C. Mina Elizabeth Leadbitter born on 13th April 1919 in Oxford.
90. Note: A letter from T.C. Lethbridge sent to C.F. Tebbutt on 15/09/69 reveals that Mina had a younger brother, Mathew, but it appears that he died in 'suspicious' circumstances whilst living in Moretonhampstead.
91. Letter from T.C. Lethbridge to Sir Cyril Fox dated 01/11/39.

92. Letter from T.C. Lethbridge to Sir Cyril Fox dated 11/03/44.
93. Letter from T.C. Lethbridge to Sir Cyril Fox dated 11/03/44.
94. Letter from Barbara Heath to Nicholas Leadbitter dated August 2004.
95. Lethbridge, T.C. – undated notebook.
96. Source: Interview with Mary Rose Rogers, Somerton, Somerset 17/02/06.
97. Letter from T.C. Lethbridge to Sir Cyril Fox dated 10/09/45.
98. Letter from T.C. Lethbridge to Sir Cyril Fox dated 17/03/46.
99. Letter from T.C. Lethbridge to Sir Cyril Fox dated 16/01/47 'Belinda is sticking pots together.'
100. Letter from T.C. Lethbridge to Sir Cyril Fox dated 11/03/44.
101. Lethbridge T.C. 'The Ivory Tower' (unpublished) ch.7.
102. Letter from T.C. Lethbridge to Sir Cyril Fox dated 11/03/44.
103. Letter from T.C. Lethbridge to Sir Cyril Fox dated 29/02/52.
104. Letter from T.C. Lethbridge to Sir Cyril Fox dated 10/05/46.
105. Lethbridge, T.C. (1948) 'Merlin's Island' Methuen and Co. p.2
106. Letter from E. Hodgkin of *The Spectator* to Daniel ?, dated June 17th 1948. Terry Welbourn letters: Box #1.
107. Lethbridge, T.C. (1949) 'Further Excavations at the War Ditches' Proceedings of the Cambridge Antiquarian Society Volume XLII, Bowes & Bowes, p.117.
108. Lethbridge, T.C. (1950) 'Byzantine Influence in Late Saxon England' Cambridge Antiquarian Society Volume XVLIII.
109. Lethbridge, T.C. 'The Ivory Tower' (unpublished) ch.5.
110. Ibid. ch.4.
111. Lethbridge T.C. 'Logbook of 1929 cruise around the Western Isles', Entry, 1 Aug-4 Sept 1929 (Gadd Collection).
112. Lethbridge, T.C. 'Logbook of 1925 cruise around the Western Isles', Entry, 22 Aug 1925.
113. Lethbridge, T.C. 'Logbook of 1927 cruise around the Western Isles', Entry, 7–29 January 1927.
114. Lethbridge T.C. 'Logbook of 1925 cruise around the Western

Isles', Entry, 31 Aug 1925.

115. Lethbridge, T.C. 'Logbook of 1927 cruise around the Western Isles', Entry, 7–29 January 1927

116. Lethbridge, T.C. (1950) 'Herdsmen and Hermits' Bowes and Bowes, pp. xviii-xix.

117. Letter from T.D. Kendrick to T.C. Lethbridge dated, 06/09/38 (Gadd Collection: Kendrick Letters, series 1, letter 30).

118. Letter from T.D. Kendrick to T.C. Lethbridge (Gadd Collection: Kendrick Letters, series 1, letter 28, n.d.). NB. The underlined words in the text are triple underlined in the original letter.

119. Lethbridge, T.C. (1950) 'Herdsmen and Hermits' Bowes and Bowes, p.136.

120. MYTH OR LEGEND? : Series #1; Broadcast Spring 1953.

LYONESSE AND THE LOST LANDS OF ENGLAND by G.E. Daniel, Fellow of St. John's College, Cambridge, University Lecturer in Archaeology.

THE CITY OF TROY by D.L. Page, F.B.A., Fellow of Trinity College, Regius Professor of Greek in the University of Cambridge.

GLASTONBURY AND THE HOLY GRAIL by R.F. Traharne, Vice-Principal and Professor of History in the University in the University College of Wales Aberystwyth.

THE FLOOD by Sir Leonard Woolley, Kt., Hon. D. Litt. Dublin, Hon. LL.D. St. Andrews, Hon. A.R.I.B.A., F.S.A.

THESEUS AND THE MINOTAUR by C.T. Seltman, Litt.D., Fellow of Queen's College Cambridge, formerly University Lecturer in Classics.

TARA by S.P. Ó'Ríordáin, Professor of Archaeology in University College, Dublin.

121. MYTH OR LEGEND? Series #2; Broadcast Winter 1953/54.

TRISTAN AND ISOLT by J.M. White, M.A., Author, and a Member of Her Majesty's Foreign Service.

ST. GEORGE AND THE DRAGON by E.R. Leach, Lecturer in

Anthropology in the University of Cambridge.

THE ISLES OF THE BLESS'D by T.C. Lethbridge, Hon. Keeper of Anglo-Saxon Antiquities at the University Museum of Archaeology and Ethnology, Cambridge.

THE DRUIDS AND STONEHENGE by S. Piggott, F.B.A., Abercronby Professor of Prehistoric Archaeology in the University of Edinburgh.

THE 'LOST CONTINENT' OF ATLANTIS by J.S.P. Bradford, F.S.A., University Demonstrator and Lecturer in Ethnology in the University of Oxford.

NEMI AND THE GOLDEN BOUGH by H.J. Rose, F.B.A., formerly Professor of Greek in the United College of St. Salvador and St. Leonard in St. Andrews.

122. Note: The Pillars of Hercules are referred to in the Bible as Tarshish. They are known in the classical world as Tartesso. They were visited by the ships of King Solomon at a time one hundred or so years before the poems of Hesiod. Nelson knew the Straits of Gibraltar as the 'Gut'.

123. Note: Eric the Red and his family settled in Greenland sometime towards the end of the tenth century. Leif the Lucky was known as 'lucky', not because he discovered America, but because he picked up a shipwrecked crew off a reef.

124. Note: Thorfinn Karlsefini's account makes reference to how and when his party arrived in America. It also tells of how the party dug pits below the high water mark to enable them to catch halibut. It was a practice still used in the Hebrides up until the end of the nineteenth century.

125. Kendrick, T.D. (1927) 'The Druids – A Study in Keltic Prehistory' Methuen & Co. p.191.

126. Whitley Stokes, (1887) 'Tripartite Life of St. Patrick' London, p.91.

127. Ettlinger, Ellen, (1953) 'The Stone Sculptures on White Island, Lower Lough Erne, Co. Fermanagh. Man, 53, Art. 53.

128. Murray, M.A., (1934) 'Female Fertility Figures' J.R. Anthrop.

Inst., No. 7. 16pp.

129. Lethbridge, T.C. (1953) 'Christian Saints or Pagan Gods? The Lough Erne Figures' Royal Anthropological Institute Journal, pp. 175-181.

130. Ibid. p.181.

131. Lethbridge T.C. 'Logbook of 1925 cruise around the Western Isles', Entry 19 Aug 1925: 'Tried to find the earth houses at Kilpheder. No success.' (Gadd Collection.)

132. Note: The joint owners of *Zoraida II*: D.B. Scampton and J.W. Trebble of Rhy, provided Tom with a detailed history of the boat, and were more than helpful in describing Zoraida's condition and offering a demonstration sail. Zoraida II was built at Looe, Cornwall in 1935. Walkers Marine of Ramsgate provided technical details and a plan of the boat. In 1948 they carried out a major refit costing nearly £956 (today's money: £17, 208: Munby, 1996).

In 1949, Camper and Nicholson of Gosport quoted for transporting her from Portsmouth to Gourock by road for £165 (£2805). Thus, by the time of the first post-war cruise, Tom had invested about £40,000 in today's money in getting her ready. About 10 years later, he was to sell her for only £300 (today's money: £3,300: Munby, 1996).

The insurance cover for her in 1957 at £2000 (today's money: £ 24,000: Munby, 1996) was £17-20 p/a., (today's money: £188: Munby, 1996). In 1959 the cost of overwintering her at Henderson's slipway at Mallaig was £80 (today's money: £880: Munby, 1996). Source: John Gadd Archive: Coastwise Craft Box: correspondence concerning purchase and sale of *Zoraida II*.

133. Bristowe, W.S. 'A Book of Islands' (1969) G. Bell & Sons, p.44.

134. Source: Obtained from a conversation with Jo Erskine-Collins 16/02/06.

135. Lethbridge T.C. (1954) 'The Painted Men' Andrew Melrose, p.13.

136. Letter from J. Whittaker (Andrew Melrose) to T.C. Lethbridge undated.
137. Note: The Cambridgeshire antiquarian William Cole (1714-82) was an important figure in the local history of the county. Born in Cambridge, William Cole was educated at Cambridge University: he eventually became rector of Milton (a village north of Cambridge). He spent the greater part of his life preparing a county history of Cambridgeshire: this would have been one of the magisterial multi-volume studies that could have ranked alongside Blomefield's *Norfolk*. Unfortunately, he was never able to discipline himself to organise his work for publication. Fortunately, William Cole left his manuscripts (50 or so volumes) to the British Museum: they are now in the British Library and can be consulted there. Microfilm copies of some of Cole's manuscripts can also be seen in the Cambridgeshire Record Office.
138. Letter from T.C. Lethbridge to Sir Cyril Fox dated 05/02/28. The letter was posted from 'Marybourne', Manor Road, Bournemouth.
139. Letter from T.C. Lethbridge to Sir Cyril Fox dated 18/05/55.
140. Letter from T.C. Lethbridge to Sir Cyril Fox dated 18/05/55.
141. Letter from H.U. Willink to T.C. Lethbridge dated 13/5/55.
142. Note: Further articles on the Gogmagog discoveries featured in: The New York Times on 8 May 1955, The Toronto Weekly on 25 February 1956, Manchester Guardian on 28/5/57 and The Daily Express and The Daily Telegraph in September 1957.
143. Letter from C.F. Tebbutt to The Council of British Archaeology dated 20/8/58.
144. Lethbridge, T.C. 'The Ivory Tower' Chapter Four (unpublished).
145. Letter from M. Murray to The Times published on 10/5/57.
146. Letter from C. Fox to T.C. Lethbridge dated 25/5/57.
147. Letter from M. Murray to T.C. Lethbridge dated 14/9/57.

148. The Listener: review of 'Gogmagog – The Buried Gods' dated 19/9/57.
149. Letter from V.J. Gaster to T.C. Lethbridge dated 25/7/57 (Gadd Archive).
150. Letter from V.J. Gaster to T.C. Lethbridge dated 15/1/58 (Gadd Collection).
151 Lethbridge, T.C. (1959) 'Excavations on the Wandlebury Figures' Proc. Camb. Ant. Soc. Vol. LII p.58.
152. Clark, W.A. (Autumn 1997) 'Dowsing Gogmagog' Article in '3rd Stone' Magazine.
153. Letter from T.C. Lethbridge to Sir Cyril Fox dated 09/06/55.
154. Letter from M. Maples to T.C. Lethbridge dated 12/10/58.
155. Letter from M.A. Murray to T.C. Lethbridge dated 27/05/58.
156. Letter from M.A. Murray to T.C. Lethbridge dated 31/05/58.
157. Letter from C.F. Tebbutt to T.C. Lethbridge dated 22/10/57.
158. C.L. Forbes 'Report on Examination of a Sediment' Sedgewick Museum: handwritten x2pp report dated, 04/10/57.
159. Note: Simon Holcomb's grandson was John Holcomb who fought under King Richard in the Third Crusade to Palestine.
160. Lethbridge, T.C. (1961) 'Ghost and Ghoul' Routledge & Kegan Paul, p.118.
161. Letter from Mina Lethbridge to Colin Wilson dated 12/11/76.
162. Lethbridge, T.C. (1961) 'Ghost and Ghoul' Routledge and Kegan Paul, p.7.
163. Letter from Mina Lethbridge to Colin Wilson dated 10/01/81.
164. Letter from Michael Norris to Colin Wilson dated 05/07/85.
165. Lethbridge, T.C. – undated notebook (Gadd Collection).
166. Note: Personally, I have always thought that Lethbridge's illustration ('Witches' p. 70) of the animal depicted on the mid-fourteenth century tile looks more like a goat than a white 'dog'.
167. Note: Nodens – Nuada, Ludd or Lugh in Irish tales– Nudd (Welsh); he was lord of the land of sleep, the childhood 'Land of Nod or Nudd'. He was also the 'Lord of Hounds'.

168. Letter from T.C. Lethbridge to Geoffrey Bushnell dated 12/09/59.
169. Letter from T.C. Lethbridge to Geoffrey Bushnell dated 16/07/59.
170. Letter from T.C. Lethbridge to C.F. Tebbutt dated 29/04/68.
171. Lethbridge, T.C. (1957) 'Gogmagog: The Buried Gods' Routledge & Kegan Paul p. 44.
172. Note: Lethbridge describes the stone as being 17' X 11' ('Witches' p.111). He also mentions finding a similar stone with the carving of a dog.
173. Letter from T.C. Lethbridge to Geoffrey Bushnell dated 12/09/59.
174. Letter from T.C. Lethbridge to C.F. Tebbutt dated 30/10/67.
175. Note: The seven short stories feature in 'Ghost and Ghoul: The Squint' p.50; 'Unwanted Visitors' p.1 & 38; 'M'Bulazi's Bones' p.59; 'The Spirit' p.93; 'The Ghoul' p.41; 'Fear on the Cliff' p.28 and the first written 'The Edge of the Crater' p.66.
176. Yeats, W.B. (1901) 'Ideas of Good and Evil' A.H. Bullen, pp. 29-69.
177. Jung, C. (1964) 'Man and his Symbols' Aldus Books.
178. Note: Aby Warburg: b. Hamburg 13 June 1866/d. Hamburg October 1929.
179. Note: I use the term 'artist' in its widest possible context; incorporating the mystic, poet and, like T.C. Lethbridge, the visionary.
180. Yeats, W.B. (1901) 'Ideas of Good and Evil' A.H. Bullen.
181. Gombrich, E.H. (1970) 'Aby Warburg – An Intellectual Biography' The Warburg Institute/University of London, pp. 239-259.
182. Lethbridge, T.C. (1963) 'Ghost and Diving Rod' Routledge and Kegan Paul, pp. 65-67.
183. Dunne, J.W. (1927) 'An Experiment with Time' A. & C. Black Ltd.
184. Letter from T.C. Lethbridge to C.F. Tebbutt dated, 02/11/63.

185. Letter from T.C. Lethbridge to Geoffrey Bushnell dated 16/07/59.
186. Letter from T.C. Lethbridge to Sir Cyril Fox dated 18/07/61.
187. Letter from T.C. Lethbridge to Sir Cyril Fox dated 27/09/62.
188. Source: Interview with Jo Erskine Collins – 16/02/06.
189. Letter from Barbara Heath to Nicholas Leadbitter dated August 2004.
190. Letter from T.C. Lethbridge to C.F. Tebbutt dated 30/09/63.
191. An extract from 'Ghost and Ghoul' featured in the January 1963 publication FANTASTIC Stories of Imagination: Vol. 12 No. 1, pp.49-55.
192. Note: Irvine outlined the programme's objectives in a letter to Lethbridge dated 4th May 1966.
193. Note: Lethbridge describes this occurrence in 'Ghost and Divining Rod', pp.31-34.
194. Lethbridge, T.C. (1967) 'A Step in the Dark' Routledge & Kegan Paul pp. 106-109 & Wilson C. (1978) Hodder and Stoughton 'Mysteries', pp.145-146.
195. Lethbridge, T.C. (1967) 'A Step in the Dark' Routledge & Kegan Paul, pp106-109 & Wilson C. (1978) 'Mysteries' Hodder and Stoughton, pp.145-146.
196. Note: In the second letter Mr. Irving makes a more intriguing remark, 'Thank you so much for your most amusing letter. I think I now have a clearer idea of the function of a sporran!'
197. Irvine's third letter to Lethbridge dated 25 May.
198. Letter from T.C. Lethbridge to C.F. Tebbutt dated 27/05/65.
199. Note: On page 154 of 'A Step in the Dark', Lethbridge mentions that a crew of eight BBC staff visited *Hole* House between 22nd and 26th August 1956. This is clearly an error, as Lethbridge and Mina didn't move to *Hole* until 1957. The year of course should have been 1966 NOT 1956.
200. '...provision of transcript of your new book ('A Step in the Dark') for use as basis for programme script and the right to use excerpts and information from your published and

unpublished works for consultation with and advice to producer and help with programme script as necessary; for provision of and right to show drawings, charts etc. as agreed; for taking part in filmed and/or recorded sequences with Mrs. Lethbridge and for facilities afforded.'

201. Letter Dated, 26/08/66.

202. Note: Grumpiness as a necessity applies not only to artists and writers; Isaac Newton, possibly the greatest scientist of all time, was also known to be extremely grumpy!

203. Letter from T.C. Lethbridge to Frank Glynn dated 13/10/51.

204. Lethbridge, T.C. (1950) Herdsmen and Hermits' Bowes & Bowes, p.129.

205. Blegen, T. C. (1968) 'The Kensington Rune-stone; New Light on an Old Riddle' St Paul: Minnesota Historical Society. Note: Theodore Blegen was one of many who consider *The Kensington Stone* to be a hoax.

206. Holland, H.R. (1919) 'The Kensington Rune Stone: The Oldest Native Document of American History' Ephriam, WS: (Private Printing?). Note: The stone was in the possession of Hjalmar Holand for some time and his publications defend its authenticity.

207. Note: The discovery of 'Wineland the Good' and other lands on the eastern coast of North America appear in two mediaeval Icelandic sagas, 'The Saga of Eiríkur the Red' and 'The Saga of the Greenlanders'. It is likely that both were written around, or shortly after 1200AD, just over two centuries after the events they record had taken place. It is likely that much has been distorted or altered through the course of time, as many of the sagas were oral tales passed down through the generations. However, these two sagas do contain a central body of facts including events, people and the new lands cited.

208. Note: An alternative account exists that suggests that it was Goodwin himself who identified the carving as a sword, but

one of a Norse origin, not British. This account also suggests that it was Lethbridge and Goodwin who corresponded until Goodwin's death, where on his associate, Frank Glynn, resumed correspondence with Lethbridge.

This, however, was a myth created by Samuel Eliot Morison. He stated that Goodwin found the face of Henry Sinclair on the rock. Researcher Dave Goudsward suggests that Goodwin, as far as we can tell, never actually visited Westford; his data was provided by Harry Cheney and Malcolm Pearson with drawings by Vincent Fagen based on the Pearson photos.

Glynn and Goodwin met only once, with minor correspondence on either side of the meeting in April 1949. Discussion was about a series of small, carved stones Glynn had discovered in Guilford, Connecticut. Neither man made a good impression on the other.

209. Email correspondence to the author 8/12/09.
210. Letter from T.C. Lethbridge to Frank Glynn dated 08/06/54.
211. Note: In 1558, the Venetian Nicoló Zeno 'Junior' published a narrative to recount the discoveries of his Zeno ancestors, who claimed to have mapped the coastlines of Greenland and North America near Labrador. In 1898, F.W. Lucas set out to discredit these narratives but recorded geographical evidence suggests otherwise.
212. Letter from Frank Glynn to T.C. Lethbridge dated 01/08/63.
213. Letter from Frank Glynn to T.C. Lethbridge dated 20/05/66.
214. Lethbridge, T.C. (1976) 'The Power of the Pendulum' Routledge & Kegan Paul p.44.
215. Source: Interview with Joy Kiddle – 17/02/06.
216. Letter from T.C. Lethbridge to C.F. Tebbutt dated 07/10/69.
217. Letter from T.C. Lethbridge to C.F. Tebbutt dated 15/09/69.
218. Letter from T.C. Lethbridge to C.F. Tebbutt dated 15/09/69.
219. Lethbridge, T.C. (1971) 'Legend of the Sons of God' Routledge & Kegan Paul p.72.
220. Lethbridge, T.C. (1969) 'The Monkey's Tail – A Study in

Evolution and Parapsychology' Routledge & Kegan Paul, p.2.

221. Letter from T.C. Lethbridge to C.F. Tebbutt dated 21/04/70.
222. Letter from T.C. Lethbridge to C.F. Tebbutt dated 21/04/70.
223. Letter from T.C. Lethbridge to C.F. Tebbutt dated 14/05/70.
224. Letter from T.C. Lethbridge to Sir Cyril Fox dated 12/04/71.
225. Letter from T.C. Lethbridge to C.F. Tebbutt dated 12/04/71.
226. 'Antiquity' vol. 47 (1973) p.4.
227. Letter from T.C. Lethbridge to C.F. Tebbutt dated 02/12/68.
228. Lethbridge, T.C. (1971) 'The Power of the Pendulum' Routledge and Kegan Paul p.6.
229. Letter from Mina Lethbridge to Colin Wilson dated 03/06/75.
230. Hawkes, C. The Times: Article in response to Obituary (2 October, 1971) dated 06/10/71.
231. 'Antiquity' vol. 46 (1972) pp. 5-6.
232. Letter from T.C. Lethbridge to C.F. Tebbutt dated 25/09/64.
233. Letter from T.C. Lethbridge to C.F. Tebbutt dated 03/10/67.
234. Lethbridge, T.C. (1967) 'The Monkey's Tail – A Study in Evolution and Parapsychology' Routledge and Kegan Paul, p.2.
235. Lethbridge, T.C. (1962) 'Witches – Investigating an Ancient Religion' Routledge & Kegan Paul, p. ix.
236. See plates i-iv (8 paintings in all) opp, pp. 4, 10, 16 and 30.
237. Ambrose Lethbridge, examples in his 9 volumes of diaries (Gadd Collection).
238. Lethbridge Archive.
239. Ibid.
240. A full set is in the Lethbridge Archive.
241. Lethbridge Archive, Watercolour Drawings, Vol.1.
242. Ibid. 2 vols, bound cases '1st and 2nd Voyages in Passat'.
243. Ibid. Two volumes of photographs, 'NW Greenland Expedition'.

References

Details of the present whereabouts of the Lethbridge Archive cited below can be obtained from the author of this book through the publishers.

T.C. Lethbridge – A Chronology

1900	**October**	Tom's first wife, Sylvia Frances Robinson, born.
1901	**23/03/01**	Thomas Charles Lethbridge born to Ambrose and Violet (nee Murdoch) Lethbridge at *Knowle House*, Timberscombe in Somerset.
		Family move to *Trevissome*, Flushing, Cornwall.
1904	**07/06/04**	Sister, Jacintha, born.
		Family move to Heytesbury, Wiltshire.
1907	**06/04/07**	Brother, Ambrose William Speke Lethbridge, born.
1909	**11/09/09**	Father, Ambrose, dies of Tuberculosis at Heytesbury, Wiltshire, aged only 34.
1919	**15/03/19**	Brother, Ambrose William Speke Lethbridge, dies of meningitis, aged only 11 years.
13/04/19		Second wife, Mina Elizabeth Leadbitter, born in Oxford.
		Enters Cambridge as an undergraduate.
1921		Jan Mayen Expedition with James Wordie onboard *Isflugen*.
1923		Graduates.
		East Greenland Expedition with James Wordie onboard *Heimen*.
1924	**06/02/24**	Marries Sylvia Frances Robertson at

		Salisbury Cathedral.
		Moves to *The Lodge,* Waterbeach, Cambridgeshire.
1925	**06/05/25**	First son born; Christopher John Lethbridge.
		Becomes Honorary Curator of Anglo-Saxon Antiquities at Cambridge.
1926	**06/01/26**	Mother, Violet, remarries; Laurence George Frank Gordon.
	21/07/26	Second son born; Hugh Periam.
		Moves to *Mount Blow,* Shelford, Cambridgeshire.
1930	**12/04/30**	Daughter born; Belinda.
1937		Baffin Bay Expedition with James Wordie onboard *Isbjorn.*
1938		Moves into new *Mount Blow,* Stapleford, Cambridgeshire.
		Mina Elizabeth Leadbitter moves to Cambridge to take up post of secretary at the Cambridge Museum of Archaeology and Ethnology.
1939		Death of Sister, Jacintha.
		Travels to Iceland with C.F. Tebbutt.
		ARP warden and Major in Home Guard.
1943	**06/06/43**	Decree of Divorce from Sylvia Frances Robertson.
		Moves to *Church Farm,* Little Evesden, Cambridgeshire.
1944	**18/07/44**	Marries Mina Elizabeth Leadbitter in Oban.
1944		Moves to *Ardantrive* on Kerrera Scottish West Coast Island off Oban.
1945		Returns to *Church Farm,* Little Evesden, Cambridgeshire.
1946	**18/03/46**	Moves to *Treverbyn,* 12 Sedley Taylor Road, Cambridge.

1948	**07/01/45**	Son, Hugh, commits suicide in Scotland.
1957		Moves to *Hole House*, Branscombe, Devon in wake of controversy regarding *Gogmagog*.
1970	**09/05/70**	Violet Gordon (Tom's mother) dies aged 96 years.
1971	**30/09/71**	Dies in the Nuffield Nursing Home, Exeter, aged 71 years.
2000	**02/11/00**	Mina Lethbridge dies in Cambridge aged 81 years.

T.C. Lethbridge – Bibliography

1920 – *A Burial of the Viking Age on Skye* – Arch J – xxvii – 135-6

1923 – *An Upper Palaeolithic Site near Fen Ditton – (with Prof. J.E. Marr, and W.B.R. King)* — PCAS - xxxv

1924 – *An Upper Palaeolithic site near Fen Ditton* (with others) – PCAS – xxv – 16-20

1926 – *The La Tene and Romano-British Cemetery, Guilden Morden, Cambs. (with Cyril Fox) – PCAS – xxvii – 49-63*

Battle site in Gorten Bay, Kentra, Ardnamurchan – PSAS – xi – 105-13

Exploration of a cairn on Canna – PSAS – xi – 238-9

The Anglo-Saxon cemetery, Burwell, Cambs — PCAS – xxvii – 72-9

1927 – *A Settlement Site of the Beaker Period at Sana Bay, Ardnamurchan, Argyll* – Man – XXVII – 173-4

The Anglo-Saxon Cemetery at Burwell, Cambs — POAS – XXVII – 116-23

An Anglo-Saxon Hut on the Car Dyke, at Waterbeach – Ant J – vii – 141-6

1928 – *The Anglo-Saxon cemetery, Burwell, Cambs* — PCAS – xxix – 84-94

Excavations in the Anglo-Saxon cemetery at Little Wilbraham (With H.G. Carter) PCAS – xxix – 95-104

Archaeological notes – PCAS – xxix – 105-15

Shell mounds and winkle pins (with H.E. David) – Arch Camb – LXXXIII – 175-81

A brooch of the Dark Ages from Kenfig – Arch Camb – LXXXIII – 200-O2

1929 – *Excavations in the Cambridgeshire Dykes* (With W. M. Palmer) – PCAS – xxx – 78-93

The Anglo-Saxon cemetery, Burwell, Cambs — PCAS – xxx – 97-109

Archaeological notes (With others) – PCAS – xxx – 110-12

An attempt to discover the site of the Battle of Aldreth – PCAS - Vol. xxxi

1930 – *Bronze Age Burials at Little Downham, Cambs* – Ant J – x – 162-4

Excavation of a house site on Gateholm, Pembs – Arch Camb – LXXXV – 366-74

East Angles, an account of recent fieldwork in Cambridgeshire and Suffolk – Ipek – 69-76

1931 – *Recent Excavations in Anglo Saxon Cemeteries in Cambridgeshire and Suffolk – A Report* – PCAS

Archaeological notes – PCAS – XXXL – 150-6

Distribution of Romano-British and Saxon elements of population in the sixth century – Man – XXXI – 244-8

A skeleton of the Early Bronze Age found in the Fens — PPSEA – vi – 362

1932 – *Further excavations at the Bran Ditch (With W.M. Palmer and C.S. Leaf)* – PCAS – xxxii – 54-6

Archaeological notes (With M. M. O'Reilly) – PCAS – xxxii – 59-66

SHANTY – Self-published

1933 – *Excavations in the bed of the Old Cam at Quaveney Rollern Lode* (With G. Fowler) – PCAS – XXXIII – 129-32

Huts of the Anglo-Saxon period (With C.F. Tebbutt) – PCAS – XXXIII – 133-51

Anglo-Saxon burials at Soham, Cambridgeshire – PCAS – XXXIII – 152-63

Archaeological notes (With M. M. O'Reilly) – PCAS – XXXIII – 165-7

Pottery of the Roman Period from Isleham Fen – PCAS - Vol xxxiv

SOME WEST COUNTRY COASTERS – Self-published

1934 – *Archaeological notes* (With M. X. O'Reilly) – PCAS – xxxiv – 88-93

FROM DUBLIN TO ELSINORE IN A SAILING SHIP – Self-published

1935 – Medieval iron arrowheads found in Britain – MHAC – 77-9

Investigation of the Ancient Causeway in the Fen between Thetford and Little Wordy – PCAS – xxxv – 86-9

The Car Dyke, the Cambridgeshire ditches and the Anglo-Saxons – PCAS – xxxv – 90-6

Ancient limekilns at Great Paxton – PCAS – xxxv – 97-105

Report on the excavation of two sites in Mildenhall Fen – PCAS – xxxv – 106-27

Archaeological notes (With others) – PCAS – xxxv – 141-6

NORTH ABOUT – NOTES ON A PASSAGE FROM THE CLYDE TO THE ÅLAND ISLANDS – Self-published

1936 – *A Cemetery at Shudy Camps, Cambridgeshire* – PCAS

Further excavations-in-the Early Iron Age and Romano-British cemetery at Guilden Morden – PCAS – XXXVI – 109-20

Excavations at Burwell Castle, Cambridgeshire – PCAS — XXXVI – 121-33

SHORT SPLICES – SOME NOTES ON SHIPS AND BOATS – Self-published

1937 – ***UMIAK – THE EUROPEAN ANCESTRY OF THE WOMANS BOAT*** – Self-published

Romano-British burials at Linton Cambridgeshire – PCAS – XXXVII – 68-75

1938 – *Anglo-Saxon Cambridgeshire* – VCH Cambridgeshire

FISHERMEN OF DURNESS – Self-published

1939 – *Archaeological data from the Canadian Arctic* – JRAI – LXIX – 187-233

Southoe Manor – PCASI – XXXVIII – 158-62

Archaeological notes – PCASI – XXXVIII – 164-9

NOTES FROM TILI – Self-published

1947 – *Treasure Trove in Britain* – CJ – XLII – 282-6

1948 – *Sutton Hoo* – Archaeology 1 – 8-12

MERLIN'S ISLAND – ESSAYS ON BRITAIN IN THE DARK AGES – METHUEN & CO.

1949 – *Further excavations at the War Ditches* – PCAS – XLII – 117-27
Archaeological notes (With others) – PCAS – XLII – 128-30

1950 – **HERDSMEN AND HERMITS – CELTIC SEAFARERS IN THE NORTHERN OCEAN** – BOWES AND BOWES
Byzantine influence in Late Saxon England – PCAS – XLIII – 2-6
Excavation of the Snailwell Group of Bronze Age Barrows – PCAS – XLIII – 30-49
Boredom in Archaeology – ANL – 111 – 89-92
Excavations on the Castle Site Known as 'The Hillings' at Eaton Socon, Bedfordshire (With C.F. Tebbutt) – PCAS – ? – 48-60

1951 – *A Cemetery at Lackford, Suffolk* (Proc. Camb. Arch. Soc. New Series No. VI)
Roman Finds at Arrington Bridge – PCAS – 45
Roman Pewter from the Old Croft River at Welney – PCAS – XLIV – 18-21
Herewardisbeche – 22-5
Bronze Bowl of the Dark Ages from Hildersham Cambridgeshire (Camb. Arch. Soc. 45)

1952 – **COASTWISE CRAFT** – FIELD STUDY BOOKS
BOATS AND BOATMEN – THAMES AND HUDSON
Excavations at Kilpheder, South Uist, and the Problem of Brochs and Wheelhouses – PPS – XVIII – 176-93
Bronze Age bowl of the Dark Ages from Hildersham, Cambs — PCAS – XLV – 44-7
Excavations at Eaton Socon, Beds (With C.F. Tebbutt) – PCAS – XLV – 48-60
Roman finds at Arrington Bridge – PCAS – XLV – 61-2

1953 – *Christian Saints or Pagan Gods? The Lough Erne Figures* – RAIJ
Jewelled Saxon pendant from the Isles of Ely – PCAS – XLVI – 1-3
Burial of an Iron Age Warrior at Snailwell, Cambs — PCAS – XLVII – 25-37

1954 – ***THE PAINTED MEN – A HISTORY OF THE PICTS*** – ANDREW MELROSE

1955 – *Myth or Legend? G.E. Daniel et alii – Essay: 'The Isles of the Bless'd'* – G Bell & Sons – pp.89-96

1956 – *The Anglo-Saxon settlement in Eastern England Dark Age Britain*

1957 – ***GOGMAGOG – THE BURIED GODS*** – ROUTLEDGE & KEGAN PAUL

The Riddle of the Dykes (Camb. Arch. Soc. 51)

1958 – *The Riddle of the Dykes* – PCAS – LII – 1-5

Excavations on the Wandlebury Figures (with C.F. Tebbutt) (Proc. Camb. Arch. Soc. 52)

PCAS – LII – 58-68

1961 – **GHOST AND GHOUL** – ROUTLEDGE & KEGAN PAUL

1962 – **WITCHES – INVESTIGATING AN ANCIENT RELIGION** – ROUTLEDGE & KEGAN PAUL

Pagan Saxon Burials at Little Paxton, Huntingdonshire (with C.F. Tebbutt) – PCIS – LV – 8-12

1963 – **GHOST AND DIVINING ROD** – ROUTLEDGE & KEGAN PAUL

Fantastic Stories of Imagination – Essay: 'Ghost & Ghoul' – Vol. 12 #1 – Doubleday & Co. inc.

1965 – **ESP – BEYOND TIME AND DISTANCE** – ROUTLEDGE & KEGAN PAUL

1967 – **A STEP IN THE DARK** – ROUTLEDGE & KEGAN PAUL

1969 – **THE MONKEY'S TAIL – A STUDY IN EVOLUTION AND PARAPSYCHOLOGY** – ROUTLEDGE & KEGAN PAUL

1972 – **THE LEGEND OF THE SONS OF GOD – A FANTASY?** – ROUTLEDGE & KEGAN PAUL

1976 – **THE POWER OF THE PENDULUM** – ROUTLEDGE & KEGAN PAUL

1980 – **THE ESSENTIAL T.C. LETHBRIDGE** – ROUTLEDGE & KEGAN PAUL

1997 – The Mildenhall Roman Treasure: A first-hand account – ANT J – 71 – 721-728

2003 – A GIANT – THE DEFINITIVE T.C. LETHBRIDGE – Aegir Recording Company

Abbreviations

ANL: Archaeological Newsletter

ANT J.: Antiquaries Journal

ARCH CAMB: Archaeologia Cambrensis

ARCH J: Archaeological Journal

CJ: Classical Journal

JRAI: Journal of the Royal Anthropological Institute

MHAC: Montgomeryshire Historical and Archaeological Collections

PCAS: Proceedings of Cambridge Archaeological Society

PPSEA: Proceedings of Prehistoric Society of East Anglia

PSAS: Proc. Scottish Archaeological Society

RAIJ: Royal Anthropological Institute Journal

VCH: Victoria County History

T.C. Lethbridge – Unpublished works

1933: Proposed book with T. D. Kendrick

1949-1952: 'Mss Notes on the Picts'

1951: 'The Natural Supernatural' – eventual incorporated within 'Ghost and Ghoul'

1950s?: 'Beasts, Bird, Man and Monster' (unfinished)

Mid 1950s: 'Who Were the English?' (unfinished)

1960s: 'The Ivory Tower' (autobiography of Cambridge years – unfinished)

Sources

Interviews and Meetings

Numerous: 1998-2007 Gorran Haven, Cornwall – Colin Wilson
21/01/06: Friston, East Sussex – Nicholas Leadbitter
21/01/06 & 13/05/07: Fishbourne, West Sussex – Andrew David
15/02/06: Dumblane, Perthshire – Peter Wordie
16/02/06: Colyton, Devon – Jo Erskine-Collins
17/02/06: Branscombe, Devon – Jeff Pathe
17/02/06: Branscombe, Devon – Joy Kiddle
18/02/06: Somerton, Somerset – Mary Rose Rogers
28/03/06: Much Hadham, Hertfordshire – Elizabeth Clark
21/06/06: Headbourne Worthy, Hampshire – Mark Walford
16/08/06: Ashmolean, Oxford – Dr. Pamela Jane Smith & Dr. Mathias Alfred Jaren
07/04/07 & 12/05/07: Fontmell Magna, Dorset – John Gadd
20/12/07: Hinxton, Cambridgeshire – Peter Gathercole

Letters and Correspondence

Letters from T.C. Lethbridge to Sir Cyril Fox: Cambridge Museum of Archaeology and Ethnology
Letters from T.C. Lethbridge to C.F. Tebbutt: University Library Cambridge
Letters from T.C. Lethbridge to Margaret Murray: University Library Cambridge
Letters from T.C. Lethbridge to Geoffrey Bushnell: University Library Cambridge
Letters from F.A.C. Boothby to T.C. Lethbridge: University Library Cambridge
Letters from G.B. Gardner to T.C. Lethbridge: University Library Cambridge
Letters from C. Franklin to T.C. Lethbridge: University Library Cambridge

Letters from Mina Lethbridge to Colin Wilson: Colin Wilson's personal archive

Letter from Barbara Heath to Nicholas Leadbitter: Nicholas Leadbitter's personal archive

Letter from T.C. Lethbridge to Sir James Wordie: Peter Wordie's personal archive

Letters from J. Whittaker to T.C. Lethbridge: John Gadd Collection – University Library Cambridge

Letters from T.D. Kendrick to T.C. Lethbridge: John Gadd Collection – University Library Cambridge

T.C. Lethbridge Sailing Logs: John Gadd Collection – University Library Cambridge

Letter/Notes from Edward Hodgkin (The Spectator): Terry Welbourn Archive

Selected Bibliography

Bell, A.H. (Edited by) (1965): *Practical Dowsing – A Symposium,* G. Bell & Sons

Branston B. (1957): *The Lost Gods of England,* Thames and Hudson

Bristowe, W.S. (1969): *A Book of Islands,* G. Bell & Sons

Carmichael H. & Dymond E.G. (1939): *Upper Air Investigations in North West Greenland,* Reprinted from the Proceedings of the Royal Society of London. Series A No. 946 Vol. 171

Conybeare Rev E. (1910): *Highways and Byways in Cambridge* and Ely MacMillan and Co.

Daniel G.E. et alii (1955): *Myth or Legend?* G. Bell and Sons Ltd.

Day, L./Warr, de la G. (1956): *New Worlds Beyond the Atom,* Stuart

Dunne J.W. (1962): *An Experiment with Time,* A & C Black Ltd.

Fox, C. (1923): *The Archaeology of the Cambridge Region,* Cambridge University Press

Gimbutas, M. (1974): *The Gods and Goddesses of Old Europe,* Thames and Hudson

Graves, R. (1948): *The White Goddess,* Faber and Faber

Graves, T. (1976): *Dowsing – Techniques and Applications*, Turnstone Books
Haddon, A.C. (1925): *Races of Man and Their Distribution*, MacMillan & Co.
Hobbs, R. (2008): *The Secret History of the Mildenhall Treasure*, The Antiquaries Journal 88, 2008, pp 376-420
Johnson G./Whittall J.P. (1980): *T.C. Lethbridge – Frank Glynn Correspondence 1950-1966*, Early Sites Research Society
Leftwich, R.H. (1976): Dowsing – *The Ancient Art of Rhabdomancy*, The Aquarian Press
Mercanton P.L. (1924): *La Premiere Ascension de Beerenberg de Jan Mayen*, Extrait de l'Echo des Alpes No. 8
Mowat, F. (1998): *The Farfarers*, Key Porter
Murray, M.A. (1931): *The God of the Witches*, Sampson Low
Murray, M.A. (1921): *The Witch Cult in Western Europe*, Oxford Clarendon Press
Naylor, P. (1980): *Discovering Dowsing and Divining*, Shire Publications
Newman, P. (1987): *Lost Gods of Albion – The Chalk Hill-Figures of Albion*, Robert Hale Ltd.
Nicolson A. (2002): *Sea Room*, Harper Collins
Palmer, W.M. (1935): *William Cole of Milton*, Galloway and Porter
Patterson T.T. (1949): *Eskimo String Figures and their Origin*, Ejnar Munksgaard
Phillips C.W. (1987): *My Life in Archaeology*, Alan Sutton
Robertson D.H. (1938): *Sarum Close – A History of the Life & Education of the Cathedral Choristers for 700 years*, Jonathan Cape
Scott-Fox, C. (2002): *Cyril Fox – Archaeologist Extraordinary*, Oxbow
Smith P.J. (2009): *A Splendid Idiosyncrasy: Prehistory at Cambridge 1915-1950*, Archaeopress
Smith, M. (2004): *Sir James Wordie – Polar Crusader*, Birlinn
Various (Apr-62): *Scotland's Magazine*, pp.37-28

Various (1963): *Fantastic Stories of Imagination Vol. 12 No. 1 (January 1963)*, Ziff Davis/Doubleday and Company Ltd.

Wilson, C. (1978): *Mysteries*, Hodder & Stoughton

Wilson, C. (1983): *Strange Talents*, Orbis Publishing

Wordie J.M. (1926): *The Cambridge Expedition to Greenland in 1926*, The Geographical Journal for Sept 1927 pp. 247-249

Wordie J.M. (1922): *Jan Mayen Island*, The Geological Journal for March 1922

Wordie J.M. (1938): *An Expedition to North West Greenland and the Canadian Arctic 1937*, Reprint from the Geographical Journal Vol XCII No. 5 Nov. 1938

Yeats W. B. (1907): *Ideas of Good and Evil*, A. H. Bullen

Index

P

R

S

T

BOOKS

O is a symbol of the world, of oneness and unity. In different cultures it also means the "eye," symbolizing knowledge and insight. We aim to publish books that are accessible, constructive and that challenge accepted opinion, both that of academia and the "moral majority."

Our books are available in all good English language bookstores worldwide. If you don't see the book on the shelves ask the bookstore to order it for you, quoting the ISBN number and title. Alternatively you can order online (all major online retail sites carry our titles) or contact the distributor in the relevant country, listed on the copyright page.

See our website **www.o-books.net** for a full list of over 500 titles, growing by 100 a year.

And tune in to myspiritradio.com for our book review radio show, hosted by June-Elleni Laine, where you can listen to the authors discussing their books.

MySpiritRadio